Introduction to
United States
International Taxation

Series on International Taxation

This book 'Introduction to United States International Taxation' is the third in the 'Series on International Taxation' published by Kluwer Law and Taxation Publishers.

This series of books is intended for use by those engaged in the practice of international taxation. The books are of high quality and limited size.

The series is edited by a board of fiscal specialists from all parts of the world. They are:

Other titles in this series:

1. Professor Alberto Xavier. The Taxation of Foreign Investment in Brazil
2. Professor Hugh J. Ault / Dr. Albert J. Rädler. The German Corporation Tax Law with 1980 Amendments.

Introduction To United States International Taxation

by

PAUL R. MCDANIEL

Professor of Law,
Boston College Law School,
Boston/Mass.

HUGH J. AULT

Professor of Law,
Boston College Law School,
Boston/Mass.

Second revised edition

SERIES ON INTERNATIONAL TAXATION, NO. 3

1981
KLUWER – Deventer – The Netherlands
Boston • Antwerp • London • Frankfurt

Distribution in USA and Canada
Kluwer Law and Taxation
190 Old Derby Street
Hingham MA 02043
USA

Cover design: Pieter J. van der Sman

ISBN 90 6544 025 9

Table of contents

Preface

The 1981 edition of *Introduction to United States International Taxation*, as did its predecessor edition, presents the basic principles and rules of the United States international tax system in a relatively brief and manageable form. We would emphasize the word 'Introduction' in the title. The book is not intended to serve as an exhaustive treatise that discusses in depth the wealth of technical detail involved in applying U.S. tax rules in an international context. Instead, the purpose is to provide an overview of the principles adopted by the U.S. in taxing U.S. or foreign individuals and corporations as they invest, work, or carry on a trade or business in the U.S. or abroad.

The book seeks to provide a structural framework within which a U.S. tax problem can be placed. As a general matter, tax practitioners outside the U.S. whose clients have activities in the U.S. will rely on their U.S. tax advisors for technical advice on the U.S. tax aspects of their clients' transactions. However, it is our hope that this book will enable the foreign tax advisor to place the material he receives from his U.S. counterpart in the overall structure of the U.S. international tax system and thus be in a position better to evaluate the advice received and to relate it to his own tax system.

It is also our hope that the book will prove useful to professors and students both within and outside the U.S. who desire to obtain a grasp of the fundamentals of U.S. international tax principles and rules. The book can serve as a text or supplement to courses that deal in whole or in part with the U.S. tax system.

In line with these objectives, we have included references to the Internal Revenue Code provisions under discussion and to the more important Treasury Regulations that are issued interpreting the statutory rules. In addition, we have also included significant administrative announcements of the Internal Revenue Service (Revenue Rulings and Revenue Procedures) as well as illustrative principal cases that have arisen. We fully realize that our readers abroad frequently will not have access to the reference materials cited in the footnotes. Accordingly we have attempted to insure that the text discussion of a provision is self-contained so that the reader will be able to obtain a general understanding of the matter under discussion without resort to the footnote references. On the other hand, we did feel it important to provide sufficient reference materials so that the tax practitioner, professor or student would have a starting point to examine in greater technical detail the explanation offered in the text.

The 1981 edition, in general, follows the pattern of the 1977 edition, with materials updated to reflect developments in legislation, court decisions, and administrative regulations and rulings. One organizational change has been made by moving the material formerly in Chapter 9 to Chapter 11. This change permits the consideration of all technical material prior to analysis of selected tax policy issues in the U.S. international tax system.

The statutory references throughout the book are to the Internal Revenue Code of 1954, as amended, and are given without further explanation as, for example, 'Section 954.' Regulations issued by the Treasury Department are cited, for example: 'Treas. Reg. sec. 1.954-1.' Citations to the Internal Revenue Code and to the Treasury Regulations issued thereunder are current as of January 1, 1981. Accordingly, the discussion in the book fully reflects the Revenue Act of 1978, the Foreign Investment in Real Property Tax Act of 1980, and other recent legislation.

The book originated in work done by Professor McDaniel at the Institute for Fiscal Studies, Erasmus University, Rotterdam. A special word of appreciation is due to Professor Dr. Jan H. Christiaanse for his encouragement and support of the work that is reflected in this volume. Our thanks also to Dr. J. C. L. Huiskamp and the members of the staff at the Institute who have provided assistance and support for the project. In addition, Dr. Albert J. Rädler, Munich, made many helpful suggestions which we gratefully acknowledge.

We are indebted to Robert J. Pomerene and A.L. Spitzer for research and editiorial assistance and to Donna Teehan for aid in preparing the manuscript for printing.

PAUL R. MCDANIEL
HUGH J. AULT

May, 1981

Chapter 1
Introduction

This book is intended to provide an introduction to the application of the U.S. income and wealth transfer tax systems to taxpayers investing or transacting business in the U.S. and other countries. The bulk of the materials deals with the income tax since this is the tax that affects most directly the day-to-day conduct of business and investment affairs by individuals and corporations. The wealth transfer tax system is dealt with in less detail, both because within the U.S. context it is a less fully developed tax than the income tax and because it is more limited in its application to international transactions. Other U.S. taxes such as the social security tax, the unemployment tax, various excise taxes, tariff duties and State taxes are not considered in this book although, of course, it is possible for a particular taxpayer engaged in international transactions to encounter these taxes.

A grasp of the outlines of the U.S. income tax system as it is applied in its purely domestic context is essential to an understanding of the U.S. international income tax system. These basic rules are always applied to U.S. citizens and corporations in their international transactions and to foreign individuals or corporations engaged in a trade or business in the U.S. Accordingly, Chapter 2 provides a general description of the U.S. income tax system, briefly describing the corporation income tax, the individual income tax, the tax treatment of partnerships, and accounting aspects of the U.S. income tax. The purpose of the general description is not to provide a detailed analysis of the U.S. income tax system, but instead to provide a structural framework against which the international tax rules may be considered. Where particular provisions have special significance in the international context, they are only cursorily considered in Chapter 2, with more detailed analysis deferred until subsequent chapters. This approach is adopted, for example, in the case of the provisions dealing with the accumulated earnings tax, the personal holding company tax, and the various forms of tax-free corporate reorganizations (considered in Chapter 8).

The basic jurisdictional principles adopted by the U.S. with respect to application of its income tax to international investments and business transactions are considered in Chapters 3 and 4. These provisions are fundamental and cut across all the situations dealt with in subsequent chapters. That is, the basic provisions governing jurisdiction and the source of income are applied alike to U.S. taxpayers investing, working, or carrying on a trade or business abroad, and to foreign individuals and corporations investing, earning income, or carrying on a trade or business in the U.S.

Chapter 5 then turns to the specific application of the income tax to foreign corporations and nonresident alien individuals. The material in this chapter examines the U.S. rules for taxing foreign corporations, foreign partnerships and nonresident aliens on their business and investment income derived from U.S. sources. Procedural aspects in the application of the tax are also considered.

The basic mechanism adopted by the U.S. to alleviate international double taxation on foreign source income derived by U.S. persons is the foreign tax credit. The credit is discussed in detail in Chapter 6. Special rules applicable to foreign source income derived by U.S. persons are also considered in Chapter 6, including the domestic international sales corporation (DISC) provisions, the taxation of income earned abroad by U.S. individuals, and the tax treatment of income derived from U.S. possessions.

From a tax policy standpoint, one of the most controversial aspects of the U.S. international tax structure over the past three decades has been the income tax treatment of foreign corporations controlled by U.S. shareholders. These provisions are contained in 'subpart F' of the Internal Revenue Code. The operation of subpart F and the role it plays in the overall U.S. international income tax structure are discussed in Chapter 7.

Special provisions to insure that the basic structural rules of the U.S. international income tax system are correctly applied are considered in Chapter 8. These provisions may be regarded as anti-tax avoidance mechanisms. Included are the provisions dealing with the formation, reorganization and liquidation of foreign corporations and transfers to foreign entities including partnerships and trusts. The intercompany pricing rules of section 482, which are of importance to multinational corporations, are also discussed. As noted above, the special rules to deal with corporate accumulations used to avoid the tax on shareholders – the accumulated earnings tax and the personal holding company tax – are also dealt with in Chapter 8. The utilization of foreign trusts to accumulate income in a manner designed to avoid U.S. tax on U.S. grantors or beneficiaries of such trusts are likewise examined in the chapter.

Chapter 9 then turns to a consideration of the income tax treaties entered into by the United States to resolve on a bilateral basis particular aspects of the application of the tax systems of the treaty countries to particular transactions, types of income and categories of taxpayers. The basic approach of the U.S. in its income tax treaties is considered. Particular emphasis is then placed on typical treaty provisions that deal with the matters considered in Chapters 3 through 8. The purpose of this discussion is to examine those situations in which U.S. income tax treaty provisions modify the basic rules discussed in the preceding chapters.

Chapter 10 deals with the U.S. wealth transfer tax system. As in the case of the income tax, a very general description is provided of the U.S. wealth transfer tax system. The jurisdictional bases of the tax are considered. Then the three separate transfer taxes – estate tax, gift tax, and generation-skipping tax – are examined in their application to property owned abroad by U.S. citizens and property owned in the U.S. by nonresident alien individuals. The limited number of estate and gift tax treaties entered into by the U.S. is also discussed, again with the focus centering on the situations in which the treaty provisions modify the otherwise applicable wealth transfer tax rules.

The materials in Chapters 3 through 10 discuss the U.S. international tax rules in a traditional manner. That is, the provisions in the Internal Revenue Code dealing with international transactions are discussed purely as tax provisions. In recent years, the U.S. has adopted an analytic technique which regards special tax provisions – those varying from the normal structure of an income tax – as federal expenditure programs effected through the tax system. This analytic technique is known as the 'tax expenditure concept' and is now incorporated into the US. budget process. In Chapter 11, the concept is examined briefly and the tax expenditures in the U.S. international income tax system are identified and quantified.

Chapter 2
The U.S. income tax system: general description

2.1. Scope

The following material outlines the basic principles of the U.S. income tax system as it applies to corporations, to individuals, and to partnerships. These rules apply to all taxpayers, both foreign and domestic. The material provides the necessary background for an understanding of the specifically international rules which are discussed beginning in Chapter 3.

2.2. The corporation income tax

2.2.1. Tax rates

Corporations[1] are subject to graduated tax rates on the first $100,000 of taxable income: 17% on the first $25,000 of taxable income, 20% on the next $25,000, 30% on the next $25,000, and 40% on the next $25,000. A flat 46% rate is imposed on taxable income in excess of $100,000.[2]

1. 'Corporations' include associations, joint-stock companies, and insurance companies. Treas. Reg. sec. 1.7701-2 prescribes rules to determine when an entity such as a trust or partnership will be treated as a 'corporation' for tax purposes. See 2.4. Special tax rules apply to certain categories of corporations such as banks, insurance companies, regulated investment companies (mutual funds), and real estate investment trusts. Those special rules are not discussed.
2. Sec. 11. In addition, a 'minimum tax' is imposed on a corporation's 'tax preference' income. The minimum tax is equal to 15% of a corporation's tax preference income in excess of an exemption equal to the greater of $10,000 or the amount of the corporation's taxes computed under section 11. For corporations, the principal tax preferences are the special 28% rate for capital gains, the excess of accelerated over straight-line depreciation for real estate, and the excess of percentage over cost depletion. See sec. 56-58.

2.2.2. The tax base

The corporate tax rates are applied to *taxable income*. The starting point in computing taxable income is *gross income* (gross receipts minus the cost of goods sold). Unlike many European systems, no distinction is made in general between sources (Quellen) of income. From this figure are subtracted the allowable *deductions*. The difference is taxable income.[3]

2.2.2.1. Gross income

Most receipts constitute gross income to a corporation. The notable exceptions are interest from state and local bonds, life insurance proceeds, contributions to the capital of the corporation, certain cancellation of indebtedness income and gifts or bequests.[4]

2.2.2.2. Deductible expenditures

The deductions allowed in arriving at taxable income fall into two broad classifications:
1. Those deductions that constitute costs of producing income for the year in question, with accounting and economic principles providing the norms for determining the proper amount.
2. Special deductions that are permitted to be taken in amounts in excess of those otherwise allowable for the year under the principles developed in classification one above.

In the first classification, the principal deductions are for the ordinary and necessary expenses incurred in a trade or business (wages, overhead, advertising, etc.), contributions to qualified employee retirement plans, interest, taxes, and depreciation (declining balance method for machinery and equipment; straight-line method for improved real estate).[5] Losses on business assets are deductible when the asset is

3. Sec. 61, 63(a).
4. In the case of non-shareholder contributions to capital and cancellation of indebtedness income, the corporation must, as the corollary to nonrecognition of income, reduce its basis in corporate assets. Sec. 362(c), 1017. As to shareholder contributions to capital, the corporation takes as its basis the basis of the property (other than cash) in the hands of the contributor. Sec. 362.
5. See in general sec. 162-167, 401-415.

disposed of or becomes worthless.[6] Similar rules apply to bad debts.[7] In the case of inventory a loss may be deducted for a decline in value.[8]

Capital expenditures – outlays the benefits of which extend beyond the year the costs are incurred – must be added to the cost basis[9] of the asset to which they relate and recovered over the useful life of the asset either through annual depreciation (or amortization) deductions or, if the useful life is not determinable, upon ultimate sale of the asset (through decreased taxable gain or increased deductible loss). In the second classification are a large number of provisions that permit certain capital expenditures to be recovered for tax purposes more rapidly than would be allowed under the principles applicable to items in classification one. The total amount deductible is not changed; but the timing of the deductions is altered. Various techniques are employed to accelerate the deductions.

In some cases, the entire capital cost may be deducted in the year paid or incurred. Principal examples of such items are intangible drilling and development costs incurred by companies involved in oil and gas or hard mineral exploration and development; reseach and development expenditures; circulation costs incurred by newspapers or other periodicals; certain costs incurred by farmers for fertilizer and clearing land; and certain expenditures to remove architectural barriers to the handicapped and the elderly.[10]

In other situations, capital expenditures are permitted to be amortized and deducted over an arbitrary period – usually five years – even though the useful life of the asset to which the expenditure relates is longer (or indeterminate). Examples of costs that qualify for special five-year amortization include those for trademarks and tradenames, organization of a corporation or partnership, pollution control facilities, rehabilitation of low-income housing, and rehabilitation of certain historic structures.[11] Ten-year amortization is provided for interest and taxes incurred during the construction period of a building.[12] Costs of railroad grading and tunnel bores may be amortized over fifty years.[13]

6. Sec. 165.
7. Sec. 166. In some cases, a deduction for partial worthlessness is allowed.
8. Treas. Reg. sec. 1.471-4.
9. 'Cost basis', as the name implies, is the original cost of the asset, sec. 1012. This figure is adjusted for various items during the time the asset is held, e.g., the cost basis is reduced by depreciation, increased by capital improvements. Sec. 1016. The 'adjusted basis' is then a kind of running balance of the tax attributes of an asset.
10. See, respectively, sec. 263(c), 617, 174, 173, 175, 182, and 190.
11. See, respectively, sec. 177, 248, 709, 169, 167(k), and 191.
12. Sec. 189.
13. Sec. 185.

Another technique adopted by the U.S. to permit more rapid recovery of asset costs than would be available under normal depreciation rules is to provide accelerated rates of depreciation for certain assets. As indicated above, in the U.S. tax system straight-line depreciation is the basic depreciation rate for improved real estate and the declining balance method for machinery and equipment. The permissible accelerated methods for real estate (and the basic methods for tangible personal property, i.e., machines, equipment, etc.) are:

1. The declining balance method, using a rate not in excess of 200% of the rate that would have been used had the depreciation deduction been computed under the straight-line method.
2. The sum-of-the years digits method.
3. Any other method that does not produce annual depreciation allowances in excess of those allowable under 1 during the first two-thirds of the useful life of the asset.[14]

In the case of real estate, however, the 200% declining balance method is available only for new residential rental property. All other new improved real estate is limited to the 150% declining balance method. If used residential real estate is purchased with a remaining useful life of 20 years or more, the maximum allowable depreciation rate is the 125% declining balance method; if the useful life is less than 20 years, only straight-line depreciation may be used.[15] Under the Tax Reform Act of 1976, property constructed on the site of a demolished 'historic structure' is limited to straight-line depreciation; on the other hand, certain costs of rehabilitating a 'certified historic structure' can be depreciated under the 200% or 150% methods, as applicable, even though the structure would otherwise constitute used real estate.[16]

In 1971 another technique for accelerating depreciation deductions was introduced in the form of the 'asset depreciation range' (ADR) system. The ADR system permits a taxpayer to reduce (or increase) the useful life of an asset for depreciation purposes. A 20 percent variation is permitted from 'guidelines' published by the Treasury Department by types of assets. Thus if the guideline life for an asset is ten years, a taxpayer is permitted under the ADR system to elect to treat the useful life of the asset as eight years. The various depreciation rates described above are then applied utilizing the shorter useful life.[17]

Another important deduction concerns intercorporate dividends.

14. Sec. 167(b).

15. Sec. 167(j). Used commercial real estate may be depreciated only on a straight-line basis.

16. Sec. 167(n), (o).

17. Sec. 167(m).

Dividends received by a corporation on stock of another corporation are includible in income. A deduction is then granted equal to 85% of the dividend received (100% if the payor and payee corporation are members of an affiliated group, i.e., subject to 80% common control).[18]

2.2.2.3. Expenditures not deductible

A limited group of expenditures are disallowed as deductions. In some cases, deduction is not permitted because the expenditure incurred often may constitute a disguised dividend. Principal examples include amounts paid as 'excessive compensation'; premiums for life insurance on the life of any officer or shareholder of the corporation if the corporation is the beneficiary under the policy; certain travel and entertainment costs; and corporate gifts in excess of $25 per donee.[19] In addition, losses incurred in sales or exchanges between a corporation and a shareholder owning 50% or more of the stock of the corporation (or between two corporations owned by such a shareholder) are not deductible.

Deductions are also disallowed where the expenditures constitute a cost of producing tax-exempt income (including interest incurred to purchase or carry tax-exempt state and local bonds).[20] In this category too may be placed the limitation on the deductibility of interest incurred in making certain acquisitions of the stock or assets of another corporation (dividends from the acquired corporation being in general non-taxable).[21]

In other instances, deductions are disallowed for nontax policy reasons. Examples include the limitation on deductible charitable contributions to 5% of taxable income; limitations imposed on costs of lobbying; and denial of deduction for the costs of demolishing certain historic structures.[22]

2.2.2.4. Net operating loss carryforward and carryback

If the corporation's deductions for the year exceed its income, the resulting 'net operating loss' can be carried back against the income of the preceding three years and, if not exhausted by the carryback,

18. Sec. 243. Special rules apply for foreign corporations. See note 37.
19. See, respectively, sec. 162(a)(1), 264, 267 and 274.
20. Sec. 265.
21. Sec. 279. The acquisition must involve convertible securities.
22. See, respectively, sec. 170(b)(2), 162(e), 280B.

carried forward for seven years.[23] Special rules apply for foreign expropriation losses.

2.2.3. Credits against tax

The tax rates prescribed in section 11 are applied to taxable income determined under the foregoing rules. Against the resulting tax liability, however, certain credits are allowed. Again, the credits are of two types.

The first group of tax credits is structural in nature. Included are the credits for estimated taxes previously paid and for taxes paid to other countries.[24]

In the second group are credits provided to encourage or subsidize particular activities. The most important of these is the investment tax credit for the costs of acquiring U.S. depreciable tangible property used in a trade or business. The credit is 10% of the cost of a qualified asset. For most corporations, the amount of the allowable credit is limited to $25,000 of U.S. income tax liability plus 90% of the corporation's U.S. income tax liability in excess of $25,000. Allowable credits in excess of the limits may be carried back three years and forward seven years.[25] The investment tax credit has become a primary fiscal tool by which the U.S. government seeks to stimulate or slow down capital investment activity. As a result, frequent changes in the credit have become commonplace and this pattern appears likely to continue.

Tax credits of lesser importance are provided to corporations that employ workers who are members of specified 'target' groups or who are enrolled in government sponsored work incentive programs.[26] The

23. Sec. 172. At the taxpayer's election, product liability losses may be carried back for a ten year period in lieu of the normal carryback and carryover periods described in the text. Sec. 172(b)(1) (H), (i).

24. Sec. 6315, 33. Estimated tax payments do not technically give rise to a tax credit. They are treated as payments 'on account of' final income tax liability. The effect is the same as a tax credit.

25. See sec. 38, 46-48. The Revenue Act of 1978 increased the former 50% limitation to 90% over a four year period, with the applicable limitations being 60% in 1979, 70% in 1980, 80% in 1981 and 90% in 1982 and thereafter. The limitations temporarily do not apply to railroads, airlines, and public utilities.

26. Sec. 40, 44B, 50A-53. In general, the maximum credit is $3,000 per employee for the first year of employment and $1,500 for the second year. The credit for wages paid to welfare recipients is permanent; the credit for employing members of 'targeted' groups is scheduled to expire after 1981. The normal deduction for wages must be reduced by the amount of the jobs tax credit claimed by a taxpayer. Sec. 280C. The result of this reduction is the same as if the amount of the tax credit constituted taxable income.

avowed purpose of these tax credits is to encourage employers to employ individuals who are members of groups which have experienced chronic unemployment or who have been on state or federal welfare rolls. In 1978 and 1980, temporary additional tax credits were provided for investments in qualified energy conservation or conversion property or in qualified alternative energy property, such as solar or wind energy devices.[27]

2.2.4. Capital gains and losses

Sales or exchanges of 'capital assets' by corporations qualify for a special alternative tax rate of 28% of the gain if the asset has been held for one year or more.[28] The alternative rate is optional and is therefore availed of by corporations that otherwise would pay a 46% rate on the gain. If the gain would otherwise be taxable only at a 17% or 20% rate, those regular rates are used rather than the 28% alternative rate. 'Capital' losses may be deducted only against capital gains. If capital losses exceed capital gains, in general the excess can be carried back three years and forward five years.[29]

'Capital assets' include tangible and intangible assets owned by a corporation other than (1) inventory, (2) property held primarily for sale to customers in the ordinary course of business, (3) copyrights, and (4) accounts receivable.[30]

Depreciable property is not a capital asset under the basic definition. Section 1231, however, provides that if the total transactions for the year concerning such property result in a net gain, that gain is treated as a capital gain. If a net loss is produced, an ordinary loss deduction results.

However, gain that would otherwise qualify as capital gain under section 1231 may be treated as ordinary income if one of the various 'recapture' provisions is applicable. Thus, under section 1245, the gain on the sale of depreciable personal property (e.g., machinery and equipment) is taxed as ordinary income to the extent of depreciation previously taken with respect to the property. That is, despite section 1231, the prior depreciation deductions are recognized as ordinary income upon sale at a gain (because the sale at a gain has demonstrated that the taxpayer's prior depreciation deduction exceeded economic

27. Sec. 46(a), 48(l). The energy tax credits are scheduled to expire after 1985.
28. Sec. 1201(a), 1223.
29. Sec. 1211, 1212.
30. Sec. 1221.

depreciation). Similar recapture rules apply to gain on the sale of depreciable real estate, oil and gas interests as to which the deduction for intangible drilling and development costs has been taken, and farm land with respect to which certain special deductions or exclusions have been claimed.[31]

Certain sales or exchanges of capital assets are tax-free. For example, no tax is imposed on gain realized on exchanges of like-kind property (involving properties other than corporate stock, notes, etc.); gain realized on an involuntary conversion of property (e.g., through condemnation by the government, fire, etc.) if the proceeds received are reinvested in similar property; and gain realized on the transfer by a corporation of its own stock in exchange for property or services.[32] In each case, the corollary of non-recognition of gain is that the property acquired takes the same tax basis as that of the property transferred (the so-called 'substituted basis' rule). As a result, the 'tax-free' exchanges are actually tax-deferred exchanges, since the gain will be subsequently realized on the ultimate disposition of the property acquired.

2.2.5. Transactions between corporations and shareholders

Under U.S. tax rules, a corporation is an entity separate and distinct from its shareholders. As a result, corporate earnings are taxed to the corporation; distributions from the corporation are taxed to the individual shareholders.

The *formation* of a corporation is generally accomplished tax-free. That is, the transfer of property to a corporation results in no current tax to the shareholders if the transferor-shareholders are in control (80%) of the corporation immediately after the transfer. The corporation realizes no gain on the issuance of its stock. The shareholders have a tax basis in their stock equal to the aggregate bases of the property transferred to the corporation.[33]

Distributions of cash or property by a corporation to its shareholders constitute taxable dividends to the shareholders to the extent of the corporation's earnings and profits (current and accumulated).[34] In general terms, 'earnings and profits' (a technical tax concept) correspond closely to the accounting concept of 'earned surplus' of a

31. Sec. 1250, 1254, 1252 and 1255.
32. Sec. 1031, 1033.
33. Sec. 351, 358, 362, 1032.
34. Sec. 316.

corporation.[35] In the case of an *individual* shareholder, the amount of the dividend is the cash or fair market value of the property distributed. If the distribution is not out of earnings and profits, then the individual shareholder reduces basis in his stock by the amount of the dividend and, if the distribution is in excess of that basis, such excess is taxed as capital gain income. A $100 dividend exclusion is available for individual recipients of corporate dividends.[36] The same rules apply to dividends received by *corporate* shareholders, except that a distribution of property constitutes a dividend only to the extent of the lesser of the fair market value of the property or the distributing corporation's adjusted basis in the property increased by the amount of any gain recognized to the distributing corporation on the distribution. A dividends received deduction of either 85 percent or 100 percent of the dividend received is provided, as noted above.[37]

As to the distributing corporation, a dividend distribution reduces its earnings and profits account by the amount of the dividend. Thus, in the case of dividend distributions of property other than cash to a corporate shareholder, the reduction in the earnings and profits account is only to the extent of the distributing corporation's adjusted basis in the property (or fair market value if less). In general, a corporation that distributes appreciated property does not realize gain on that distribution, and hence earnings and profits are reduced only by the basis of the property distributed. The Code does, in the case of certain types of property, require that the corporation include the amount of potential gain on the distributed property in income and, correspondingly, the earnings and profits account is then reduced by the full fair market value of the property distributed.[38]

In most cases, a distribution of the corporation's own stock (a 'stock dividend') is nontaxable to the shareholder. However, in certain circumstances, the receipt of a stock dividend does constitute ordinary income to the shareholder.[39]

A *redemption* of stock (i.e., a purchase by the corporation of its own stock from a shareholder) results in capital gain to the redeemed shareholder provided that the distribution by the corporation is not essential-

35. Sec. 312.

36. Sec. 301(a), (c); 116. For the period 1981-1982, a $200 exclusion ($400 for married couples filing joint returns) is provided for dividend and interest income.

37. Sec. 301(b), 243. Special rules apply for foreign corporations. See Chapter 5, footnote 58.

38. Sec. 311, 312.

39. Sec. 305. See also sec. 306 as to the treatment of preferred stock distributed by a corporation.

ly equivalent to a dividend. Rules are provided for determining whether a particular distribution falls on the ordinary dividend or on the capital gain side of the line. In general, the transfer of appreciated property by a corporation to redeem its own stock will give rise to recognition of gain on the appreciation by the distributing corporation.[40]

Distributions in *partial* or *complete liquidation* of a corporation also are treated as *exchanges* which qualify for capital gains treatment. Again, in general, a corporation does not recognize gain on the distribution of appreciated property in liquidation. The double tax that otherwise would result on the liquidation of a corporation which sold its assets and distributed the proceeds to its shareholders is eliminated if the transaction meets certain formal requirements; only a single capital gain tax is imposed on the shareholder in the liquidation. The liquidation of an 80 percent owned subsidiary is tax-free to the corporate parent; correspondingly, the parent takes a carryover basis in the assets acquired in the liquidation. An exception to this rule, however, is provided where the parent corporation has acquired the stock of a subsidiary and liquidates the acquired corporation within a two-year period; in such a case, the parent may step-up the basis in the acquired assets to reflect the purchase price paid for the stock.[41]

To insure that the corporate form is not utilized to avoid high individual income tax rates, the Code imposes two penalty taxes on the failure to distribute dividends on a current basis. A special 'accumulated earnings tax' is imposed on accumulations of earnings in excess of the reasonable needs of the business if the principal purpose of the accumulation is tax avoidance. Where the corporation's assets consist of passive investments, the personal holding company tax imposes a special 70 percent tax on undistributed income of the corporation.[42]

The Code permits a variety of corporate *reorganizations* to be effected on a tax-free basis. In general, these sections are designed to permit business transactions involving certain corporate readjustments to be consummated without a tax being incurred by the participating corporations or their shareholders at the time of the transaction. The theory of these provisions is that the readjustments, while they may produce changes in the structure of a business enterprise, do not involve such fundamental changes in the nature or character of the

40. Sec. 302, 311(d). See also sec. 304 for rules on the treatment of purchases by one corporation of stock in a second corporation that is controlled by the same shareholders who control the purchasing corporation.

41. Sec. 331-337.

42. Sec. 531-537; 541-547. The accumulated earnings tax is discussed in 8.4.1. and the personal holding company tax in 8.4.2.

relation of the owners of the enterprise to the enterprise as to warrant a tax on the accrued gain or allowance of a loss deduction. The nonrecognition provisions cover a wide range of transactions ranging from statutory mergers to exchanges of stock for stock, stock for assets, recapitalizations of a single corporation, or a mere change in the form or name of the corporation.

In a qualifying reorganization, neither the shareholders of the corporations involved nor the corporations themselves recognize any gain or loss. As a corollary, special basis rules are required to reflect the nonrecognition of gain. In general, the shareholders substitute the basis in their old stock as the basis in the new stock. At the corporate level, assets acquired in a reorganization carry over the same basis to the acquiring corporation as they had in the hands of the transferring corporation. In certain types of reorganizations, the receipt of cash or other property is permitted in addition to the receipt of stock in the acquiring corporation. In such cases, the value of the cash or other property is taxed at the time of the reorganization, the gain generally qualifying for capital gain rates.[43]

Special rules are also provided to permit certain tax-free divisions of existing corporations. But these rules are in general quite restrictive since corporate divisions present the possibility that cash and other liquid assets may be distributed to shareholders at capital gain rates rather than at ordinary income rates applicable to dividends.[44]

In qualifying reorganizations, special rules are provided to carry over the corporate attributes of the transferring corporation, such as its earnings and profits account, net operating loss carryovers, etc.[45]

The reorganization provisions are discussed in greater detail at 8.1.1. where reorganizations involving U.S. and foreign corporations are considered.

Consolidated returns may be filed by corporate groups where the parent corporation owns at least 80 percent of the stock of its subsidiary corporations. Under the consolidated return rules, income and deductions of the various members of the group are consolidated and the net income of the group is subject to tax. Dividends within the corporate group are not taxable. The Regulations provide detailed rules for the tax treatment of inter-company transactions. A foreign corporation in general may not be a member of a consolidated return group and,

43. See sec. 354, 356-368.

44. Sec. 355.

45. Sec. 381. Limitations on the availability of net operating loss carryovers are imposed by sec. 269, 382, 383.

therefore the significance of the consolidated return rules is limited to domestic corporate groups.[46]

A number of other aspects of domestic corporate taxation are discussed in Chapter 8.

2.3. The individual income tax

2.3.1. Tax rates

Individuals are subject to tax rates ranging from 14 to 70 percent of taxable income. Separate rate schedules are provided for married couples filing joint returns, married couples filing separate returns, heads of households, and single persons. In general, single person tax rates range from 5 to 40 percent higher than those applicable to the same brackets of income for married persons filing joint returns. Head of household rates (generally involved where a single parent maintains a household with dependent children) are about halfway between joint return rates and single person rates.[47]

A special 50 percent maximum marginal rate of tax applies to earned income. Under this provision, a taxpayer's earned income (i.e., wages, professional income, etc.) cannot in general be taxed at a rate higher than 50 percent, although other income received by the taxpayer, such

46. See Treas. Reg. sec. 1. 1502. However, a foreign taxpayer may own the stock of a U.S. parent with U.S. subsidiaries and the U.S. group may file a consolidated return.
47. Sec. 1. In addition, individuals are subject to two separate 'minimum taxes'. Sec. 55-58. As in the case of corporations, individuals are subject to an 'add on' minimum tax equal to 15% of 'tax preference' income less the greater of $10,000 or one-half of the individual's regular tax liability computed under section 1. The most important of the tax preference items subject to the 'add on' minimum tax are the excess of accelerated over straight-line depreciation and the excess of percentage over cost depletion. As its name implies, the 'add on' minimum tax is simply added to the taxpayer's regular tax liability. The Revenue Act of 1978 provided an 'alternative' minimum tax for individuals. The alternative minimum tax is in general computed by adding back to the taxpayer's regularly computed taxable income the sum of the excluded portion of capital gains (discussed below) and 'excess itemized deductions'. The result is 'alternative minimum taxable income' to which three rates of 10%, 20%, and 25% are applied (after substracting a $20,000 exemption). The resulting 'alternative minimum tax liability' is then compared to the sum of the taxpayer's regular tax plus 'add on' minimum tax, and the taxpayer must pay the greater of the two figures. In general, the alternative minimum tax will apply only to taxpayers with both large amounts of capital gain income and very large itemized personal deductions.

as dividends, interest, and rents, may be subject to tax up to the general maximum 70 percent rate.[48]

2.3.2. The tax base

The individual tax rates are applied to *taxable income*. The starting point in computing taxable income is *gross income* (gross receipts minus the cost of goods sold). From this figure are first subtracted allowable *business deductions* to arrive at *adjusted gross income*. From adjusted gross income are then subtracted certain *personal deductions*. The taxpayer is then allowed a deduction for *personal exemptions* to arrive at the final figure for taxable income.

2.3.2.1. Gross income

Gross income includes income 'from whatever source derived'.[49] However, certain statutory exceptions are provided. The principal exclusions are interest on state and local bonds; certain fringe benefits of employees; certain prizes and awards; the gain on property transferred by gift or bequest; receipts of gifts or bequests; compensation for injuries or sickness; income from the discharge of indebtedness (if a corresponding reduction in basis is made); scholarships and fellowship grants; and all or part of the gain on the sale or exchange of residences by individuals over age 55.[50] By administrative action, social security benefits and benefits paid under other programs to further social welfare objectives of the government are also excluded from gross income.

2.3.2.2. Deductible expenditures – Business

The deductions allowed to an individual from gross income in arriving

48. Sec. 1348. The amount of earned income that qualifies for the maximum 50% rate is reduced (and hence the income is taxed at rates in excess of 50%) by one dollar for each one dollar of 'tax preference' income received by the individual. 'Tax preferences' are the same items that are subject to the minimum tax (see note 47, above), except that the excluded portion of capital gains is not an item of tax preference for purposes of the maximum tax.
49. Sec. 61.
50. The provisions excluding receipts from gross income appear generally in sec. 71-127.

at adjusted gross income are the same as those allowed to corporations described in 2.2.2.2., above.

In addition to the ordinary and necessary expenses of a trade or business, an individual is allowed as a deduction all ordinary and necessary expenses paid or incurred for the production or collection of income, and for the management, conservation, or maintenance of property held for the production of income.[51]

2.3.2.3. Expenditures not deductible

The group of expenditures that are disallowed as deductions, described in 2.2.2.3. above, are in general also disallowed as to individuals. In addition, individuals are denied deductions for personal, living, or family expenses except as provided in 2.3.2.4. below. Limitations are imposed on the deduction of interest by individuals paid to purchase or carry investments (the deduction being limited to net investment income plus $10,000); on interest to maintain certain life insurance contracts; and on losses, expenses and interest incurred in transactions with related taxpayers, such as members of the same family or controlled corporations.[52]

2.3.2.4. Deductible expenditures – Personal

Certain deductions are permitted even though they do not represent costs of producing income.

The expenses which are deductible regardless of the nature of the expenditure – the 'itemized personal deductions' – include interest, certain state, local and foreign taxes, casualty losses, charitable contributions, medical expenses, and certain contributions to qualified individual retirement plans. In several instances, limitations are imposed on the deductible amounts.[53]

Most taxpayers do not itemize the above personal deductions by virtue of a 'standard deduction' that is built into the rate schedules as a bracket of income to which a zero rate is applied. For married taxpayers filing a joint return, the zero bracket amount is $3,400 ($1,700 for married persons filing separate returns) and $2,300 for single persons. If

51. Sec. 162, 212.
52. See sec. 263, 163(d), 264, 267, and the provisions cited in note 19, above.
53. See sec. 163, 164, 165(c), 170, 213, 219-220.

a taxpayer's itemized personal deductions described above exceed the applicable zero bracket amount, he may subtract the excess from adjusted gross income. If the itemized personal deductions are less than the zero bracket amount, the zero bracket amount constitutes, in effect, the taxpayer's 'standard deduction' for personal expenditures.[54] The zero bracket amount, when added to the personal exemptions discussed below, insures that persons with incomes below governmentally established poverty levels of income will not incur any income tax liability.

Special rules are provided for a category of 'mixed' business-personal expenditures. These expenditures involve activities in which there is a significant personal element, but as to which there is also a business element. The personal element should not be deductible; the business element should be deductible. Generally speaking, the Code provides arbitrary rules for determining the extent of deductibility (and hence the business-relatedness) of these types of expenses. Examples of mixed business-personal expenditures, which are partly deductible, include moving expenses, travel and entertainment expenses, work clothing, offices maintained in a personal residence, vacation homes which are rented out for part of the year, and so-called 'hobby' situations where it is unclear whether the taxpayer is actually engaged in the activity to make a profit.[55] The amounts that are allowed as deductions under these rules generally are subtracted from adjusted gross income to arrive at taxable income.

After the foregoing deductions have been subtracted from adjusted gross income, the taxpayer is then entitled to one $1,000 deduction for himself, his spouse and each dependent. These deductions are the so-called *personal exemptions*.[56]

With the subtraction of the personal deductions from adjusted gross income, the individual taxpayer has arrived at taxable income.[57]

54. Sec. 3, 63. The zero bracket concept was introduced in The Tax Reduction and Simplification Act of 1977. It replaced the prior 'general standard deduction' (16% of adjusted gross income or $2,800 for joint returns) and the 'minimum standard deduction' ($2,100 for joint returns).

55. See sec. 217, 274, 280A, 183.

56. Sec. 151-152.

57. As a result of the 1977 legislation, most taxpayers simply determine their tax from a table after arriving at adjusted gross income, the tables having built in the personal exemptions. Certain taxpayers, however, including nonresident alien individuals, must itemize personal deductions and follow a special procedure to arrive at taxable income. Sec. 63(e).

2.3.3. CREDITS AGAINST TAX

The tax rates described in section 1 of the Code all apply to taxable income determined under the foregoing rules. Against the resulting tax liability, however, certain credits against tax are allowed. As in the case of corporations, the credits are of two types.

The first group of tax credits are structural in nature and include the credits for taxes withheld by the individual's employer, estimated taxes previously paid, and income taxes paid to other countries.[58]

In the second group are credits provided to encourage or subsidize particular activities. These include the investment tax credit, the work incentive tax credits, and the targeted jobs tax credit discussed in 2.2.3., above. In addition tax credits are allowed to individuals for costs of child care incurred to enable the taxpayer to work outside the home and for certain political contributions.[59] A temporary tax credit for investment in energy conservation equipment or renewable energy sources (such as wind or solar equipment) is provided to individuals who install such equipment in their personal residences.[60] An earned income credit is granted to individuals in an amount equal to 10 percent of the earned income of the taxpayer up to $5,000. The credit is gradually phased out at income levels between $6,000 and $10,000. The earned income credit is *refundable*, so that if the amount of the credit exceeds the individual's tax liability, a refund check is issued by the Treasury.[61] Finally, a tax credit for the elderly is provided. In general, the purpose of the tax credit for the elderly is to exempt from tax an amount of retirement income that approximates the exclusion from income that is provided for social security benefits.[62]

2.3.4. CAPITAL GAINS AND LOSSES

A special rate of tax is provided for gains realized on the sale or exchange of a 'capital asset' if the individual has held the asset for one year or more. In general, the preferential treatment is provided by means of a deduction equal to 60 percent of the realized gain. In effect,

58. Sec. 31, 6315 (see note 24, above), 33.
59. Sec. 44A, 41.
60. Sec. 44C. The credit equals 15% of energy conservation expenditures up to $2,000; in the case of renewable energy source equipment, the credit is 30% of the first $2,000 and 20% of the next $8,000 of expenditures. The credits are due to expire after 1985.
61. Sec. 43.
62. Sec. 37.

this means that an individual pays tax on his capital gain income at 40 percent of the rates applicable to this other income.[63]

The capital gain rules described in section 2.2.4. above apply equally to individuals, except that capital losses in excess of capital gains may not be carried back, but may be carried forward indefinitely.

2.3.5. Trusts and estates

In very general terms, trusts and estates are treated as conduits for tax purposes. As a result, each individual beneficiary includes his share of estate or trust income in his individual tax return when it is distributed to him. The character of the income and deductions, and any limits imposed thereon, are generally determined and applied by the individual beneficiary in his own individual income tax return.[64] The rules governing the taxation of estates and trusts are, however, quite complex, especially in the case where all income is not distributed annually. The treatment of trusts, especially in the international context, is described in more detail in 8.5.

2.4. Partnerships

Under U.S. tax principles, the partnership is not treated as a separate taxpaying entity. Partnership income and deductions 'flow through' to the individual partners, whether natural persons or juridical entities, and are taxed to them in accordance with the principles outlined in the preceding sections. The partnership itself is treated as an accounting entity for purposes of computing the partnership's net income or loss which is then apportioned to its partners. Accordingly, the partnership must file a tax return which fundamentally operates as an information return with respect to the items of partnership income and deduction.

In general, income and deductions realized at the partnership level retain their tax character when passed through to the partners.[65] Thus, for example, if the partnership realizes an item of tax exempt income,

63. Sec. 1201-1202. As a result, the maximum rate of tax an individual can incur on capital gain income is 28% (40% × 70%). The excluded 60% of capital gain is treated as an item of tax preference for purposes of the 'alternative minimum tax' described in note 47, above. The top rate under the alternative minimum tax is 25%.

64. Rules governing estates and trusts are set forth in sec. 641-678; those applicable to partnerships are contained in sec. 701-761.

65. Sec. 702(b).

that income remains tax exempt in the hands of the partner. Since the partnership earnings are taxed to the partners whether distributed or not, a partnership distribution to a partner ordinarily does not generate any further tax to the partner when received.[66]

The U.S. tax rules applicable to partnerships treat the partnership in some cases as simply an aggregate of the individual partners while for other purposes the partnership is treated as a separate entity, independent of its individual members. For example, certain tax elections are made by the partnership as an entity rather than by the individual partners.[67] On the other hand, some limitations on deductions are applied to the individual partners rather than to the partnership itself, treating the partnership as an aggregate of the partners involved.[68]

Detailed Regulations are provided for the classification of organizations as partnerships.[69] The status of the organization as a partnership for federal tax purposes is determined by applying federal standards and the State or foreign law characterization of the organization is not controlling. The most difficult classification issues involve limited partnerships which can be structured to have many of the characteristics of corporations. If a limited partnership is found to have too much 'corporate resemblance' it will be treated as a corporation for federal tax purposes and corporation rather than partnership principles will determine its tax treatment.[70]

2.5. Accounting aspects

Income and deductions are accounted for in the U.S. tax system under a special set of tax accounting rules. While there are many instances in which tax and financial accounting methods correspond, the tax accounting principles nonetheless represent a separate body of rules. There is no general *Maßgeblichkeitsprinzip*.

66. This is not true if the total of partnership distributions to the partner exceeds the partner's share of partnership income and the partner's original investment in the partnership. In such cases gain may be recognized by the partner.
67. See, e.g., sec. 754.
68. See Treas. Reg. sec. 1.702-1(a)(8)(iii).
69. Treas. Reg. sec. 301.7701-1 to 5.
70. In general, the Regulations focus on four factors in distinguishing partnerships from corporations: (1) limited liability; (2) continuity of life; (3) free transferability of interests; (4) centralization of management. If an organization has more than two of these so-called 'corporate characteristics', it will be treated as a corporation for federal tax purposes. See also 5.6.1.

There are two general methods of accounting for income and deductions: the cash method and the accrual method. Under the *cash method* an item of income is recognized in the year in which cash (or its equivalent) is received and an item is deductible in the year in which it is paid. The expense must constitute a currently deductible expense rather than a capital expenditure. Under the *accrual method* of accounting, the taxpayer includes items of income in the year in which a right to the payment arises and subtracts deductions in the year in which an expense is incurred. The accrual method of accounting is used by most business operations and is required if the business operates with an inventory.[71] While the accrual method corresponds in general outline to financial accounting there are important differences. An overriding principle in the tax accounting area is that the accounting method chosen must 'clearly reflect income'.[72] Whatever the general accounting method, there are a number of rules covering specific situations. For example, whether on the cash or accrual method, the taxpayer may account for certain sales of assets under the so-called 'installment sale' method whereby the purchase payment received each year on the sale of an asset is treated in part as return of investment and in part as income.[73] Special rules also apply for the accounting of transactions such as long-term construction contracts.[74]

Income must be accounted for on an annual basis, usually the calendar year, though the taxpayer is free to choose a fiscal year differing from the calendar year. By and large, the annual accounting concept is followed quite rigorously and events which change the tax treatment of an item in a subsequent year are reflected in that year rather than through a recomputation of the tax liability for the earlier year. Here too, however, there are a number of exceptions which treat integrated transactions on a unified basis even where they take place over several tax years.[75]

Income must be calculated and the tax paid in U.S. dollars.[76] This is true both for U.S. taxpayers taxable on their worldwide income and foreign taxpayers taxable on income from U.S. sources. The taxpayer may elect among a variety of methods for accounting for transactions which take place in foreign currency. Some of these methods take into account currently gain or loss attributable to currency fluctuation,

71. Treas. Reg. sec. 1.446-1(c)(ii).
72. Sec. 446(b).
73. Sec. 453, 453A and 453B.
74. Treas. Reg. sec. 1.451-3.
75. See, e.g., sec. 1341.
76. Sec. 6316.

while others defer the recognition of the exchange rate gain or loss until the underlying economic transaction is completed.

2.6. Statute of limitations

In general, a three year statute of limitation applies to tax matters.[77] A special six year period applies if the taxpayer omits from gross income an amount in excess of 25 percent of the income shown on the return and the omitted amount is not disclosed in the return.[78] There is no time limit if a return is not filed or if the return is false or fraudulent. The taxpayer likewise has three years from the time the return was filed or two years from the time the tax was paid, whichever is later, to file a claim for refund.[79] Tax deficiencies carry an interest rate geared to the prevailing interest level as do successful refund claims.

There are a variety of civil and criminal penalties for tax fraud and tax evasion.[80]

77. Sec. 6501(a).
78. Sec. 6501(e).
79. Sec. 6511(a).
80. See, e.g., sec. 6653(b).

Chapter 3
Jurisdictional principles

As noted in Chapter 2, section 1 of the Internal Revenue Code imposes a tax on the 'taxable income' of every individual. Taxable income in turn is derived from the section 61 definition of gross income, i.e., 'all income from whatever source derived'. The term 'source' embraces within its meaning both the type of income derived and the geographical location within which the income is produced. As a result, in the first instance, the literal scope of the United States income tax on *individuals* is to tax all individuals in the world on their worldwide income! However, subsequent provisions make it clear that the assertion of worldwide taxing jurisdiction is only meant to include individuals who are U.S. citizens or residents. For these taxpayers, U.S. taxing jurisdiction is based on their personal relationship or status with respect to the U.S.; the geographic source of their income is irrelevant. Trusts and estates, whose taxation in very general terms approximates that of individuals, are likewise subject to U.S. worldwide taxing jurisdiction if they are 'domestic' entities, i.e., if they have substantial contacts with the U.S.[1]

The remaining class of potential taxpayers, nonresident aliens and foreign trusts and estates, are also subject to U.S. tax. For such taxpayers, however, the U.S. tax jurisdiction is based on the *geographic source* of the taxpayer's income. These taxpayers are in general only subject to tax on income from sources within the U.S. Their business income from U.S. sources is taxed in much the same way as that of a U.S. citizen or resident, while their investment income is subject to a special set of tax rules.

As respects *corporations*, the assertion of U.S. worldwide tax juris-

1. Some of the relevant factors in determining whether an estate or trust is 'domestic' or 'foreign' include the residence of the trustee or executor, the domicile of the decedent, the country under whose laws the trust or estate is created, and the location of the assets. See, e.g., Rev. Rul. 60-181, 1960-1 Cum. Bull. 257, which classified a trust as a U.S. resident based on its investment activities in the U.S.

diction is based solely on the place of incorporation. A corporation incorporated in the U.S. is subject to tax on its worldwide income just as are U.S. citizens and residents. Correspondingly, a corporation incorporated under the laws of some other country is treated for U.S. tax purposes as a foreign corporation. Foreign corporations, like non-resident alien individuals, are subject to U.S. tax on the basis of the *U.S. source* of their income.

While the U.S. asserts taxing jurisdiction over the foreign income of its citizens and residents, it alleviates the so-called 'international double taxation', which may arise when another country also attempts to tax a portion of that income, through a foreign tax credit. The credit is available to U.S. citizens and residents and domestic corporations who pay taxes on foreign income to other countries. In addition, an indirect credit is provided to U.S. domestic corporations which receive dividend income from foreign corporations in which they own at least 10% of the voting stock.

The U.S. in some situations also looks to the nationality or residence of a foreign corporation's shareholders in determining the appropriate pattern of taxation. In the case of *controlled foreign corporations* (that is a foreign corporation more than 50 percent of whose voting stock is owned by U.S. individuals or corporations), the normal U.S. jurisdictional rules, which would allow deferral of U.S. tax on the foreign income earned by a foreign corporation until its distribution to its U.S. shareholders, are modified for certain types of undistributed income of the foreign corporation. In such cases, the U.S. shareholders of the 'controlled foreign corporation' are subject to tax on their allocable share of the described income, even though it is not distributed as a dividend to the U.S. shareholders.[2] Special treatment is also provided for 'foreign personal holding companies', again with the object of currently taxing to the U.S. shareholders the undistributed taxable income of the foreign corporation.

A number of provisions are intended to prevent avoidance of U.S. tax jurisdiction, for example, section 482 (dealing with allocation of income and deductions among enterprises controlled or owned by the same interests in order clearly to reflect income) and section 367

2. In one sense the controlled foreign corporations provisions introduce a different test to determine whether a corporation is a 'domestic' corporation, i.e., the place of incorporation test gives way to one focusing on the residence or nationality of the shareholders. However, this generalization is not completely accurate, since it is the *U.S. shareholder* and not the corporate entity which is subject to U.S. tax. Some of the policy considerations behind the controlled foreign corporation provisions are considered in 7.9.

(requiring the approval of the Secretary of the Treasury or his delegate when a U.S. person enters into a tax-free organization, reorganization or liquidation involving a foreign corporation).

The U.S. has entered into a number of bilateral tax treaties which modify the above general pattern of United States income taxation of international transactions.

The foregoing discussion describes in the broadest terms the general pattern of U.S. rules dealing with foreign income and foreign taxpayers. That general description masks technical provisions that are extraordinarily complex in interpretation and operation. This, of course, is only to be expected since international transactions themselves – especially as conducted by multinational corporations – are necessarily complex. In the following Chapters, we turn to an analysis of the most important of these provisions and the technical problems that have arisen in implementing them, viewed both from the standpoint of the tax administrator and from the standpoint of taxpayers who must live and operate within those rules.

Chapter 4
Source rules

4.1. General

The Code in sections 861–864 and the Regulations issued thereunder set forth with considerable specificity the rules for determining the source of income for U.S. tax purposes. The exclusive function of these rules is to establish whether income is derived from sources within the United States ('U.S. source income') or from sources without the United States ('foreign source income'). Other sections of the Code dictate the operative results that flow from the source determination.

The two most important substantive provisions that depend on the source rules are: (1) the tax treatment of nonresident aliens and foreign corporations, which in general are taxed only on U.S. source income; and (2) the limitations applicable to the foreign tax credit which are fixed by the amount of the taxpayer's foreign source income, determined under U.S. source rules. In addition, the applicability of a number of other Code provisions depends on whether income is determined to be from U.S. or foreign sources.

4.2. Application of source rules to specific items of gross income

Sections 861 and 862 set forth rules for determining the source of specified types of *gross income*.[1] Section 863 then provides source rules for items of income that are not listed in sections 861 and 862.

1. The reader should be aware that lurking behind the seemingly straightforward list of income items set forth in 4.2.1. through 4.2.8. are a host of difficult definitional problems. For example, the term 'interest' includes not only direct interest paid but also imputed interest under section 483 and original issue discount under section 1232. 'Dividend' is a term of art in U.S. tax law being defined in sections 301 and 316. Since Treas. Reg. sec. 1.861-3(a)(1) refers to section 316, it is possible for some distributions to be treated as dividends for corporate law purposes, but still not constitute 'dividends' for source rule →

4.2.1. Interest

In general, interest received on an obligation issued by any U.S. debtor constitutes U.S. source income.

There are, however, several exceptions to this general rule:

First, interest on bank deposits in U.S. banks received by a non-resident alien or foreign corporation is foreign source income.[2]

Second, if less than 20% of the U.S. obligor's gross income from all sources is derived from U.S. sources, the interest is foreign source income. The determination is made by considering the ratio of the U.S. source income to the total income of the obligor for the three years preceding the year in which the interest was paid. If the obligor's U.S. gross income is less than 20% of gross income from all sources, then all the interest is foreign source income; conversely if the 20% limit is exceeded, all the interest is U.S. source income.

Third, interest received from a foreign corporation engaged in a trade or business in the U.S. is foreign source income if less than 50% of its gross income from all sources was, for the three years preceding the year of payment, 'effectively connected' with the conduct of a trade or business in the U.S. (See 5.3. for the rules applicable to determine whether income is effectively connected with the conduct of a trade or business in the U.S.). If this test is met none of the interest is U.S. source income. If more than 50% of the obligor's gross income from all sources was effectively connected with the conduct of a trade or business in the U.S., then a portion of the interest constitutes U.S. source income. In the latter situation, the interest income from U.S. sources is determined by applying to the interest a ratio, the numerator of which is the obligor's 'effectively connected' income for the three preceding years and the denominator of which is the obligor's gross income from all sources for the same period. For example, if a foreign

→

purposes; conversely, a distribution which is treated as a dividend under section 316 (even though in corporate law terms it is not a dividend) is a dividend for source rule purposes. There is also an uncertain and much litigated line in U.S. tax jurisprudence between compensation for personal services and receipts from royalty income or the sale of property. The classification of the receipt under U.S. tax principles will affect whether the source rules described in paragraphs 4.2.3., 4.2.4., or 4.2.6. will be applicable. Detailed analysis of these intricacies is beyond the scope of this work.

2. The exception only applies to bank interest which is not 'effectively connected'. See 5.3. The exception for interest on deposits with persons carrying on a banking business was scheduled to expire on December 31, 1976. However, the Tax Reform Act of 1976 made the exemption permanent. In addition, the Senate Finance Committee had recommended that the exception be extended to apply to interest on all U.S. debt obligations. The full Senate, however, rejected this proposed change.

corporation for the three preceding years derived $300 of gross income from all sources and $200 of the income was effectively connected with the conduct of a U.S. trade or business, then 2/3 of the interest paid in the current year would be U.S. source income.

Miscellaneous exceptions to the general rule that interest from a U.S. obligor constitutes U.S. source income are provided for foreign central banks, foreign banking branches of U.S. corporations and partnerships, and certain obligations subject to the now expired interest equalization tax.

4.2.2. Dividends

All dividends from U.S. corporations constitute U.S. source income if 20% or more of the corporation's gross income from all sources was, for the three years preceding the year of declaration of the dividend, derived from sources within the U.S. If the 20% test is not met none of the dividends constitute U.S. source income.[3]

Dividends paid by a foreign corporation conducting a trade or business in the U.S. constitute U.S. source income only if 50% or more of the corporation's gross income from all sources was, for the preceding three years, effectively connected with the conduct of a trade or business in the U.S. If the 50% limit is exceeded, only a portion of the dividend is U.S. source income, determined by applying the ratio described in 4.2.1.

4.2.3. Personal service income

In general, U.S. source income includes all income derived from personal services performed in the U.S., regardless of the residence of the payor, where the contract was entered into, or where the payment was made.[4]

3. If two companies merge, their respective U.S. and total gross incomes for the preceding three years must be combined for purposes of applying the 20% test applicable to interest and dividends. Rev. Rul. 76-300, 1976-2 Cum. Bull. 217.

4. Treas. Reg. sec. 1.861-4(b)(1) was amended effective January 1, 1976, to provide that where services are performed in part within and in part without the U.S. an apportionment of the amount paid between U.S. and foreign sources must be made 'on the basis that most correctly reflects the proper source of income under the facts and circumstances of the particular case'. Prior to 1976, the apportionment had been made on a time basis, a method that is one, but not the only, acceptable method of apportionment under

→

However, compensation derived from services performed within the U.S. will constitute foreign source income if (1) it is received by a nonresident alien who is temporarily in the U.S. for not more than 90 days in a year, (2) it does not exceed $3,000, and (3) the services are performed for a foreign payor not engaged in a trade or business in the U.S. (or for a foreign business operation of a U.S. person).[5]

Compensation for personal services performed outside the U.S. is foreign source income.

4.2.4. Rents and royalties

All rents and royalties from property, tangible and intangible, located or used in the U.S. are U.S. source income. Included are rents or royalties for the use in the U.S. of patents, copyrights, secret processes, etc.

Rents and royalties from property located or used outside the U.S. are foreign source income.

4.2.5. Gains from disposition of real property

Gains from the disposition of 'United States real property interests' constitute U.S. source income.

If real estate is located outside the U.S., gains from sales are foreign source income.

4.2.6. Gains from sale of purchased personal property

U.S. source income includes gains from personal property sold within the U.S. (even if the property was purchased in another country). Gains from personal property sold outside the U.S. are foreign source income (even though purchased in the U.S.).

→

the revised Regulation. For examples of application of the allocation rules in personal services situations, see Rev. Rul. 74-108, 1974-1 Cum. Bull. 248 (payments by U.S. soccer team to foreign player); Rev. Rul. 77-167, 1977-1 Cum. Bull. 239 (payments to international airline pilot); Rev. Rul. 79-388, 1979-2 Cum. Bull. 270 (payments to a non-resident alien from a pension plan established by a U.S. employer).

5. The foreign employer will not be regarded as engaged in a U.S. trade or business by virtue of the activities of the employee for purposes of applying the source rule. Treas. Reg. sec. 1.861-4(a)(3).

The Regulations provide that the place of sale is generally the country in which the rights, title and interest of the seller pass. If the seller retains a bare legal title, then the sale occurs where the risk of loss passes. If tax avoidance was the primary purpose for structuring a transaction in a particular manner, the Treasury will look to all the surrounding circumstances to determine where the substance of the sale occurred.[6]

4.2.7. Underwriting income

Income derived from insuring U.S. risks is U.S. source income. All other underwriting income is foreign source income.

4.2.8. Income from certain aircraft, vessels and railroad rolling stock

Section 861(e) provides that owners of certain U.S. constructed aircraft or vessels shall to treat as U.S. source income both the income derived from the lease of such property to third parties and gain from the sale thereof. Section 861(f) provides a similar rule for railroad rolling stock leased to a domestic railroad for use primarily in the United States.

4.3. Application of source rules to other items of income

4.3.1. General

Section 863(a) gives the Secretary of the Treasury broad authority to allocate or apportion between U.S. and foreign sources items of gross income other than those enumerated above.[7]

6. Treas. Reg. sec. 1.861-7(c). See U.S. v. Balanovski, 236 F. 2d 298 (2d Cir. 1956), for an example of the application of these principles. In addition, special rules apply in determining the source of income on certain sales of personal property for purposes of the foreign tax credit. See 6.2.6.3.1., below.
7. Regulations have been issued dealing only with income from natural resources. Treas. Reg. sec. 1.863-1(b). See also Rev. Rul. 66-291, 1966-2 Cum. Bull. 279, applying this authority to determine the source of income derived from winning a prize in a contest sponsored by a U.S. company.

4.3.2. INCOME PARTLY FROM U.S. SOURCES AND PARTLY FROM FOREIGN SOURCES

Section 863(b) provides a special method for determining the source of four categories of income. The Secretary of the Treasury is granted regulatory authority to allocate or apportion, between U.S. and foreign sources, taxable income (i.e. gross income minus the deductions allocable thereto) derived from the following activities:

(a) Transportation rendered partly within and partly without the U.S.

(b) Sale of personal property produced within and sold without the U.S.

(c) Sale of personal property produced without and sold within the U.S.

(d) Purchase of personal property within a U.S. possession and sale within the U.S.[8]

4.4. Allocation of deductions to arrive at taxable income

Except for the special situation described in 4.3.2., the foregoing rules have involved the determination of the source of *gross income*. The proper allocation of deductions to arrive at *taxable income* from a U.S. or foreign source is an independent question. Sections 861(b), 862(b), 863(a), and 863(b) each contain provisions granting broad authority to the Treasury Department to issue regulations to effect the allocation of deductions, losses and expenses between U.S. and foreign sources.

Prior to 1977, Treasury Regulations provided only very general allocation rules: From U.S. source income were deducted items of expense

8. In general, in the case of category (a), the allocation between U.S. and foreign sources is made on the basis of comparing the sum of the costs of conducting the business in the U.S. and a reasonable return on the property used in the U.S. to the sum of the same items for the total business of the taxpayer. Treas. Reg. sec. 1.863-4. In the case of sales of personal property described in categories (b) and (c), one-half the taxable income is allocated on the basis of comparing sales within the U.S. and the foreign country, and one-half is allocated on the basis of comparing the value of property within the U.S. to the value of property within the U.S. and the foreign country. Treas. Reg. sec. 1.863-3(a), (b). In the case of category (d), one-half of the taxable income is allocated on the basis of comparing the value of the taxpayer's property in the U.S. to the value of property within the U.S. and the possession, and the other one-half on the basis of comparing the taxpayer's business in the U.S. to the total business within the U.S. and the possession. Treas. Reg. sec. 1.863-3(c). Rev. Rul. 71-387, 1971-2 Cum. Bull. 264, illustrates the computation technique required by the Regulations.

'properly apportioned or allocated thereto' plus a ratable share of expenses that could not be definitely allocated to any particular item or class of gross income. The ratable share was based on the ratio of the taxpayer's gross income from U.S. sources to its total gross income from all sources.[9]

In 1977, the Treasury issued new Regulations under secton 861. These Regulations replace the general rules of the pre-1977 period with a set of specific and quite detailed rules for allocating various types of deductions.[10] In general terms, the result of the 1977 Regulations for U.S. corporations is to allocate a greater portion of deductible expenditures such as interest, research and development costs, overhead costs and the like to foreign source income. The resulting reduction in foreign source income could bring with it a corresponding reduction in the available foreign tax credit. On the other hand, for some foreign corporations, it is possible that the new rules may operate to allocate a greater percentage of their deductions to U.S. source income, reducing U.S. tax liability, and, at least in the case of companies operating from exemption countries, producing a lower overall tax burden.

The 1977 Regulations provide general rules applicable to all types of deductible expenditures. In addition, specific rules are detailed for certain types of deductible items, notably interest, research and development costs, and overhead expenses.

Under the general rules, deductions must first be *allocated* to a *class of gross income*. The Regulations list the classes of gross income among which deductions must be allocated. Those classes include the types of income described in 4.2. above, but, in some cases, group several of those income items into a single class (for example, gains derived from dealings in property) and add some additional classes of income. As a basic proposition, deductions are to be allocated to a class of gross income based on the 'factual relationship' between the deductions and the class of gross income. It is not necessary that in a given year the taxpayer actually have realized income in the class to which the deductions relate; it is only necessary that the property or activity has generated, or will reasonably be expected to generate, gross income.

9. For illustrative cases allocating deductions between U.S. and foreign sources under the pre-1977 Regulations, see Grunebaum v. Commissioner, 420 F.2d 332 (2d Cir. 1970); F.W. Woolworth Co. v. Commissioner, 54 T.C. 1233 (1970); and Missouri Pacific R.R. Co. v. U.S., 411 F.2d 327 (8th Cir. 1969).

10. Treas. Reg. sec. 1.861-8. The Regulations apply to taxable years beginning after 1976.

Thus, for a given year, deductions allocable to a class of income may exceed the income actually realized in that class.[11]

In summary, at the first level, deductions are to be allocated to the class of income to which they are 'definitely related' on a factual basis; deductions not definitely related to a class of income are ratably allocated to all gross income.[12]

Once deductions have been allocated to the appropriate class of gross income it may then be necessary to make an *apportionment* of the deductions. Apportionment of deductions is required between the *statutory grouping* of gross income and the *residual grouping* of gross income. A statutory grouping is comprised of the gross income from a specific source which must be determined in order to arrive at taxable income. For example, if a U.S. corporation has both U.S. and foreign source income, and it is necessary to determine its foreign tax credit, the relevant statutory grouping is foreign source income and the residual grouping in U.S. source income. Thus, the items of income assigned to a particular statutory grouping depend upon which operative section of the Code is under consideration.[13]

Apportionment of deductions between a statutory grouping and the residual grouping is required in two situations:

(1) Where a class of income to which deductions are allocated is in part in the statutory grouping and in part in the residual grouping; and

(2) Where the class of income contains more than one statutory grouping.

If a class of gross income is entirely within one grouping, no apportionment is required.

As in the case of the rules governing the allocation of deductions to particular classes of income, the apportionment of deductions between statutory and residual groupings is to be made on the basis of the 'factual relationship' of the deductions and the groupings. Factors are provided that are to be taken into account in effecting an apportionment, as for example, a comparison of the units sold that are attributable to each grouping, a comparison of the gross sales and receipts attributable to each grouping, the costs of goods sold attributable to each grouping and the like.[14] Deductions not definitely related to any class of gross income must be apportioned on the basis of gross income

11. Treas. Reg. sec. 1.861-8(a)(2), (3); 1.861-8(b). For purposes of making the allocation or apportionment required by the Regulations, gross income includes any exempt or otherwise excluded income. Treas. Reg. sec. 1.861-8(d)(2); 1.861-8(g), Example (24).

12. Treas. Reg. sec. 1.861-8(b)(5).

13. Treas. Reg. sec. 1.861-8(a)(2), (4).

14. Treas. Reg. sec. 1.861-8(c)(1).

in the statutory grouping to total gross income,[15] but given the specificity of the apportioning rules, this type of deduction will presumably occur infrequently.

The foregoing rules are modified in the case of certain specified types of deductions. The most important of these are the deductions for interest, research and development costs, and home office oversight expenses.

In the case of *interest*, the Regulations applicable to all taxpayers except foreign corporations proceed on the proposition that money is fungible. Therefore, in general, interest is allocated to all classes of gross income. (In a few narrowly defined cases, interest may be allocated to a specific class of income generated by a specific piece of property). Once interest has been allocated to a class of income, it must be apportioned between the statutory grouping and the residual group ing. The fundamental apportionment method to be applied is the *asset method*. Under this method, to determine the interest to be apportioned to U.S. source income, the taxpayer's total interest expense is multiplied by a fraction, the numerator of which is the book value of the assets used in the United States and the denominator of which is the book value of the taxpayer's total worldwide assets. (Book value is the cost of the asset minus depreciation. In some instances, the taxpayer may be permitted to use fair market values.) The balance of the interest would be apportioned to foreign source income.

Two optional methods are then provided for apportioning the interest deduction between the statutory and residual groupings. These methods are intended to provide relief for taxpayers in making the transition from the pre-1977 rules to the new Regulations. If the taxpayer meets the conditions imposed for either option and the result produced by the option is more favorable to the taxpayer than the fundamental *asset method*, the taxpayer may use the apportionment result produced by the applicable option.[16]

The method of interest expense allocation adopted in Regulations, section 1.861-8, created problems for foreign corporations with U.S. branch operations, especially when coupled with the rule that currency gains and losses generally are not taken into account in computing a foreign corporation's U.S. tax liability. Thus, a foreign corporation which could borrow at a low interest rate in a currency stronger than the dollar would reflect a lower interest cost than a foreign corporation which borrowed at a higher rate in dollars. In the period 1977-1980, this

15. Treas. Reg. sec. 1.861-8(c)(2).
16. Treas. Reg. sec. 1.861-8(e)(2); 1.861-8(g), Examples (1) and (2).

situation frequently prevailed and under the 1977 Regulations, a foreign corporation borrowing in the foreign currency would get very little of its interest expense allocated to the U.S. branch. Nor would it be able to deduct its currency loss incurred as U.S. dollars were translated into stronger foreign currencies to repay foreign loans.

To alleviate these problems, Regulations, section 1.882-5, adopted in 1980, apply a different set of allocation of interest expense rules to foreign corporations with U.S. branch activities. The 1980 rules adopt a concept of the fungibility of capital (rather than of money) and focus (1) on the relationship between the liabilities and assets of the U.S. branch as shown on the branch's books and (2) on the overall relation between the liabilities and assets in the enterprise worldwide. In general, if the book liabilities of the U.S. branch bear the same ratio to the book assets of the branch as the worldwide book liabilities of the enterprise bear to its worldwide book assets, then all of the interest paid by the U.S. branch will be deductible in the U.S. If the U.S. book liabilities-assets ratio exceeds the overall book liabilities-assets ratio of the foreign corporation, only a portion of the interest expense actually paid by the U.S. branch will be deductible in the U.S. Conversely, if the book liabilities-assets ratio of the U.S. branch is less than the overall book liabilities-assets ratio of the foreign corporation, the interest expense deducted by the U.S. branch may exceed the interest expense actually paid by the branch.

For taxable years 1977 through 1980, a foreign corporation was given the option to use either the rules applicable to other taxpayers under Regulations, section 1.861-8, or the rules applicable to foreign corporations under section 1.882-5. For periods after February 6, 1981, the regulations applicable to foreign corporations must be used. Only in the case of interest expense deductions are different rules applied to foreign corporations; in all other situations the allocation of deduction rules are the same for U.S. and foreign taxpayers.

Special rules are also provided for the treatment of *research and development expenses*. Prior to the issuance of the 1977 Regulations, it was suspected that American companies allocated virtually all of their research and development expenses to U.S. source income. As a result, the allowable foreign tax credit could be increased at no net overall increase in tax cost. The effect of the 1977 Regulations is to allocate a much greater portion of research and development costs to foreign source income of U.S. taxpayers. The Regulations proceed on the premise that research and development 'is an inherently speculative activity, that findings may contribute unexpected benefits, and that the gross income derived from successful research and development must bear the cost of unsuccessful research and development'.

As a result, research and development expenditures are considered under the Regulations to be connected to appropriate product categories and therefore are allocable to items of gross income as a class that are related to the product category. Product categories are specified and include such broad classifications as hard mineral mining, crude petroleum and natural gas, construction services, transportation services and the like. For manufactured products, the classification is in terms of broad groups such as machinery (except electrical), furniture, apparel, etc. The income that is considered related to a product category includes not only sales income but royalties and dividends as well.

Once the allocation of the deduction to classes of income related to product categories has been made, the deduction then may have to be apportioned between the relevant statutory grouping of gross income and the residual grouping of gross income. The fundamental test by which research and development costs are to be apportioned is the *geographic source* test, reflecting the view that research and development is generally most valuable in the country where it is performed. There are two elements to the geographic source test. First, a 'fixed percentage' test is applied. After 1978, 30 percent[17] of the taxpayer's total research and development costs *must* be apportioned to income from the geographic source where the activities accounting for more than 50 percent of the research and development deductions were performed. For example, if activities accounting for 75 percent of a taxpayer's total research and development deduction were performed abroad, 30 percent of the total deduction must be apportioned abroad. The balance of the research and development costs are apportioned under the *sales method*. Under the sales method, the remaining research and development costs are multiplied by a fraction, the numerator of which is sales within the statutory grouping and the denominator of which is the taxpayer's total sales. The resulting amount is apportioned to the statutory grouping and the balance of the research and development costs are then apportioned to the residual grouping. In determining the sales figures, sales of corporations controlled by the taxpayer must also be taken into account if the controlled corporation 'can reasonably be expected to benefit directly or indirectly ... from the taxpayer's research expense'. Thus, in apportioning a parent

17. The percentage was 50% in 1977 and 40% in 1978. The figures are obviously artificial and represent a compromise between the various views urged on the Treasury Department. It is expected that the 30% allocation for years after 1978 will be re-examined in the future.

corporation's research and development costs under the sales method, not only must the sales of the parent corporation be taken into account but also the sales of all of its controlled subsidiaries which are connected with the product category to which the research and development costs relate. Moreover, sales within the product category by *uncontrolled parties* must also be taken into account in making the apportionment 'if the uncontrolled party can reasonably be expected to benefit directly or indirectly . . . from the research expense connected with the product category.' If the sales of the unrelated parties cannot be determined or reasonably estimated, the figure to be used by the taxpayer is an amount equal to ten times the royalties received from the uncontrolled party.

As in the case of the apportionment of interest expense, two optional apportionment methods are provided in the case of research and development costs. The options permit apportionment ratably between gross income within the statutory grouping and within the residual grouping if the same tests are satisfied as apply to the interest expense deduction.[18]

18. Treas. Reg. sec. 1.861-8(e)(3); 1.861-8(g), Examples (3)–(16). The operation of the research and development expense rules may be illustrated by the following examples:

Foreign Corporation Y incurred 100 of general research and development expenses for the taxable year. All the research was performed in foreign country A. Y also received 100 royalty income from an unrelated licensee in foreign country B. Y's sales in the U.S. were 1500 and sales outside the U.S. were 1000. Y's U.S. gross income was 200 and its total gross income was 1000.

Under the fixed percentage element of the geographical source test, 30% (or 30) of Y's research and development expenses must be apportioned to the residual grouping (non-effectively connected income) since all the research was performed outside the U.S. The sales method element under the geographic source test is computed as follows:

Apportioned to Statutory Grouping (effectively connected income)	$\frac{\text{1500 (Sales in U.S.)}}{\text{3500 (Total sales)}} \times 70 = 30$

The balance of 40 research and development expenses are apportioned, under the sales method, to the residual grouping (non-effectively connected income). As a result, only 30 of the expenses could be apportioned to U.S. effectively connected income under the geographic source method. Note that the denominator of the fraction includes not only Y's 2,500 direct sales, but also an amount equal to 10 times the royalty received from its unrelated licensee in Country B.

The 1977 Regulations provide specific rules (although not in the detail employed for interest and research and development deductions) for home office or oversight costs attributable to dividends received from a foreign corporation; legal and accounting fees and expenses; income taxes; losses on the sale, exchange or other disposition of property; and the net operating loss deduction.[19]

As noted above, the allocation rules in the Regulations primarily affect the computation of the overall limitation to the foreign tax credit, discussed in 6.2.6. However, the rules are also important with respect to determining 'effectively connected' taxable income of foreign taxpayers (5.3.); foreign base company income under the subpart F rules (7.5.1.); and numerous other provisions discussed in succeeding chapters which rely on the determination of U.S. and/or foreign source income.[20]

19. Treas. Reg. sec. 1.861-8(e)(4)-(8). See also Treas. Reg. sec. 1.861-8(g), Examples (17)-(21), (25)-(26).

20. See the listing in Treas. Reg. sec. 1.861-8(f), and illustrations in Treas. Reg. sec. 1.861-8(g), Examples (22) and (23).

Chapter 5
Income taxation of foreign corporations and nonresident aliens

5.1. Introduction

A number of structural building blocks are involved in determining the U.S. tax liability of a foreign person. There are three basic concepts involved: (1) the nature and source of the taxpayer's income; (2) the taxpayer's activities in the U.S., i.e., whether he is engaged in a U.S. trade or business; and (3) the relation between his income and his U.S. activities, i.e., whether his income is 'effectively connected' with a U.S. trade or business. It is within the framework of these three variables that the pattern of U.S. taxation is established. Source of income and income classification problems were discussed in Chapter 4. The following materials first discuss the other two elements in the statutory pattern, the trade or business concept and the effectively connected concept, and then examine in more detail the pattern of taxation for nonresident aliens, foreign corporations and partnerships.

5.2. The 'trade or business' concept

5.2.1. Background

A foreign taxpayer who is engaged in a U.S. trade or business has achieved a substantial level of economic penetration in the U.S. He is not merely a passive investor but has become a direct participant in the economic life of the country.

The significance of a U.S. trade or business for the tax treatment of foreign persons has varied over the years. The U.S. tax system has always distinguished between the *investment income* from U.S. sources of a foreign taxpayer and the *business income* attributable to the foreign taxpayer's trade or business carried on in the U.S. The investment income has generally been subject to a flat rate of tax on gross income, withheld at the source, while the net business income has been taxed at regular individual or corporate rates. However, prior to 1966, if a foreign taxpayer was engaged in a U.S. trade or business, under the so-called force of attraction principle, the U.S. taxed investment income at regular rates, even though it had no connection with the foreign taxpayer's U.S. trade or business. The investment income was 'attracted' to the U.S. trade or business and taxed accordingly.

In the Foreign Investors Tax Act of 1966, the United States abandoned the force of attraction principle.[1] Under the 1966 legislation, only investment income that is *effectively connected* with the conduct of a trade or business in the U.S. is subjected to the full individual or corporate rates applicable to business income. The mere existence of a U.S. trade or business is not sufficient to subject the investment income to the normal tax rates. Investment income not effectively connected with a U.S. trade or business is taxed at the 30% statutory withholding rate or lower treaty rates.[2] While the existence of a trade or business in the U.S. no longer affects the taxation of unrelated investment income, the 'trade or business' concept continues to play an important role in the U.S. taxation of foreign individuals and corporations. It determines the basic pattern under which the foreign taxpayer's income will be taxed, as discussed more fully in 5.4 and 5.5.[3]

5.2.2. The existence of a trade or business

Although the term 'trade or business' is employed in several different sections of the Internal Revenue Code, the statute does not contain a general definition of the phrase. Instead, the determination whether an

1. For a discussion of the policies behind the 1966 Act, see 'Tax Policy and Tax Reform: 1961–1969, Selected Speeches and Testimony of Stanley S. Surrey' (Hellmuth and Oldman, eds., 1973) at pp. 388–396.
2. The 1966 statutory changes are discussed in Ross, U.S. Taxation of Aliens and Foreign Corporations: The Foreign Investors Tax Act of 1966 and Related Developments, 22 Tax Law Review 277 (1967); Tillinghast, The Foreign Investors Tax Act of 1966, 20 American Bar Ass'n Tax Section Bull. 87 (January, 1967).
3. The 'trade or business' concept is somewhat analogous to the 'permanent establisment' concept adopted in U.S. tax treaties. Similarly, 'effectively connected' corresponds to the notion of income 'attributable to' the permanent establishment. See 9.5. While a determination that a foreign individual or corporation maintains a permanent establishment in the U.S. will generally mean that a U.S. trade or business exists, the reverse is not the case. The trade or business concept is broader than the permanent establishment rules and, therefore, a foreign individual or corporation can often be engaged in a trade or business in the U.S., but still be found not to maintain a permanent establishment there. de Amodio v. Commissioner, 299 F.2d 623 (3d Cir. 1962).

activity constitutes a 'trade or business' is left to a case by case resolution by the fiscal authorities and the courts.[4]

In the context of the rules governing foreign individuals and corporations, the fundamental distinction to be drawn is between commercial activity carried on in the U.S. with some regularity versus passive investment. The polar models are a manufacturing plant operated in the U.S. and the simple receipt of dividends paid on stock in a U.S. company. But between these clear extremes, there are an infinite variety of activities which must be placed either in the trade or business or in the investment category. Prior to 1966 most of the disputes centered around rental real estate[5] and securities trading activities.[6]

The 1966 legislation provided guidelines for resolution of the trade or business issue in three situations. Section 864(b) excludes from trade or business status:

(1) The performance of personal services for a nonresident employer under the same conditions that determine that compensation for personal services constitutes foreign source income[7] (see 4.2.3., above).

(2) Trading in stocks, securities or commodities through a U.S. broker, if the foreign individual or corporation does not maintain a U.S. office or fixed place of business through which the transactions are effected.[8]

(3) Trading in stocks, securities, or commodities for the foreign

4. Indeed, the Supreme Court, in one of its more peculiar pronouncements, held that the term 'trade or business' in section 174 (dealing with the deductibility of research and development costs) did not have the same meaning as the term 'trade or business' in section 162 (dealing with the deductibility of costs incurred in carrying on a trade or business). Snow v. Commissioner, 416 U.S. 500 (1974).

5. See, e.g., Pinchot v. Commissioner, 113 F.2d 718 (2d Cir. 1940) (real estate holdings in U.S. required such extensive management that they constituted a trade or business); Lewenhaupt v. Commissioner, 20 T.C. 151 (1953) (same result).

6. Compare, e.g., Adda v. Commissioner, 10 T.C. 273 (1948), aff'd per curiam, 171 F.2d 457 (4th Cir. 1949) (nonresident alien was engaged in U.S. trade or business as a result of dealing in commodity futures through discretionary resident agent); Commissioner v. Nubar, 185 F.2d 584 (4th Cir. 1950) (foreign citizen who for six years lived in U.S. and actively traded stocks and commodities was engaged in a U.S. trade or business); Liang v. Commisioner, 23 T.C. 1040 (1955) (pure investment activity by a nonresident through a resident agent was not a trade or business); de Vegvar v. Commissioner, 28 T.C. 1055 (1957) (no trade or business where investment gains held in custody account for nonresident); Continental Trading, Inc. v. Commisioner, 265 F.2d 40 (9th Cir. 1959) (foreign corporation holding stock in U.S. companies not engaged in U.S. trade or business).

7. Sec. 864(b)(1); Treas. Reg. sec. 1.864-2(b).

8. Sec. 864(b)(2)(A)(i), 864(b)(2)(B)(i), 864(b)(2)(C); Treas. Reg. sec. 1.864-2(c)(1), (d)(1).

investor's own account, whether effected in the U.S. directly or through agents.[9] This exception does not apply to 'dealers' in stock or securities. In addition, if the foreign taxpayer is a foreign corporation whose principal business is trading in securities, business classification for such trading activities can be avoided only if the corporation maintains its principal office outside the U.S.[10] But a foreign corporation that is not a dealer can trade in commodities for its own account even if its principal office is in the U.S.

Other statutory provisions treat certain activities as a trade or business:

(1) Section 871(c) provides that certain foreign students, teachers and exchange visitors 'shall be treated as' engaged in a trade or business.[11]

(2) Sections 871(d) and 882(d) permit foreign individuals and corporations that own U.S. real estate to elect to treat the income therefrom as trade or business income. The election applies only to real estate investments that, absent the election, would not constitute a trade or business under generally applicable principles.[12]

(3) Section 897(a) provides that gain or loss from the disposition of a 'United States real property interest' shall be taxed 'as if' the taxpayer were engaged in a U.S. trade or business. See 5.3.3.

Apart from these specific statutory rules, the determination whether an activity constitutes a trade or business is determined on a case-by-case basis, taking into account such factors as the taxpayer's motive (profit versus personal), quantitative aspects (frequency, substantiality and duration of the activities) and qualitative aspects (business versus investment).[13]

9. Sec. 864(b)(2)(A)(ii), 864(b)(2)(B)(ii); Treas. Reg. Sec. 1.864-2(c)(2)(i) and (ii), (d)(2).
10. Sec. 864(b)(2)(A)(ii); Treas. Reg. sec. 1.864-2(c)(2)(iii) and (iv). A foreign corporation which, but for the fact that all of its stock is owned by foreign interests, would be a 'personal holding company' (see 8.4.2.) may trade in stocks or securities for its own account even if its principal office is in the U.S. But see Rev. Rul. 79–116, 1979-1 Cum. Bull. 213 (a foreign corporation was not a 'personal holding company' because its stock was treated as being owned indirectly by a U.S. citizen by virtue of attribution rules; it was a 'foreign personal holding company' and, because its principal office was located in the United States, the foreign corporation was engaged in a U.S. trade or business and was taxable on all its effectively connected income).
11. Treas. Reg. Sec. 1.871-9.
12. Treas. Reg. sec. 1.871-10 details the procedures to be followed in making the election. See also Treas. Reg. sec. 1.882-2(a). No other type of income is granted such an option. Rev. Rul. 74-63, 1974-1 Cum. Bull. 374. A similar election is provided in many U.S. income tax treaties. See 9.6.3.
13. See e.g. Rev. Rul. 73-522, 1973-2 Cum. Bull. 226 (nonresident alien who visited U.S. once during the year to negotiate leases on real estate he owned was not engaged in trade →

5.2.3. THE LOCATION OF A TRADE OR BUSINESS IN THE U.S.

There is no Code provision that offers a comprehensive definition of when a trade or business is located within (or without) the U.S. A few specific examples are given. Thus, the performance of personal services in the U.S. constitutes a trade or business located in the U.S. under section 864(b). As noted in 5.2.2., a corporation with its 'principal office' in the U.S. can be considered to have a trade or business in the U.S. when it is trading in stocks or securities for its own account.[14] In addition, section 864(c) and the Regulations issued thereunder, which set forth the 'effectively connected' definition, contain a number of examples illuminating the business location issue. Those examples are considered in 5.3.2. Again, the issue whether a trade or business is located in the U.S. is one to be determined on the basis of all relevant facts and circumstances. On the one hand, a foreign producer that ships directly to U.S. customers does not have a trade or business located in the U.S.[15] At the other extreme, if a foreign corporation has →

or business); Rev. Rul. 75-23, 1975-1 Cum. Bull. 290 (Netherlands Antilles corporation that was a limited partner in U.S. partnership involved in major commercial real estate projects was engaged in trade or business of the partnership); Rev. Rul. 73-227, 1973-1 Cum Bull. 338 (foreign corporation with its principal office in the U.S. engaged in a trade or business where it borrowed funds and relent them to other members of affiliated group of corporations).

Section 875 provides that a nonresident alien individual or a foreign corporation that is a partner in a partnership (or the beneficiary of an estate or trust) which is engaged in a U.S. trade or business is considered also to be engaged in a U.S. trade or business. On the other hand, grantors of trusts are not considered to be engaged in a U.S. trade or business *merely* because the trustee is engaged in a U.S. trade or business. Treas. Reg. sec. 1.875-2(b).

14. See Treas. Reg. sec. 1.864-2(c)(2)(iii) for examples of corporate functions that constitute a principal office. The quite detailed rules in the Regulation provide guidelines for a foreign investment company that desires to avoid U.S. trade or business status by locating its principal office outside the U.S. This guidance led to the creation of the so-called 'offshore investment funds', through which foreign investors invest in U.S. stocks, bonds and commodities. If properly structured, profits on sales will be free of U.S. capital gains tax (because, as explained in 5.3.2., only capital gains effectively connected with the conduct of a U.S. trade or business are subject to U.S. tax). In addition, if the country of incorporation selected has a favorable treaty with the U.S., the U.S. tax on dividends and interest may be reduced or eliminated. These results make the offshore funds attractive to foreign investors. U.S. investors in such funds, on the other hand, may encounter various tax avoidance provisions such as the foreign personal holding company rules (8.4.3. below); the controlled foreign corporation rules (Chapter 7); and the foreign investment company rules in sections 1246 and 1247 (8.1.2.7.).

15. See Rev. Rul. 73-158, 1973-1 Cum. Bull. 337. But if the sales are effected through the foreign corporation's resident U.S. agent, the foreign corporation may have a U.S. located business. Rev. Rul. 70-424, 1970-2 Cum. Bull. 50.

its principal office in the U.S. and conducts all its activities there, it will obviously have a business situs in the U.S.[16] But most situations will not be so clear cut and have to be resolved on the basis of the extent of the corporation's business functions carried on in the U.S.[17]

5.3. The 'effectively connected' concept

5.3.1. General

The third of the critical definitional aspects of the U.S. system for taxation of nonresident aliens and foreign corporations is the 'effectively connected' concept. *If* a nonresident alien or foreign corporation has derived income from U.S. sources (under the rules described in Chapter 4) and *if* that individual or corporation is engaged in a trade or business in the U.S. (under the rules described in 5.2.), then the actual tax treatment of the income depends on whether it is effectively connected with the conduct of a trade or business in the U.S.[18] Section 864(c) and the Regulations issued thereunder prescribe the tests to be utilized in determining whether or not income is effectively connected with a U.S. trade or business.

The 'effectively connected' rules apply to four categories of U.S. source income: (1) gain or loss from the sale or exchange of capital assets; (2) fixed or determinable annual or periodical gains, profits or income (described in sections 871(a) (1) and 881(a)); (3) gain or loss from the disposition of a U.S. real property interest; and (4) all other income, gain or loss. The U.S. system of imposing tax on such income derived by nonresident aliens and foreign corporations will be discussed in greater detail in 5.4 and 5.5. However, it will be useful to summarize he general pattern of taxation at this point to demonstrate the results that follow a determination that a particular class of U.S. source income

16. See, e.g., Rev. Rul. 73-227, supra, note 13.
17. See Bittker and Eustice, Federal Income Taxation of Corporations and Shareholders p. 17-13 (4th ed. 1979) for a listing of some of the relevant factors.
18. With certain limited exceptions, if a nonresident alien or foreign corporation at no time during the taxable year was engaged in a trade or business in the U.S., no income will be treated as effectively connected income. Sec. 864(c)(1)(B). The exceptions are for participants in certain exchange or training programs in the U.S. (sec. 874(c)), income from real estate which is treated as effectively connected (sec. 871(d), 882(d) and 897(a)), and interest on U.S. obligations received by banks organized in a U.S. possession (sec. 882(e)). See Treas. Reg. Sec. 1.864-3.

either is or is not income effectively connected with a U.S. trade or business.

Nonresident Aliens

Category of income	If income is effectively connected	If income is not effectively connected
1. Capital gains	Net income taxed at U.S. individual income tax rates (40% of normal rates)	No U.S. tax (unless the individual is in the U.S. for 183 days, in which event a flat 30% rate is imposed on the gain)
2. Fixed or determinable income	Net income taxed at full U.S. individual income tax rates	Gross income taxed at flat 30% rate
3. U.S. real property interest gains	Net income taxed at capital gain rates (minimum 20% rate)	Treated as effectively connected income
4. Other income	Net income taxed at full U.S. individual income tax rates	Treated as effectively connected income

Foreign Corporations

Category of income	If income is effectively connected	If income is not effectively connected
1. Capital gains	Net income taxed at flat 28% rate	No U.S. tax
2. Fixed or determinable income	Net income taxed at regular corporate tax rates	Gross income taxed at flat 30% rate
3. U.S. real property interest gains	Net income taxed at capital gain rates	Treated as effectively connected income
4. Other income	Net income taxed at regular corporate tax rates	Treated as effectively connected income

Thus, in general terms, the effectively connected concepts divides U.S. source income between a foreign investor's two pockets. Income that is effectively connected (or is so treated) is placed in his 'business' pocket and taxed at full U.S. rates; income that is not effectively connected is placed in his 'investment' pocket and taxed at a flat rate.[19]

5.3.2. Capital gains and fixed or determinable income

Section 864(c)(2) prescribes two tests for determining whether U.S. source capital gain income and fixed or determinable income is effectively connected with the conduct of a U.S. trade or business. The term 'capital gain income' refers to gains (or losses) derived from the sale of exchange of a capital asset.[20] The term 'fixed or determinable income' refers in general to interest, dividends, rents, salaries, wages, premiums, annuities, compensations, remunerations, emoluments and certain gains on transfers of patents, copyrights, etc.[21]

The tests to be applied to these two categories of income are (1) the 'asset use' test and (2) the 'business activities' test.

5.3.2.1. The 'asset use' test

The 'asset use' test is employed primarily to determine whether U.S. source passive investment income, such as interest or dividends, constitutes effectively connected income.[22] For example, the U.S. branch of a foreign corporation may conduct a manufacturing business and also derive dividend income from stock in a U.S. company or income from the sale of the stock.

An asset, such as the stock in the above example, will be considered to be used in the conduct of a U.S. trade or business – and the income, gain or loss derived therefrom thus effectively connected – if any one of three conditions is satisfied:[23]

19. The statutory 30% rate on income that is not effectively connected may be varied by treaty. See 9.6.
20. The term 'capital asset' is defined in section 1221. See 2.2.4 and 2.3.4. For materials on the tests employed to determine whether an asset is (or is not) a capital asset, see Surrey, Warren, McDaniel and Ault, *Federal Income Taxation*, vol. 1, pp. 988–1175 (1972) and 1979 Supplement.
21. Sections 871(a) and 881(a), discussed in 5.4 and 5.5, define 'fixed or determinable income' in detail.
22. Treas. Reg. sec. 1.864-4(c)(2)(i).
23. Treas. Reg. sec. 1.864-4(c)(2)(ii).

(1) The asset is held for the principal purpose of promoting the *present* conduct of a trade or business in the U.S. For example, assume a foreign corporation that maintains a branch factory in the U.S. acquires all the stock in a financially unstable U.S. corporation that supplies a raw material essential to the foreign corporation's U.S. manufacturing operation. The acquisition was effected to insure the continued supply of the raw material to the branch factory operation. Dividends paid on the stock, or gain or loss on the sale of the stock, will be considered effectively connected income because the asset producing the income promoted the present conduct of the U.S. business.

(2) The asset is acquired and held in the ordinary course of business conducted in the U.S. Assume that in the above example the U.S. branch factory commonly sold its products by taking trade notes receivable in payment. Interest income on the notes would constitute effectively connected income.[24]

(3) The asset is otherwise held in a 'direct relationship' to the trade or business conducted in the U.S.[25] The requisite 'direct relationship' exists if the asset is *presently needed* in the business. Thus, in the above example, assume the U.S. branch factory requires a large cash balance to conduct its business. However, the amount required varies through the year as the result of the cyclical nature of the business. The U.S. branch therefore invests the cash in short-term notes during these periods. Interest earned on the notes will be effectively connected income since the notes are required to meet present business needs. By contrast, if the cash were invested in securities in preparation for a future diversification or expansion by the U.S. branch, its interest income would not be effectively connected since the notes would not be held to meet the *present* needs of the business.[26]

In addition, the Regulations create a presumption that a 'direct relationship' exists if (1) the asset was acquired from funds generated by the U.S. trade or business; (2) the income from the asset is retained in the business; *and* (3) personnel in the U.S. who are actively involved in the business exercise significant management and control over the investment of the asset. This presumption is, however, rebuttable by the taxpayer. Therefore, in the foregoing example, even if the investment securities were acquired out of funds generated by the U.S.

24. See Rev. Rul. 73-227, 1973-1 Cum. Bull. 338 (foreign corporation with principal office in U.S. borrowed and relent funds to its U.S. and foreign affiliates; held, interest from U.S. affiliates is effectively connected income).
25. Treas. Reg. sec. 1.864-4(c)(2)(iii).
26. Treas. Reg. sec. 1.864-4(c)(2)(iv), Examples (1) and (2).

branch business, dividends were retained in the business, and the managing officers of the U.S. branch were responsible for supervising the investment, the income from the securities would not be effectively connected because the fact that the securities were acquired to meet future rather than present needs of the business would rebut the presumption of a 'direct relationship' created by the Regulations.[27]

5.3.2.2. *The 'business-activities' test*

The 'business-activities' test is applied primarily to determine if income derived by dealers in stocks or securities, investment companies, those engaged in the business of licensing patents, and service businesses constitutes effectively connected income.[28] Management of an investment portfolio does not fall within the business activities test, unless that activity is the principal activity of the U.S. trade or business. As in the case of the 'asset use' test, the objective of the 'business activities' test is to determine whether passive income – dividends, rents, royalties, etc. – 'arises directly from' the U.S. trade or business. Detailed rules are provided in the Regulations for application of the test to banking, financing and similar businesses conducted in the U.S.[29]

5.3.3. Gains from disposition of U.S. real property interests

Prior to 1980, properly advised foreign investors in U.S. real estate could generally dispose of the property free of any U.S. tax on the capital gain. A variety of techniques were used to achieve this result. These tax plans generally took advantage of the fact that, under normally applicable U.S. tax rules, the U.S. imposed no tax on capital gains, including gains from the disposition of real estate, unless the taxpayer was engaged in a U.S. trade or business or, in the case of individuals, was present in the U.S. for 183 days during the taxable year. Thus, for example, a foreign taxpayer could structure his U.S. activities so that he was not in fact engaged in a U.S. trade or business (typically through a net lease transaction) and thus avoid any gain on the disposition of the

27. Treas. Reg. sec. 1.864-4(c)(2)(iii)(*b*) and (iv), Examples (3), (4) and (5).
28. Treas. Reg. sec. 1.864-4(c)(3).
29. Treas. Reg. sec. 1.864-4(c)(5). See Rev. Rul. 73-227, note 24, above (foreign corporation with U.S. office that borrowed and relent funds to its affiliated companies was not in banking business, although it was engaged in a U.S. trade or business).

property. This technique could be combined with a tax treaty election to have the rental income taxed on a net basis in the years preceding the year in which the real property was sold. See 9.6.3. Alternatively, the foreign investor could invest in United States real estate through a corporation and no U.S. tax would be imposed on the gain from the disposition of the shares of stock.

The rapid increase in the level of foreign investment in U.S. real estate and agricultural operations which took place in the late 1970's led to closer scrutiny of these transactions by the U.S. Government. Part of the response to the situation was the enactment of the Foreign Investment in Real Property Tax Act of 1980.[30]

Under the 1980 Act, gain or loss realized by a nonresident alien individual or foreign corporation from the 'disposition' of a 'United States real property interest' is taxed as if the foreign investor were engaged in a U.S. trade or business and as if the gain or loss were effectively connected to that trade or business.[31] As a result, the ordinary U.S. rates, typically capital gain rates, apply to such gains. A special minimum tax rate of 20% is imposed on gain realized by nonresident alien individuals,[32] which in effect means that for such taxpayers the capital gain tax rates range from 20% to 28%. For foreign corporations, the regular 28% capital gain rate generally will be applicable.

A 'United States real property interest' may be either (1) a direct interest in real property (including a mine, well or other natural deposit) located in the U.S., or (2) an interest (other than solely as a creditor) in a domestic 'United States real property holding corporation' (RPHC). An RPHC is a corporation in which the fair market value of U.S. real property interests owned by the corporation equals or exceeds 50% of the sum of the fair market value of the corporation's U.S. real property interests plus its foreign real property interests plus all other assets used in its trade or business. If, under the foregoing test, a corporation was a domestic RPHC at any time during the five years preceding the

30. Prior to the 1980 tax legislation, the International Investment Survey Act of 1976 and the Agricultural Foreign Investment Disclosure Act of 1978 had required extensive reporting to the Departments of Commerce and Agriculture, respectively, by foreign investors in U.S. property and agricultural land. See Report of Committee on Foreign Investment in U.S. Real Estate, American Bar Association Section of Real Property, Probate, and Trust Law, 'Foreign Investment in U.S. Real Estate: Federal and State Laws Affecting the Foreign Investor', 14 Real Property, Probate and Trust Journal 1, 42 (1979).

31. Sec. 897(a)(1).

32. Sec. 897(a)(2).

disposition of the taxpayer's interest (or, if shorter, between June 18, 1980 and the date of disposition), gain (or loss) is recognized and taxed by the U.S.[33]

Thus, where a foreign investor owns U.S. real estate directly or through a U.S. corporation which is an RPHC, gain on a sale or exchange of either the property or the stock will be fully subject to U.S. tax. Moreover, the techniques discussed in 2.2.4. and 2.2.5. for exchanging property on a tax-free basis generally are not available unless the property received in the exchange is such that the gain on its sale would be subject to U.S. tax. The Act gave the Treasury broad authority to issue Regulations which will determine the extent to which the various nonrecognition provisions discussed in Chapter 2 will or will not apply to exchanges of U.S. real estate interests or stock in a domestic RPHC.[34]

Different rules apply where the U.S. real property interest is owned by a foreign corporation. The gain on disposition of stock in a foreign corporation which owns a U.S. real property interest is not subject to tax under section 897. Instead, tax is deferred until the corporation itself disposes of the interest whether by sale or exchange, dividend distribution, or distribution pursuant to a redemption or liquidation. The tax is then imposed *on the corporation* despite the fact that a similar distribution by a U.S. corporation would not be subject to tax.[35] The gain subject to tax is the difference between the fair market value of the interest at the time of distribution and its adjusted basis. Neither statutory tax-free exchanges nor the use of tax treaty elections, discussed above, can be used to avoid U.S. tax on disposition of U.S. real property interests by a foreign corporation.

The 1980 Act provisions are reinforced by extensive reporting requirements, as discussed in 5.7.1. Treaty implications of the legislation are considered in Chapter 9.

5.3.4. OTHER INCOME

U.S. source income other than capital gains and fixed or determinable

33. Sec. 897(c). Special 'look through' rules are applied so that a corporation is treated as owning its pro rata share of the relevant assets of corporations controlled (50%) by it. Attribution rules are applied to determine whether the requisite 50% control exists.

34. Sec. 897(e) empowers the Treasury to treat as taxable, transactions that otherwise would be nontaxable if 'necessary or appropriate to prevent the avoidance of federal income taxes.'

35. Sec. 897(d). See 2.2.5. for a description of the rules applicable to distributions by U.S. corporations.

income is effectively connected income if the taxpayer conducts *a* trade or business in the U.S. Such income will therefore be taxed at full U.S. rates even though it has no actual connection at all with the trade or business actually conducted in the U.S. To this extent the 'force of attraction' principle still has a limited application even after 1966. For example, suppose a foreign corporation sells two products. It establishes a U.S. branch to sell one of the products in the U.S. The other product is sold directly to U.S. customers by the home office abroad, with the home office shipping directly to the U.S. customers. The sales income at the home office is treated as effectively connected income even though it in fact has no connection with the business actually conducted by the U.S. branch.[36]

5.3.5. Foreign source income effectively connected with a U.S. business

Paragraphs 5.2 and 5.3. have discussed the rules applied by the U.S. to determine whether its full tax rates should be applied to U.S. source income derived by nonresident aliens or foreign corporations. The detailed nature of those rules is intended to provide guidance and a relatively high degree of certainty so that foreign investors can determine in advance the tax consequences of U.S. investment. In addition, the particularity of the rules is designed to insure that the modification of U.S. tax jurisdiction effected by the 1966 Act does not convert the U.S. into a tax haven.

In furtherance of this latter objective, the 1966 Act established certain categories of foreign source income that are treated as effectively connected with the conduct of a U.S. trade or business and hence subject to full U.S. tax rates. In general, foreign source income is not treated as effectively connected income. Section 864(c)(4)(A). However, section 864(c)(4)(B) details specific types of income that will be

36. Treas. Reg. sec. 1.864-4(b). As discussed in note 13, above, an alien individual who is a partner in a U.S. partnership which is engaged in a U.S. trade or business is also considered to be engaged in a U.S. trade or business. Under Treas. Reg. sec. 1.875-1, such a nonresident alien partner is subject to full U.S. income tax on any effectively connected income if the partnership 'at any time during the taxable year' was engaged in a U.S. trade or business. As a result, a nonresident alien who becomes a limited partner on the last day of a taxable year could subject previously earned 'other income' to full U.S. tax since such income is treated as effectively connected income if the taxpayer is engaged in *a* U.S. trade or business. See Vitale v. Commissioner, 72 T.C. 386 (1979), for an application of this result under pre-1966 law.

treated as effectively connected with a U.S. trade or business even though the income is determined to arise from a foreign source under the rules discussed in Chapter 4. The types of foreign source income selected for this special treatment include those that are especially susceptible to manipulation by taxpayers to obtain tax advantages. In the absence of section 864(c)(4)(B), transactions could be arranged so that the income was treated as from a foreign source under the source rules, even though the transaction in fact had substantial economic ties to the U.S. In a sense the results with respect to effectively connected foreign source income can be seen as a modification of the otherwise applicable source rules discussed in Chapter 4. Put another way, the types of income covered have such a relationship to the U.S. that they should be treated as U.S. source income and taxed accordingly. However, instead of formally changing the source rules in these situations, the 1966 legislation applied the effectively connected concept to what was still technically foreign source income. This choice of technique has some important implications. For example, in some of its income tax treaties, the U.S. has obligated itself to tax only the U.S. source income of foreign taxpayers. In such cases, the treaty provisions prevent the application of the effectively connected concept to what is still technically foreign source income.[37]

Foreign source income will be treated as effectively connected with a U.S. trade or business if it is 'attributable' to an 'office or other fixed place of business' in the U.S. Both of the quoted terms are defined in the statute (section 864(c)(5)) and given detailed content by the Regulations.

The foreign source income that can be treated as effectively connected income if the above conditions are satisfied includes (1) rents or royalties and gain or loss from intangible property which is located or used outside the U.S. if derived from the active conduct of a trade or business in the U.S.;[38] (2) dividends or interest and gain or loss from stocks or securities which are derived in the conduct of a U.S. trade or business either by banks or other financial institutions or by a corporation whose principal business is trading in stocks or securities for its own account;[39] (3) income from the sale of inventory items (or other

37. See Rev. Rul. 74-63, 1974-1 Cum. Bull. 375.

38. Treas. Reg. sec. 1.864-5(b)(1).

39. Treas. Reg. sec. 1.864-5(b)(2). The Regulations exempt income derived from incidental investment activity – portfolio investments – and specifically state that a holding company is not a corporation whose principal business is trading in stocks or securities. In addition, income described in categories (1) and (2) in the text does not constitute →

property held primarily for sale to customers in the ordinary course of trade or business) where the sale occurs outside the U.S. but is effected through the U.S. office (however, if a foreign office of the taxpayer participated materially in the sale, the income is not effectively connected regardless of the extent of participation by the U.S. office).[40]

Under section 864(c)(5)(B), foreign source income of the types specified above is 'attributable' to a U.S. office only if (1) that office is a material factor in the production of the income, and (2) the income is realized in the ordinary course of the trade or business of the office. The term 'material' is defined by examples in Regulations, section 1.864-6. In very general terms, the 'material factor' test is met if the U.S. office made a 'significant contribution' to or was an 'essential economic element' in the realization of the income. For example, simply holding meetings of the board of directors in the U.S. would not constitute a 'material factor' in producing income. On the other hand, the Regulations also make clear that the activities of the U.S. office need not be a 'major' factor in the production of income in order for them to be 'material'.[41] The Regulations do provide guidelines and examples with respect to each of the categories of income specified in the preceding paragraph which give considerable guidance in determining the types of activities that will and those that will not be considered to be 'material' to the production of income.[42]

Similar guidance is provided by the Regulations to determine whether a nonresident alien or foreign corporation has an 'office or fixed place of business' in the U.S. In general, the Regulations look to whether a 'fixed facility' (such as a factory or store) is maintained in the U.S. or whether active day-to-day management activity is conducted in the U.S.[43] However, the most difficult problems arise in connection with the activities of U.S. agents for a foreign business. Here the Code in section 864(c)(5)(A) specifies that the office or fixed place of business of

→

effectively connected income if the recipient owns more than 50% of all the voting stock of the corporate payor of if the income constitutes subpart F income (see Chapter 7, below).

As to interest, compare Rev. Rul. 73-227, note 24, above (interest received by the foreign corporation from its foreign affiliates was not effectively connected with its U.S. business); Rev. Rul. 75-253, 1975-1 Cum. Bull. 290 (foreign source interest income was effectively connected where received by a foreign financial corporation that performed in the U.S. all significant activities concerning negotiation and purchase of, and collection of interest and principal on, its securities).

40. Treas. reg. sec. 1.864-5(b)(3).

41. Treas. Reg. sec. 1.864-6(b)(1).

42. See Treas. Reg. sec. 1.864-6(b)(2) and (3).

43. Treas. Reg. sec. 1.864-7(a), (b) and (c).

an agent will not constitute the office or fixed place of business of a nonresident alien or foreign corporation unless (1) the agent possesses and regularly exercises the authority to negotiate and conclude contracts for the principal or maintains a stock of merchandise from which he regularly fills orders on behalf of the principal, *and* (2) the agent is not an independent agent (that is, he is like an employee whose activities are controlled by his foreign principal). Again the Regulations provide numerous examples to illustrate when an agent will be considered independent of his foreign principal and when not.[44]

5.4. Taxation of nonresident aliens

5.4.1. General

The resolution of the definitional issues discussed in the preceding materials defines the tax base to which U.S. rates will be applied. The U.S. then imposes a tax on all U.S. source income and all income that is effectively connected with the conduct of a U.S. trade or business.[45] The rate of tax applied to U.S. source income of a nonresident alien[46]

44. Treas Reg. sec. 1.864-7(d), (e), (f) and (g).
45. Treas. Reg. sec. 1.871-1.
46. The term 'nonresident alien' means an individual who is neither a resident nor a citizen of the U.S. The determination of citizenship is usually a relatively straightforward matter. Residence, however, involves a much more complicated factual inquiry. Treas. Reg. sec. 1.871-2 through 6 provide some detailed guidelines for the resolution of the residency question. In general an alien is presumed to be a nonresident alien. On the other hand, if an alien has been residing within the United States for one year there is a presumption that he is a resident for United States tax purposes. The presumption may be rebutted, however, by appropriate evidence demonstrating the transient nature of the alien's stay. Rev. Rul. 69-611, 1969-2 Cum. Bull. 150. The determination as to resident status is based on the alien's intention with regard to the length and nature of his stay in the U.S. A number of factors are considered, among them the type of visa under which the alien has entered the U.S., the length of time he is physically present in the country, and the nature and extent of his activities within the U.S. As might be expected the question has been the subject of substantial litigation. The following are some representative cases: Siddiqi v. Commissioner, 70 T.C. 553 (1978) (resident alien status where taxpayer entered the United States for an expected stay of 4-5 years to study architecture; compensation earned from temporary employment taxable at full U.S. tax rates); Jellinek v. Commissioner, 36 T.C. 826 (1961) (nonresident alien status despite filing a declaration of intention to become a U.S. citizen where the taxpayer returned to the foreign country within a short period of time because of lack of U.S. employment opportunities); Brittingham v. Commissioner, 66 T.C. 373 (1976) (presumption of nonresidency rebutted where the taxpayer regularly lived in the United States for a period of over 20 years →

varies depending on the type of income involved, whether the taxpayer is engaged in a trade or business in the U.S., and whether the income is effectively connected with that trade or business.

5.4.2. Income taxed at 30% rate

If the nonresident alien individual is not engaged in a U.S. trade or business, a flat rate of 30% is imposed on four categories of income from U.S. sources:

(1) Fixed or determinable annual or periodic income (generally passive investment income such as dividends or interest plus royalties for patents, copyrights, etc.);[47]

(2) Income from certain types of transactions that are given preferential capital gain treatment;[48]

(3) Original issue discount on debt obligations;[49]

→

despite the fact that the stay was limited to a definite period by the immigration laws).

47. The items of income are specified in sec. 871(a)(1)(A). See also Treas. Reg. sec. 1.871-7(b). Sec. 1441 requires that U.S. payors of fixed or determinable income that is not effectively connected income withhold U.S. tax on that income at a rate of 30%. See 5.7.2. Thus, the withholding tax is the tax imposed. By virtue of the source rules, discussed in 4.2.1., interest paid by U.S. banks to nonresident aliens is generally foreign source income and therefore is not subject to the 30% withholding tax.
With respect to transactions involving patents, know-how, and other intangibles, royalties paid under a license agreement are subject to the 30% withholding tax. In addition, if the transfer of the intangible is formally structured as a sale rather than a license, but payments are contingent on the productivity or use of the intangible, the transaction is treated as a license and the payments are subject to withholding as royalties. See sec. 871(a)(1)(D) and 871(e).

48. The income in category (2) is income that is accorded capital gain treatment by special statutory provisions ('deemed' capital gain) even though it would not qualify under the generally applicable capital gain rules. This income includes (a) certain lump sum distributions from qualified employee retirement plans; (b) gains from the sale of patents granted capital gain treatment under sec. 1235; and (c) timber, coal and iron ore royalties. Because the gains in this category do not qualify as 'capital' gains under the general rules, they are subject to the 30% rate regardless of the length of time the recipient is present in the U.S. during the taxable year. 'Normal' capital gains of the type specified in category (4) are taxed at the 30% rate only if the recipient is present in the U.S. for the prescribed period of time.

49. In the Tax Reform Act of 1969, Congress revised the method of taxing orginal issue discount, requiring in general that the holder of the debt obligation include the discount in income ratably over the term of the obligation. No rules were prescribed, however, for the treatment of nonresident aliens who realized original issue discount income on U.S. debt obligations. This oversight was remedied in the Revenue Act of 1971. Sec. 871(a)(1)(C) prescribed rules to determine when the original issue discount must be

→

(4) the excess of capital gains over capital losses if the taxpayer has been present in the U.S. for 183 days or more during the taxable year.[50]

The 30% rate is applied to income of the type discussed above even though the nonresident alien is engaged in a U.S. trade or business, as long as the income is not 'effectively connected' under the tests outlined in 5.2.[51]

Where the income is subject to the 30% rate, the tax is imposed on *gross* income.[52] Thus, no deductions are allowed even though attributable to the income subject to tax. In the case of capital gains, the tax is imposed on the full amount of net gain.[53]

5.4.3. Income taxed at full U.S. tax rates

All income of a nonresident alien that is (or is treated as) effectively connected with the conduct of a U.S. trade or business is subject to the progressive U.S. tax rates from 14–70%.[54] As in the case of U.S.

→

reported currently (and tax withheld currently) and when reporting can be deferred until the redemption of the obligation. See also Proposed Treas. Reg. sec. 1.871-7(b)(2), (c)(1)(ii) and (4) (1976).

50. Treas. Reg. sec. 1.871-7(d). If the 183 day requirement is met, the gains are subject to U.S. tax even though the taxpayer was not in the U.S. when the sales occurred. Conversely, if the taxpayer was in the U.S. for less than 183 days, no tax is imposed even if he was in the U.S. when the sale occurred. In situations where the 183 day test is not satisfied, only gains that would constitute 'effectively connected' income are subject to tax.

51. Treas. Reg. sec. 1.871-8(b)(1).

52. Commissioner v. Wodehouse, 337 U.S. 369 (1969), held, under pre-1954 Code law, that lump sum payments received by a nonresident alien author for the exclusive series and book rights in the U.S. constituted 'gross income' from U.S. sources. Rev. Rul. 74-555, 1974-2 Cum. Bull. 202, as modified by Rev. Rul. 76-283, 1976-2 Cum. Bull. 222, held similarly under current law.

Sec. 872 defines 'gross income' for purposes of sec. 871 and specifically excludes: (1) earnings from foreign ships and aircraft if the country of registration grants the same exemption to a U.S. citizen, see Rev. Rul. 75-459, 1975-2 Cum. Bull. 289; and (2) compensation paid by a foreign employer to a nonresident alien under designated international exchange or training programs. Likewise excluded are (1) income exempt from tax under a treaty (sec. 894(a)); (2) certain distributions from qualified employee retirement plans (sec. 871(f)); and (3) foreign source income that is not 'effectively connected' income (sec. 864(c)(4)(A)).

53. Thus the deduction for 60% of long-term capital gains under section 1202 and the unlimited carryover for capital losses under section 1212(b) are denied. However, the gains may be reduced by capital losses incurred during the year.

54. A nonresident alien individual may utilize the 50% maximum rate on earned income provided in sec. 1348 if the income is 'effectively connected' income and the individual is

→

individuals, the rates are applied to taxable income (rather than to gross income as in the case of items described in 5.4.2.). Thus, gross income (as defined in section 872) is reduced by the deductions that are 'connected with income' which itself is 'effectively connected' income (as specified in section 873).[55] In addition, section 873 allows gross income to be reduced by one personal exemption and the deductions for charitable contributions and personal casualty losses even though these items are not so 'connected'.[56] Finally, credits against tax, such as the investment tax credit, are allowed.

→

single. If the nonresident alien individual is married, the maximum tax cannot be utilized because its benefits are made available to married individuals only if they file a joint return. Under section 6013(a)(1), a joint return normally may not be filed if either spouse is a nonresident alien. Accordingly, a married nonresident alien can utilize the 50% maximum tax only if his or her spouse is a U.S. citizen or resident and the spouses elect to file a joint return under the procedure discussed in note 56, below. Wages are subject to the full U.S. withholding rates. Other 'effectively connected' income is not subject to the 30% withholding rate specified in sec. 1441. See 5.7.2. For a discussion of the U.S. tax treatment of compensation paid to alien individuals, see Harllee, U.S. Income Taxation of Aliens on Current and Deferred Compensation, 37 New York University Institute on Federal Taxation sec. 21.00 (1979).

55. The rules for allocating and apportioning deductions are those set forth in Treas. Reg. sec. 1.861-8 and 1.863-1 through 5, discussed in 4.4. No deduction is allowed for an expenditure that is allocable to an item exempt from tax. See Treas. Reg. sec. 1.873-1(a)(1), (5).

56. The Internal Revenue Service held in Rev. Rul. 58-434, 1958-2 Cum. Bull. 110, that the deduction for child care expenses could likewise be taken by a nonresident alien even though it was an itemized personal deduction like the charitable contributions deduction and personal casualty loss deduction. Presumably the same result will be reached under the present credit for child care costs. Deductions for costs of producing income, such as the moving expense deduction and state and local taxes on U.S. earnings, are deductible by nonresident aliens. See, e.g., Rev. Rul. 73-402, 1973-2 Cum. Bull. 227. A nonresident alien is not given the benefit of the zero bracket amount (standard deduction) discussed in 2.3.2.4. because personal deductions are generally not allowed to such taxpayers. Sec. 63(e)(1)(B).

If a nonresident is married to a U.S. citizen or resident, sections 6013(g) and (h) permit the spouses to elect to treat the nonresident spouse as a U.S. resident and file a joint return. The spouses must consent to be taxed on their worldwide income for the taxable year. They then are entitled to claim personal exemptions for themselves and qualified dependents, the zero bracket amount, excess itemized personal deductions, the 50% maximum tax on earned income, tax credits, etc., just as in a joint return filed by married U.S. citizens or residents.

Sec. 874 requires a nonresident alien to file a return in order to obtain the benefit of the deductions allowed by sec. 873. Brittingham v. Commissioner, 66 T.C. 373 (1976), held that even though some return is filed, no deductions are allowed if it is not a 'true and accurate' return.

5.4.3.1. Real estate gains taxed at U.S. capital gain rates

Typically, gain from the disposition of a U.S. real property interest would be subject to tax at the capital gains rates (40% of the otherwise applicable regular rate). A special 20% minimum tax is applicable if normal rules would produce a lower rate.

5.4.4. TREATIES

Treaty provisions agreed to by the U.S. and another country may modify the rules described above. See Chapter 9.

5.5. Taxation of foreign corporations

5.5.1. GENERAL

The U.S. method of taxation of foreign corporations follows in most respects the rules applicable to nonresident alien individuals. Thus, in general, U.S. source investment income is taxed at a flat 30% rate if it is not effectively connected with the conduct of a U.S. trade or business or at the normal corporate rates (generally 46%), if it is effectively connected.

5.5.2. INCOME OF FOREIGN CORPORATIONS TAXED AT 30% RATE

If a foreign corporation is not engaged in a U.S. trade or business during the taxable year, a tax of 30% is imposed on its gross income[57] from U.S. sources that consists of (1) fixed or determinable annual or periodic income;[58] (2) timber, coal or iron ore royalties; (3) original issue

57. Sec. 883 excludes from gross income of a foreign corporation (1) earnings from the operation of foreign ships, aircraft and certain railroad rolling stock if the country of registration grants a similar exemption to U.S. corporations; and (2) earnings by a foreign entity that is designated by its government to participate with the U.S. in the ownership or operation of a global communications satellite system.
58. The definition in sec. 881(a) follows that in sec. 871(a) discussed in 5.4.2. As to dividends paid in property (rather than cash) by a U.S. corporation to a foreign corporation, the amount of the dividend is the fair market value of the property if the dividend is not effectively connected income to the foreign corporation; if it is effectively connected, →

discount;[59] and (4) gains from the sale or exchange of patents, copyrights, etc. to the extent that the gains are contingent on the productivity, use or disposition of the property sold.[60]

Even though a corporation is engaged in a U.S. trade or business, income of the type described in the preceding paragraph is taxed at the 30% rate if it is not effectively connected with the conduct of the U.S. trade or business.

5.5.2.1. Capital gains

Unlike nonresident alien individuals, the capital gains realized by a foreign corporation that are not effectively connected with a U.S. trade or business are exempt from U.S. tax. Capital gains of a foreign corporation that are effectively connected generally are taxed at the 28% corporate capital gain rate.[61]

5.5.2.2. Gains from disposition of U.S. real property interests

Gains from the disposition of U.S. real property interests by a foreign corporation are treated as effectively connected with the conduct of a U.S. trade or business. The term 'disposition' includes dividend distributions and distributions pursuant to a redemption or liquidation. Gains are thus generally taxed at the 28% corporate capital gain rate.

5.5.3. Income of foreign corporations taxed at normal corporation tax rates

The taxable income of a foreign corporation that is (or is treated as) effectively connected with the conduct of a U.S. trade or business is taxed at the normal U.S. corporate rates: 17% on the first $25,000 of taxable income, 20% on the next $25,000, 30% on the next $25,000, 40% on the next $25,000, and 46% on all taxable income in excess of $100,000.

→

the amount of the dividend is the lower of the fair market value of, or the distributor's cost basis in, the property. Sec. 301(b)(1)(D), (d)(3).

59. See note 49, above; Proposed Treas. Reg. sec. 1.881-2(b)(2), (c)(1)(ii) (1976).

60. See note 47, above.

61. See 5.3.2.

In determining taxable income, the starting point is gross income[62] which is effectively connected with the U.S. trade or business. Deductions are allowable to the extent that they are 'connected with income' that is itself effectively connected income.[63] A charitable contribution deduction is allowed whether or not it is so connected. In addition, credits against tax, such as the investment tax credit, are allowed.

5.5.4. Treaties

Treaty provisions agreed to by the U.S. and another country may modify the rules described above. See Chapter 9.

5.6. Taxation of partnerships

Since the U.S. does not treat the partnership as a separate taxable entity, the partnership, whether foreign or domestic, simply serves to pass through the partnership income and loss to the partners. Thus, the rules outlined above with respect to nonresident aliens and foreign corporations determine the taxability of partnership income.

5.6.1. Foreign partnership with U.S. partners

As indicated above, the foreign partnership[64] is not itself a taxable

62. See note 57.
63. Sec. 882(c)(1). See note 55, above.
64. Sec. 7701(a)(5) defines a foreign partnership as one which is not a domestic partnership, which in turn means a partnership which is not organized under U.S. law. As indicated in 2.4., the status of a foreign entity as a partnership or as a corporation for U.S. tax purposes is determined by applying U.S. standards. Although foreign law determines the relationships of the individual investors to the entity, the foreign law classification of the organization is not controlling for U.S. tax purposes. The tests to be applied are those listed in note 70 to Chapter 2. See Rev. Rul. 77-214, 1977-1 Cum. Bull. 408, where a German GmbH formed by two U.S. subsidiaries of a U.S. parent corporation was held to constitute a corporation. The Ruling stated that a German GmbH is not automatically classified as either a partnership or as a corporation; the proper classification depends on all the relevant facts and circumstances, including the provisions of the memorandum of association. Under German law, a GmbH has the U.S. corporate characteristics of limited liability and centralized management. Although the memorandum of association provided for a disolution upon bankruptcy of any of the quotaholders and quotas were not freely transferable without the consent of all quotaholders, the Ruling held that the →

entity. The U.S. partners are subject to tax on their share of the partnership's worldwide income and are entitled to a foreign tax credit for any taxes paid by the foreign partnership.

5.6.2. Foreign partners in a U.S. or foreign partnership

The taxation of a foreign partner on the income of a U.S. or foreign partnership depends on the nature of that income. Under the conduit principle of partnership taxation, the partnership income retains its character in the hands of the individual partner. Thus, for example, if the partnership has income which is effectively connected with its U.S. trade or business, the partner is taxable on his share of such income under the rules described in 5.4.3 and 5.5.3. The partnership's U.S. trade or business is attributed to the foreign partners.[65] If the partnership has income which, if received by the foreign partner directly would not be subject to tax, for example, noneffectively connected income from foreign sources, the foreign partner is not subject to tax on his share of such income.

5.7. Procedural aspects

5.7.1. Return requirements

Every nonresident alien or foreign corporation which is engaged in a U.S. trade or business must file a U.S. tax return.[66] This return must be filed even though the taxpayer has no taxable income in his U.S. trade

→

corporate characteristics of free transferability of interest and continuity of life nonetheless existed because the U.S. parent could make any transfer decisions for the quotaholders and there were no separate interests to compel dissolution upon the occurance of any of the stated dissolution events. Private rulings have been issued by the Internal Revenue Service classifying a particular foreign juridical entity as a partnership for U.S. tax purposes where the facts and memorandum of association indicated that free transferability of interests and continuity of life were not present. A number of seemingly contradictory private rulings have been issued in this area and it is understood that the Internal Revenue Service is re-examining the whole question of the classification of foreign entities. See also MCA, Inc. v. U.S. 80-2 USTC 9617 (C.D. Calif., 1980), holding various foreign limited liability companies taxable as corporations and not as partnerships.

65. Sec. 875(1).

66. Treas. Reg. sec. 1.6012-1(b), 2(g).

or business. A U.S. return must also be filed if the foreign taxpayer's U.S. tax liability has not been completedly covered by withholding at source. The filing of a return is a prerequisite for the allowance of any deductions otherwise available under the Code and in addition there are penalties for failure to file.[67] The return is generally due on or before the 15th day of the sixth month following the close of the taxable year (June 15th for calendar year taxpayers). Special rules apply for employment income. In some cases estimated tax payments may be required.

Departing aliens in certain visa classifications must procure a certificate that they have complied with the income tax laws before departing ('sailing permit').

Extensive reporting requirements were instituted as part of the 1980 legislation subjecting to U.S. tax the gains on dispositions of U.S. real estate by foreign investors. (See 5.3.3.) If a domestic corporation has a foreign person as a shareholder and qualifies as a 'United States real property holding corporation' (RPHC) at any time during the current calendar year or any of the four immediately preceding calendar years, it is required to file a return identifying the foreign shareholders and supplying the tax administrator with such other information as may be required.[68] A foreign corporation or a partnership, trust or estate (foreign and domestic) is required to file an annual return identifying all foreign persons who have a substantial indirect investment in U.S. real property interests through the entity. A substantial interest investor is one whose pro rata share of U.S. real property interests held by the entity exceeds $50,000.[69] As an alternative to the reporting requirement, the entity may furnish the tax administrator adequate security to insure that any U.S. tax attributable to dispositions of U.S. real property interests will in fact be paid. Finally, any foreign person who holds a direct investment in U.S. real estate which does not constitute a trade or business (and who is not required to file a return under the rules described above) must file an annual information return if the value of his interest equals or exceeds $50,000.[70] Monetary penalties are imposed for failure to comply with the reporting requirements.

67. Sec. 874(a); sec. 882(c)(2).

68. Sec. 6039C(a). The reporting requirement does not apply to publicly traded corporations. Nominees holding stock for foreign persons are also subject to the reporting rules.

69. Sec. 6039C(b). The entity is also required to furnish such other information as the tax administrator may request. Similar information must be provided to each substantial foreign investor in the entity.

70. Sec. 6039C(c).

5.7.2. Withholding at Source

Section 1441 imposes a 30% withholding tax on interest, dividends, wages, etc., and other fixed or determinable annual or periodic income paid to a nonresident alien or foreign corporation from U.S. sources. In the normal situation, this withholding at source fully satisfies the nonresident taxpayer's U.S. tax liability and no tax return need be filed.

No withholding is required for income which is effectively connected with a U.S. trade or business.[71] This mirrors the fact that effectively connected income is not subject to the 30% tax, but is taxed at normal individual or corporate rates. Wages received by a nonresident alien employee for services performed in the U.S. are subject to the usual wage withholding tax imposed on U.S. citizens and residents rather than the 30% rate.[72]

To be subject to withholding under section 1441, amounts must be from sources within the U.S. and thus no withholding is required on non-U.S. source income, e.g., wages paid by a foreign employer to a nonresident alien employee who is only temporarily present in the U.S. and meets the tests of section 861(a)(3) (see 4.2.3.). On the other hand, if the income is from U.S. sources, withholding is required even if the foreign employer is not otherwise engaged in a U.S. trade or business.

The 30% withholding rate is often reduced or eliminated in United States tax treaties. See Chapter 9.

In general, for any exemption from or reduction in withholding tax to apply, various certifications of the recipient's qualification for the reduction or exemption must be supplied to the U.S. withholding agent.[73]

71. Sec. 1441(c)(1).
72. Treas. Reg. sec. 1.1441-4(b).
73. See, e.g., Treas. Reg. sec. 1.1441-4(a)(2).

Chapter 6
Taxation of foreign source income of U.S. persons

6.1. General

U.S. citizens and residents and corporations organized in the U.S. are subject to tax on their worldwide income. However, a number of rules apply to the income from foreign sources of such taxpayers. By far the most important is the foreign tax credit, which allows such taxpayers a credit against their U.S. income tax liability for foreign income taxes paid on income from foreign sources. In addition, there are a number of other special provisions which are applicable to the foreign income or foreign activities of U.S. taxpayers. The effect of these special rules on U.S. taxpayers is discussed after consideration of the foreign tax credit.

6.2. The foreign tax credit

6.2.1. Treatment of foreign taxes in general

U.S. citizens, resident aliens and domestic corporations who pay income taxes to foreign countries may elect either:

(1) To deduct those taxes from income as prescribed by section 164(a)[1]; or

(2) To claim foreign income taxes paid or accrued as a credit against U.S. income taxes[2] as allowed under sections 901–908 and 960. If the

1. A deduction also is allowed for foreign real property taxes and any other foreign taxes incurred in profit-seeking activities.
2. Section 901 precludes utilization of the foreign tax credit to offset certain special U.S. penalty taxes as, for example, the 'add on' minimum tax, the accumulated earnings tax and the personal holding company tax. The foreign tax credit may be used by individuals, however, to offset the 'alternative' minimum tax.

taxpayer elects to utilize the foreign tax credit as to *any* income taxes, no foreign *income* taxes may be deducted under section 164. However, the deductibility of all other types of taxes described therein is not affected by the election.

Generally speaking, it is to the taxpayer's advange to elect the foreign tax credit rather than the deduction. The credit produces a dollar-for-dollar offset against U.S. tax liability; the benefit of a deduction is limited to the amount of the foreign income taxes multiplied by the taxpayer's marginal U.S. tax bracket (i.e., a maximum reduction for an individual of 70 cents in U.S. tax for each dollar of foreign tax paid).

6.2.2. Objectives of the foreign tax credit

Detailed rules are provided in the Code and Regulations to implement the foreign tax credit mechanism.[3] In considering these rules, it is important to keep in mind the various functions which the foreign tax credit plays in the U.S. international tax system.

Given the fact that the U.S. taxes the foreign source income of its tax residents in full, some recognition must be given to the existence of foreign taxes which are also imposed on that income by foreign countries or else (1) a U.S. taxpayer with foreign source income will bear a total tax burden greater than that of a taxpayer with only income from the U.S., and (2) because of the multiple burden, foreign investment will be less attractive for a U.S. taxpayer than domestic investment. The first point is essentially a question of equity in the treatment of U.S. taxpayers regardless of the source of their income; the second is a question of the attitude to be adopted regarding the impact that the tax system should have on investment decisions.

As to the first point, from the point of view of the U.S., equity is achieved if the foreign taxes paid by the U.S. taxpayer with income from abroad are treated as equivalent to the payment of U.S. taxes up

3. The discussion of the foreign tax credit is necessarily brief and is intended to provide a general outline of the structure and operation of the credit. The classic work on the subject is Owens, The Foreign Tax Credit (1961). See also Surrey, Current Issues in the Taxation of Corporate Foreign Investment, 56 Columbia Law Review 815 (1956); Surrey, The United States Taxation of Foreign Income, 1 Journal of Law and Economics 72 (1958). Recent legislative changes in the foreign tax credit are discussed in Dale, The Reformed Foreign Tax Credit: A Path Through the Maze, 33 Tax Law Review 175 (1978).

to the level of taxation imposed by the U.S. on a similar amount of income received by a taxpayer with income from sources within the U.S. The foreign tax liability replaces all or a portion of the U.S. tax liability on the foreign source income and equality of treatment is assured.

Suppose, however, that the foreign taxes exceed the U.S. taxes which would be applicable on the same amount of income. Here the taxpayer with income from abroad bears a higher tax burden than a U.S. taxpayer with the same amount of income from U.S. sources, if the credit is limited to the amount of U.S. tax liability on the income. This result does not occur because of the failure of the U.S. to recognize the foreign tax liability. It simply reflects the fact that the foreign tax rate is higher than that selected by the U.S. for the taxation of the income, whether domestic or foreign, of its tax residents. In such a case, the U.S. is treating its taxpayers equally when viewed from the perspective of the general level of *U.S.* taxation. Put another way, there is no international double taxation as long as the U.S. recognizes the foreign tax liability up to the level of U.S. taxation.

However, when considered from the perspective of the second point, the impact of total tax burden on foreign investment decisions, failure to credit (or refund) foreign taxes when they exceed the level of U.S. taxation results in an additional tax burden on foreign investment by a U.S. taxpayer when compared with purely domestic investment. Here a policy of tax neutrality ('capital export' neutrality) with respect to investment decisions would require a full crediting of foreign taxes without regard to their level in comparison with U.S. domestic taxation. As will be seen, because of special limitations and special preferences, this result is not achieved by the U.S. foreign tax credit mechanism.

The foreign tax credit mechanism of dealing with the existence of a foreign tax liability can of course be contrasted with the exemption method used by many European countries. Under the exemption system, the foreign tax liability is recognized by exempting the foreign source income from domestic taxation. As a result, international double taxation is by definition avoided, but at the price of losing (1) equality of treatment of domestic taxpayers regardless of the source of their income when viewed from the perspective of the domestic system, and (2) tax neutrality with respect to foreign versus domestic investment decisions. Countries which have utilized the exemption method have insured that the foreign operations of their domestic taxpayers will not bear any other tax burden than that imposed by the country of foreign operation. This benefit (capital import neutrality) is seen by those countries as outweighing the equity and capital export neutrality factors.

The above discussion illustrates the fact that no mechanism has been developed to deal with the problem of overlapping tax jurisdictions which will by itself accommodate all three of the considerations here discussed. Therefore, many countries including the U.S., provide subsidies (either directly or through the tax system) to achieve the objectives which cannot be realized through their basic structural mechanism for dealing with the problem of multiple jurisdictions taxing the same income.[4]

6.2.3. The direct foreign tax credit in general

6.2.3.1. Eligibility for tax credit

6.2.3.1.1. Persons eligible

Section 901(b) describes the categories of taxpayers eligible for the credit. U.S. citizens and domestic corporations may credit income taxes paid to any foreign country. Alien residents, subject to the limitation described in 6.2.5.2., below, are also entitled to the credit for taxes paid to any foreign country. As discussed in more detail in 6.2.3.4., section 906 allows a credit to nonresident alien individuals and foreign corporations for taxes paid to any foreign country or U.S. possession with respect to income that is effectively connected with a U.S. trade or business (see 5.3., above). Any of the above categories of eligible taxpayers that are members of a partnership or beneficiaries of a trust may also claim as a credit their proportionate share of the qualifying foreign taxes paid by the partnership or trust.[5]

4. For discussions of the issues, see U.S. Treasury Department, U.S. Taxation of Undistributed Income of Controlled Foreign Corporations (Treasury Department News Release WS-778, April, 1976); Bergsten, Horst and Moran, American Multinationals and American Interests (1978), pp. 165-212, 461-467.

5. If a partnership or trust is determined to be an association taxable as a corporation (under U.S. tax principles), then no foreign tax credit is allowable to the individual U.S. investors under section 901 even though the entity may be a valid partnership or trust under foreign law. Rev. Rul. 72-197, 1972-1 Cum. Bull. 215.

6.2.3.1.2. Taxes eligible

The credit for foreign taxes is limited to *income* taxes.[6] In general, the character of the foreign tax is determined by its similarity to the U.S. income tax. Detailed Regulations have been issued which deal with the question of when a foreign tax qualifies as an income tax.[7]

6. Technically the credit extends to war profits and excess profit taxes as well but in practice it is the income tax aspect of the credit which is important. The theoretical justification for limiting the credit to income taxes is that such taxes in general are not economically passed on by the U.S. taxpayer and thus, with respect to those taxes, true economic double taxation has occurred. Rather than examining each situation to determine if in fact the tax has been passed on, the statute assumes that all (and only) income taxes are borne by the U.S. taxpayer and are thus eligible for the credit. For a discussion of these issues, see Owens, note 3, at 83.

7. The determination whether a foreign tax qualifies as an income tax is a crucial part of the foreign tax credit mechanism. After a number of years of relatively little activity in this area, the Internal Revenue Service in 1978 began issuing a number of rulingsetting forth the tests that a foreign tax must meet before it qualifies as an 'income tax'. See, e.g., Rev. Rul. 78-61, 1978-1 Cum. Bull. 221 (Ontario mining tax was not a creditable income tax because unrealized income was included in the base, deductions were not allowed to permit the taxpayer to recover capital investment and other costs of producing the mining income; the tax was in fact a severance tax on the privilege of mining); Rev. Rul. 78-63, 1978-1 Cum. Bull. 222 (Lybian and Saudi Arabian oil taxes imposed on 'posted prices' and hence not on realized gain were likewise not creditable income taxes). In 1980, the Internal Revenue Service issued Temporary Regulations, effective for taxable years ending after June 15, 1979, which set forth detailed standards to determine whether a foreign tax is creditable. The Temporary Regulations may be modified by subsequent final Regulations.

In general, the Temporary Regulations take the position that a foreign charge is an income tax only if: (1) the charge is not compensation for a specific economic benefit; (2) the charge is based on realized net income; and (3) the charge follows reasonable rules of taxing jurisdiction. The Regulations specifically provide that a foreign tax may qualify as an income tax even if the provisions of foreign law imposing the tax differ substantially from the income tax provisions of the Internal Revenue Code. Temporary Treas. Reg. sec. 4.901-2(a). Nonetheless, the Regulations are extremely detailed and rather clearly reflect the U.S. Internal Revenue Code.

The Regulations deal with a number of specific situations. Thus, for example, Temporary Treas. Reg. sec. 4.901-2(a) takes the position that a foreign tax is not creditable if liability for the tax is related to the availability of a credit for the tax against the income tax liability of another country. This provision is aimed at so-called 'soak up' taxes which are imposed by some countries when payments are made to nonresidents of a foreign tax credit system country but not when made to other nonresidents.

The Temporary Regulations exempt, from the requirement that the tax be imposed on net income, gross withholding taxes on interest, dividends, royalties, etc., if the foreign country makes a 'reasonable distinction' between the situations in which its tax is imposed on a gross basis and the situations in which the tax is imposed on a net basis. This distinction must be based on the degree of contact that the recipient has with the foreign country or with the assets and activities in the foreign country that generate the income. →

6.2.3.2. *'In lieu of' taxes*

Section 903 also permits certain foreign taxes paid in lieu of an income tax to qualify for the credit under section 901. In general, the following conditions must be met before a tax will be considered as imposed 'in lieu of' an income tax: (1) the tax must not be a compensation for a specific economic benefit; (2) the tax must be in substitution for, and not in addition to, an income tax otherwise generally imposed; (3) the burden imposed by the tax must be comparable to the burden imposed by the otherwise applicable general income tax, over a reasonable period of time; and (4) the tax must be imposed following 'reasonable rules' of taxing jurisdiction.[8]

6.2.3.3. *Time and manner of claiming credit*

Generally the year in which a taxpayer is entitled to claim the credit is determined by its method of accounting, i.e., cash or accrual. Section 905(a), however, permits a taxpayer to claim the credit in the year the foreign taxes accrued regardless of the method of accounting employed. But, if the foreign tax ultimately determined differs from that claimed as a credit, appropriate adjustments must be made.

→

For example, a 25% withholding tax on gross interest paid by residents to nonresidents, regardless of the level of activity which the nonresident performs within the country, does not qualify as an income tax because the 'reasonable distinction' test is not met. On the other hand, if the country makes a distinction between nonresidents that are 'established' in the country and taxes them on a net basis while taxing 'nonestablished nonresidents' on a gross basis, the gross tax will qualify as an income tax. Temporary Treas. Reg. sec. 4.901-2(e), Examples (28)-(30). Despite the specificity of the Temporary Regulations, it is anticipated that rulings will be issued with respect to a number of important taxes of specific countries. In addition, the results reached in the Regulations and the rulings may be changed by tax treaty. For example, Rev. Rul. 78-424, 1978-2 Cum. Bull. 179, held that the U.K. petroleum revenue tax (PRT) was not a creditable income tax because the tax base included certain unrealized gains and was imposed on a field-by-field basis so that a taxpayer could have an overall loss on operations and still incur tax. The result in Rev. Rul. 78-424 was changed by the Third Protocol to the U.S.-U.K. tax treaty which provides a limited tax credit for the U.K. PRT. A 'foreign country' includes any political subdivision thereof that levies and collects an income tax. Treas. Reg. sec. 1.901-2(h).

8. Temporary Treas. Reg. sec. 4.903-1. The Regulations give a number of examples of taxes meeting the 'in lieu of' requirement. For example, if all business income is subject to an income tax except the income derived by insurance companies and insurance companies are subject to a charge on gross premiums, the charge on gross premiums would meet the 'substitution' requirement and, if the other requirements were met, would qualify as an 'in lieu of' tax. Temporary Treas. Reg. sec., 4.903-1(d), Example (8).

To be entitled to the foreign tax credit, the taxpayer must submit proof of (1) the amount of its total foreign source income; (2) the amount of its income from each country and the taxes paid or accrued thereto for which a credit is being taken; and (3) any other information necessary to enable the Internal Revenue Service to verify and compute the credit.[9]

6.2.3.4. Nonresident aliens and foreign corporations

As part of the Foreign Investors Tax Act of 1966, the U.S. subjected certain foreign source income to U.S. tax. See 5.3.4. above. As noted earlier, the purpose of this provision was to prevent the U.S. from becoming a tax haven as the result of the relaxation of its tax jurisdiction. However, the foreign source income that is taxed by the U.S. under its effectively connected concept may also be taxed by the country of source and/or the country of domicile. Consistent with the purposes of the foreign tax credit, therefore, section 906 was added in 1966 to grant a foreign tax credit under section 901 to nonresident aliens and foreign corporations for taxes paid or accrued (or deemed paid or accrued under section 902) to a foreign country or U.S. possession with respect to that income. The limitations applicable to sections 901 and 902 likewise apply to the credit allowable by virtue of section 906.

6.2.4. The indirect credit

The discussion in 6.2.3. concerned taxes paid directly by a U.S. (or other qualifying) taxpayer to a foreign country. Section 902 treats foreign income taxes paid by described subsidiaries of U.S. parent corporations as deemed paid by the parent. As a result, the U.S. corporation becomes entitled to a credit under section 901 for the taxes thus deemed paid by it. This is commonly referred to as the 'indirect credit'.[10]

More specifically, if a U.S. corporation owns 10 percent or more of

9. Treas. Reg. sec. 1.905-2, and Rev. Rul. 67-308, 1967-2 Cum. Bull. 254, provide guidelines on the kind of evidence that a taxpayer should submit to substantiate a claimed foreign tax credit.

10. As in the case of the direct credit, the discussion provides an outline of the structure and operation of the indirect foreign tax credit. For a detailed analysis of the mechanism, see Owens and Ball, The Indirect Foreign Tax Credit (vol. 1, 1975; vol. 2, 1979).

the voting stock[11] of a foreign corporation from which it receives a dividend[12], it will be deemed to have paid the foreign income taxes paid by the subsidiary attributable to that dividend. As a result, the U.S. parent is entitled to a foreign tax credit under section 901 for the taxes paid by the foreign subsidiary. The U.S. parent must also include the amount of the credit in its income (the 'gross-up' requirement of section 78).[13] In effect, then, the U.S. parent is treated as if the foreign subsidiary had paid it a dividend that included the tax due to the foreign country and the U.S. parent had then paid the tax to the foreign country. On this model, inclusion of the amount of the tax in the U.S. parent's income, treating the grossed-up dividend as foreign source income, and then granting a tax credit under section 901 produces a structurally correct result (and the same result that is produced if the U.S. parent operates abroad through a branch rather than a subsidiary).

The indirect credit is also extended to taxes paid on dividends distributed by second and third tier foreign corporations if the parent of each meets the 10 percent voting stock requirement. However, in the case of second and third tier subsidiaries, the U.S. parent must have an indirect ownership in such subsidiaries of at least 5 percent. For example, assume a U.S. parent owns 30 percent of the voting stock of a foreign corporation which in turn owns 10 percent of the voting stock of still another foreign corporation. Although the 10 percent test is met in each case, the U.S. parent will not be entitled to an indirect credit for foreign taxes paid by the second tier subsidiary because the U.S. parent has only an indirect 3 percent interest in it (30 percent of 10 percent).

If the 5 percent test is met with respect to second and third tier subsidiaries, then the foreign taxes paid by the first tier subsidiary include the taxes it is deemed to have paid with respect to dividends paid up by the second and third tier corporations. Accordingly, the U.S. parent will then get the benefit of those lower tier taxes as to dividend distributions it receives from the first tier subsidiary.[14]

11. See Rev. Rul. 74-459, 1974-2 Cum. Bull. 207 (indirect credit not available for dividends paid on a 75% nonvoting stock interest when the shareholder did not own 10 percent of the voting stock of the distributing corporation).

12. The 10 percent test is applied at the time the dividend is received by the U.S. shareholder. Treas. Reg. sec. 1.902-1(a)(8).

13. Prior to the Tax Reform Act of 1976, dividends received from less developed country corporations were not subject to the gross-up requirement. The Act, however, applied the gross-up requirement to dividends received from such corporations. The change generally applied to taxable years beginning after December 31, 1975.

14. Guidelines and examples of the operation of the indirect credit where second and third tier corporations are involved are set forth in Treas. Reg. sec. 1.902-1.

The amount of the indirect credit allowable to a U.S. parent corporation is the ratio of the total foreign taxes paid by the foreign subsidiary which the dividend paid[15] bears to the subsidiary's accumulated earnings and profits in excess of the foreign taxes paid.[16] For example, assume U.S. Corporation X owns all the stock of Foreign Corporation Y. Y has $100 of before tax profits for the year, pays a foreign tax of $48, and distributes a dividend to X of $26. Corporation X is entitled to a foreign tax credit with respect to the dividend of $24 ($48 times 26/52). Correspondingly, Corporation X must include in its income $50 (the $26 dividend received plus the $24 deemed taxes paid).

The operation of the indirect credit where first and second tier subsidiaries are involved is illustrated by the following example: Assume U.S. Corporation A owns all the stock of Foreign Corporation B which in turn owns all the stock of Foreign Corporation C. During the year, Corporation C had before-tax profits of 300, paid foreign tax of 90 and distributed a 100 dividend to Corporation B. During the same year, Corporation B had 300 of before-tax profits, made up of 200 from its own business operations and the 100 dividend from Corporation C. Corporation B paid 50 of foreign tax on its business income and distributed a dividend of 125 to Corporation A. Corporation B is deemed to have paid 42.857 of the foreign taxes paid by Corporation C (90 times 100/210). Corporation B thus actually paid and is deemed to have paid 92.857 of foreign taxes, composed of the 50 taxes actually paid and the 42.857 of taxes paid by Corporation C which are deemed paid by Corporation B. Corporation A then gets a credit against U.S. tax of 46.428 determined by multiplying the 92.857 taxes paid and deemed

15. The term 'dividend' means a dividend as defined under U.S. tax rules in section 316. For treatment of a dividend paid in property other than cash, see H. H. Robertson Co. v. Commissioner, 59 T.C. 53 (1972), affirmed per curiam (unpublished opinion, 3d Cir. 1974); Rev. Rul. 77-483, 1977-2 Cum. Bull. 244 (where a foreign subsidiary distributes appreciated property as a dividend to its U.S. parent, for section 902 purposes the amount of the dividend is the fair market value of the property; the basis of the property to the U.S. corporation is the fair market value of the property; but the earnings and profits of the foreign subsidiary are reduced only by the basis of the property). As to gains recognized on sales or exchanges of stock in a foreign corporation that are taxed somewhat like dividends, see section 1248, discussed in 8.1.2. See also Schoenfeld, Some Definitional Problems in the Deemed Paid Foreign Tax Credit of Section 902: 'Dividends' and 'Accumulated Profits', 18 Tax Law Review 401 (1963).

16. Treas. Reg. sec. 1.902-1(b)(2). Earnings and profits of the foreign corporation are determined under U.S. tax rules. Treas. Reg. sec. 1.902-1(g). See Rev. Rul. 74-550, 1974-2 Cum. Bull. 209, for computations where multiple years' earnings and profits are involved, some with surpluses and some with deficits.

paid by Corporation B by a fraction the numerator of which is 125 (the dividend actually paid by Corporation B) and the denominator of which is 250 (Corporation B's accumulated profits in excess of taxes). Correspondingly, Corporation A must include the 46.428 in income under section 78. The operation of the indirect foreign tax credit does require careful planning. As the foregoing example illustrates, where the tax rate of the second tier corporation is higher than the tax rate of the first tier corporation on their respective business operations, a dividend by the second tier subsidiary to the first tier subsidiary can increase the allowable foreign tax credit upon a dividend by the first tier subsidiary to the U.S. parent corporation. On the other hand, if the tax rate of the second tier subsidiary is lower than the tax rate of the first tier subsidiary, a dividend by the second tier subsidiary in effect reduces the foreign tax credit available on a dividend by the first tier subsidiary to the U.S. parent corporation.

The foreign taxes deemed paid under section 902 are treated under section 901 in the same manner as foreign taxes paid directly and are subject to the same limitations.

6.2.5. Special limitations on the foreign tax credit

6.2.5.1. General

Although a taxpayer may satisfy the requirements for the direct or indirect foreign tax credit, the amount of the credit that will actually be allowed to offset U.S. tax liability may be reduced either by certain special limitations imposed by the Code or by the overall limitation established in section 904. The special limitations are applied first to the otherwise allowable foreign tax credit, after which the remaining amount is then subject to the overall limitation of section 904. The special limitations are discussed below and the overall limitation is taken up in 6.2.6. Finally, a limitation that appears to limit even the overall limitation is considered in paragraph 6.2.7.

6.2.5.2. Resident aliens

Generally a resident alien is entitled to a credit against U.S. income taxes for taxes paid to any foreign country or U.S. possession. However, section 901(c) authorizes the President to disallow the foreign tax credit to resident aliens who are citizens of a foreign country that does not allow U.S. citizens resident therein a similar credit for taxes paid to the U.S. or other countries. Before the President can take such an action, he must make findings that (1) the foreign country involved does not allow U.S. citizens a credit similar to the U.S. foreign tax credit, (2) the U.S. has made a request to the foreign country to provide a tax credit to U.S. citizens who are residing in it, and (3) it is in the public interest of the U.S. to allow a foreign tax credit to citizens of the foreign country who are U.S. residents only if the foreign country grants a similar credit to U.S. citizens who are residents of the foreign country. The special limitation may be invoked only by a Presidential proclamation.

6.2.5.3. Foreign taxes on mineral income

The U.S. grants a tax subsidy to oil, gas and other mineral producers through the percentage depletion deduction. Different percentage depletion rates are specified for the various natural resources covered.[17] The percentage depletion deduction is allowed even though the taxpayer has already recovered its cost in a particular mine or well. In effect, the percentage depletion deduction operates to exempt from tax a percentage of income from specified natural resources (e.g., 22 percent in the case of uranium and sulphur).

The percentage depletion deduction is available for all domestic production (except major oil companies cannot take the deduction for oil and gas production). In the case of certain specified hard minerals (e.g., sulphur and uranium), the percentage depletion deduction is also available for foreign production.

Section 901(e) imposes a special limitation that prevents a taxpayer from claiming a foreign tax credit that is attributable to foreign income exempt from U.S. tax by virtue of the percentage depletion deduction. Because the percentage depletion deduction is granted by the U.S. for income from certain foreign natural resource production, Congress apparently felt that a double tax benefit resulted if a foreign tax credit could be taken with respect to the income exempted from U.S. tax by the deduction.

17. Sec. 613, 613A.

6.2.5.4. *Oil and gas payments not treated as taxes*

In the case of payments made to a foreign country with respect to income from the purchase and sale of oil and gas extracted from the country, section 901(f) imposes a special limit on the amount of the allowable foreign tax credit. Such payments will be considered costs of acquiring the oil or gas and not creditable taxes if (1) the taxpayer has no 'economic interest' in the oil and gas[18], and (2) the purchase or sale of the oil or gas is at a price which is other than fair market value. As in the case of section 901(e), the limitation under section 901(f) is applied on a country by country basis.

The special limitation in section 901(f) is designed to prevent an oil and gas company from obtaining a foreign tax credit for transactions where the oil and gas is really owned by the foreign government and the company is simply purchasing it, with the 'tax' in reality constituting part of the purchase price.[19]

6.2.5.5. *Taxes on oil and gas extraction income*

With the repeal of percentage depletion in 1975 for foreign oil and gas income[20], the limitation of section 901(e) (6.2.5.3.) ceased to be applicable to oil and gas companies. Accordingly, Congress enacted section 907(a) to impose a limit on the foreign tax credit for taxes paid by corporations on oil and gas extraction income. Under section 907(a) no foreign tax credit is allowed for such foreign taxes to the extent that the foreign tax rate exceeds the U.S. corporate tax rate (46%).

The provisions discussed in 6.2.5.4. and 6.2.5.5. were adopted by the U.S. in 1975 and 1976 in response to the enormous increase in prices charged for oil and gas by oil producing countries. These increased amounts, if denominated as 'taxes' (and the oil producing countries had no discernible interest in the label attached to them), would far exceed the U.S. 46% corporate tax rate. As a result, the oil companies could

18. 'Economic interest' is a term of art in oil and gas tax law. See Treas. Reg. sec. 1.611-1(b).

19. This provision is related to the requirement in Temporary Treas. Reg. sec. 4.901-2(b), that a payment, to qualify as an income tax (or as a tax 'in lieu of' an income tax) is not a payment for a 'specific economic benefit,' i.e., in the nature of a royalty payment. See Temporary Treas. Reg. sec. 4.903-1(f), Examples (10)-(14).

20. Section 613A(c) continues a limited percentage depletion deduction for domestic production by so-called 'independent producers', i.e., generally those that do not sell oil or gas through their own retail outlets. Section 613A(d).

use the 'taxes' paid to the oil producing countries to eliminate U.S. tax on the companies' worldwide income whether from oil or from other sources. Data showed that although oil companies usually paid high nominal taxes on worldwide income, little if any tax was paid to the U.S. Further, carryovers of excess foreign tax credits appeared likely to guarantee continuance of this situation for the foreseeable future. This allocation of revenues was unacceptable to the U.S. and the absence of tax treaties with the oil producing countries precluded resolution of the allocation problems on a bilateral basis. Accordingly the U.S. took the unilateral actions in sections 901(f) and 907(a) to protect the integrity of its foreign tax credit mechanism.

6.2.6. Overall limitation on the foreign tax credit

6.2.6.1. General rule

In addition to the special rules discussed in the preceding material, the foreign tax credit almost from its inception has been subject to a general limitation on the amount of the credit available for foreign taxes. While the forms of the limitation have varied, the basic purpose of the limitation has always been to prevent the crediting of foreign taxes against the U.S. tax on income from U.S. sources. As a result, foreign source income will be subject to the higher of the effective U.S. or foreign tax rates. Rather than tracing the actual foreign taxes paid to specific items of income, and limiting the credit to the amount of the U.S. tax on that income (thus preventing the credit from 'spilling over' to U.S. taxes on other income from U.S. sources), the U.S. system has adopted an approach which limits the credit for foreign taxes paid to a portion of the total U.S. tax liability determined by the relation between foreign source income and total income.

Following the Tax Reform Act of 1976, a single overall method of computing the limitation on allowable foreign tax credits is provided in section 904(a). Prior to the 1976 Act, a taxpayer could elect to compute the limitation either on a country-by-country basis (the per-country limitation) or by aggregating all taxes paid to all foreign countries (the overall limitation).[21] Generally the per country method was chosen by

21. The following example illustrates the difference between the two limitations. Assume U.S. Corporation A has $1000 of income from Country X, $1000 of income from Country Y and $1000 of U.S. source income. Country X imposes tax at a 60% rate, →

taxpayers with losses in some countries and profits in others, because the losses did not prevent the crediting of taxes in the profit countries. On the other hand, the overall method was preferable for taxpayers operating at a profit in different countries, some with rates of tax higher than the U.S. and some with rates lower. The overall method here allowed the taxpayer to average the high and low rate countries and thus utilize currently the excess credits form the higher rate countries.

Elimination of the per-country method in 1976 reflected a Congressional view that the interaction of the deductible losses from some countries and allowable foreign tax credits from others was creating an excessive tax benefit. Apparently, the averaging of rates achieved under the overall method was not seen as creating a similar problem. The effect of requiring that all taxpayers use the overall method is to insure that foreign losses from a country first reduce other foreign source income before the tax credit mechanism comes into play.

Technically, the limitation in section 904(a) provides that the total amount of the credit allowable under section 901 (after taking into account the special limitations previously discussed) may not exceed the proportion of the U.S. tax on a taxpayer's worldwide taxable income that its foreign source taxable income bears to its total taxable income from U.S. and foreign sources.[22] For example, assume that a corporation has $2 million foreign source taxable income from country A on which it paid $600,000 in taxes, a $1 million loss in country B, and $1 million U.S. source taxable income. The US. tax on worldwide income is $920,000. The maximum foreign tax credit that may be claimed in the current year by the corporation is $460,000 ($920,000 × $1,000,000/$2,000,000). Thus, even though the effective rate of tax in Country A is only 30%, the full amount of tax paid may not be credited because of the effect of the loss in Country B. On the other hand, if the

→

Country Y at a 40% rate, and the U.S. at 46%. The former per-country limitation would have allowed a credit for the full $400 of Country Y tax and $460 of the Country X tax (46% × $3000 = $1380; $1380 × $1000/$3000 = $460). Thus $140 of the Country X tax would be an excess foreign tax credit. Under the overall limitation, the allowable credit for both Country X and Country Y taxes would be $920 (46% × $3000 = $1380; $1380 × $2000/$3000 = $920). Hence, the excess credit is only $80 as compared to $140 under the per country method and Corporation A has in effect used most of its excess foreign tax credit from Country X against the U.S. tax on the income from Country Y.

22. Taxable income for purposes of section 904 is determined under U.S. tax concepts and accounting rules. The amount of foreign taxes naturally is determined under the laws of the foreign country. If there are substantial differences, for example, in the items included in the tax base, this will affect the amount of currently available tax credit, even if the nominal tax rates are the same.

corporation had $500,000 income from Country A on which it paid $300,000 taxes (60% rate) and $500,000 from Country B on which it paid $160,000 taxes (32% rate), the full $460,000 would be creditable ($1,000,000/$2,000,000 × $920,000 = $460,000) since the use of the overall method allows the averaging of the foreign rates.

6.2.6.2. Carryback and carryover of excess credits

Allowable foreign tax credits in excess of those creditable in the current year ($140,000 in the above example) may be carried back two years and forward five years.[23] The amount then creditable depends on the application of the section 904 limitation in the year to which the foreign taxes are carried.

6.2.6.3. Modifications of source rules

Generally both the numerator and the denominator of the section 904 fraction are determined by applying the definitional rules discussed in Chapters 4 and 5. Obviously, substantial tax stakes turn on the determination whether taxable income is from foreign or U.S. sources.[24] To the extent that a U.S. taxpayer could increase the amount of its income which is treated as foreign source, the amount of currently creditable tax could be increased accordingly. In certain situations, the U.S. has

23. Under prior law, excess credits from per-country limitation years could not be carried back or forward to years in which the taxpayer elected to utilize the overall method. The Tax Reform Act of 1976 added section 904(e) to provide limited carrybacks and carryforwards for taxpayers who were on the per-country method but after December 31, 1975 were required to change to the overall method. Under section 907(f), foreign taxes on oil and gas extraction income paid in excess of the 46% limit (see 6.2.5.5.) may only be carried over in an amount equal to 2% of foreign oil extraction income; any taxes on extraction income in excess of that amount are neither creditable nor deductible. Section 383 provides for the carryover of excess foreign tax credits from an acquired to an acquiring corporation in certain tax-free reorganizations.
24. For examples of the application of the source rules as related to income exempt from U.S. tax, see Rev. Rul. 69-622, 1969-2 Cum. Bull. 298 (foreign source income exempt from U.S. tax must be excluded from both the numerator and denominator of the section 904 fraction); Rev. Rul. 62-67, 1962-1 Cum. Bull. 128 (if entire foreign source income is exempt from U.S. tax, no foreign tax credit is allowable since numerator of fraction is zero); Rev. Rul. 72-126, 1972-1 Cum. Bull. 217, amplified by Rev. Rul. 75-268, 1975-2 Cum. Bull. 294 (any excess credits resulting from the application of the foregoing rules can be carried forward or back).

modified its source rules to eliminate what it considered potential abuses of its foreign tax credit mechanism.[25]

6.2.6.3.1. Capital gains and losses

The U.S. provides a preferential rate for long term capital gains for corporations, i.e., a 28 percent rate in lieu of the normal 46 percent rate. Prior to 1976, however, the existence of this preferential rate was not reflected in the computation of the limitation on the foreign tax credit. As a result, some taxpayers received a foreign tax credit on foreign capital gain income in excess of the applicable U.S. tax, but others, with U.S. capital gains, received as a credit an amount less than the U.S. tax on the foreign income.[26]

Another problem in the capital gain area arose from the fact that pre-1976 rules did not require the netting of U.S. capital gains and losses with foreign capital gains and losses for purposes of computing the section 904 limitation. As a result, a taxpayer with net U.S. losses could use these losses in full to reduce U.S. tax liability; but they did not reduce foreign gains for purposes of computing taxable income from foreign sources in the section 904 fraction.[27] Therefore, long term gains from foreign sources would always increase the amount of the allowable foreign tax credit, but would have no impact on the computation of pre-credit U.S. tax liability if U.S. losses existed to offset the gain.

Finally, the source rules on sales of personal property described in 4.2.6. were being manipulated to increase the allowable foreign tax credit. Under basic U.S. rules, the source of gain on the sale of personal property generally is the country where title passes to the seller. But if this country did not tax such gains, a U.S. seller could increase the foreign tax credit limitation (because the gain would constitute foreign source income) at no additional tax cost.

To deal with these problems, the Tax Reform Act of 1976 modified the treatment of capital gains in computing the limitation on the other-

25. See also 6.3.7., below, where the U.S. has modified its source rules to allow a foreign tax credit for income that otherwise would not qualify.

26. Since foreign source capital gain was included in full in the numerator of the section 904 fraction it increased the amount of the limitation as if it were taxed at the normal 46% rate. Conversely, U.S. source capital gain was also included in full in the denominator, so that a corporation with U.S. source capital gain and foreign source ordinary income would not be able to take the full credit for the foreign taxes. Thus, the impact of the limitation depended, in an irrational way, on the relation of foreign and domestic source capital gain to the taxpayer's other income.

27. This result was approved in Rev. Rul. 73-572, 1973-2 Cum. Bull. 289.

wise allowable foreign tax credit by providing in section 904(b)(2) that:

(1) Foreign and U.S. capital gains and losses must be netted. Only net foreign gains will be allowed to increase the foreign tax credit limitation. Net U.S. losses which exceed foreign gains prevent the gains from entering into the limitation computation.

(2) Foreign source capital gain that is taken into account must be reduced to reflect the rate differential between capital gain income (28%) and normal taxable income (46%). Thus, a maximum of 28/46ths of the gain is taken into account for purposes of the limitation computation (28/46 being the ratio of the U.S. corporate capital gain tax rate to the normal corporate tax rate). As a result, a taxpayer will receive neither a greater nor a lower foreign tax credit just because of the preferential U.S. capital gain rate.

(3) Gain on personal property sold outside the U.S. is to be treated as U.S. source income for purposes of computing the section 904 limitation if the country of sale imposes a tax of less than 10 percent on the amount of the gain. The 10 percent rate was selected as a test of whether a sale in a country was tax motivated or not. However, normal U.S. source rules apply to gains on the sale of personal property (even if the 10 percent tax rate test is not met) in certain situations in which the facts indicate that a sale was not tax motivated.[28]

6.2.6.3.2. Recapture of foreign losses

Another problem involved in computing the limitation on foreign tax credits arises from the fact that U.S. rules for computing taxable income differ from those applicable in a number of foreign countries. For example, if a corporation experiences current losses in its foreign operations, it may use these losses to reduce U.S. tax on other *U.S. source* income which it may have. This situation can occur not infrequently in starting up a new business operation in a foreign country or in oil and gas drilling operations abroad. However, in later years

28. See sec. 904(b)(3)(C). Treas. Reg. sec. 1.861-7(c), discussed in 4.2.6., provides that the Treasury will relocate the source of a sale if tax avoidance was the primary purpose for structuring the transaction in a particular manner. In effect Congress in section 904(b)(3)(C) provided some mechanical tests to determine when tax avoidance was likely a motive in locating a sale in a particular country. But these special source rules apply only for foreign tax credit purposes, not for determining the U.S. tax liability of nonresident aliens and foreign corporations. For a discussion of the 1976 changes with respect to capital gains, see Lokken, The Effects of Capital Gains and Losses on the Credit for Foreign Income Taxes, 30 University of Florida Law Review 40 (1977).

when income is derived from the operation or well, a foreign tax will be due unless the country allows a net operating loss carryover of the prior losses (as would the U.S. in a similar situation). If the foreign country does not provide for a carryover of losses, foreign income and a foreign tax will be generated in later years and, under normal principles, a foreign tax credit would be available for those taxes. However, this ignores the fact that the prior foreign losses have been used to reduce *U.S. source* income so that a full crediting of the subsequent foreign taxes would give the U.S. taxpayer a double benefit, i.e., a reduction of U.S. taxes in earlier years and a foreign tax credit in later years.

To deal with this problem, the Tax Reform Act of 1976 provided for a 'recapture' of previously deducted net foreign losses in the later year in which net foreign source income is realized. Technically this recapture is effected in section 904(f) by treating as U.S. source income that portion of a taxpayer's foreign source income that is equal to the lesser of (1) the amount of the prior loss, or (2) 50 percent (or such larger percent as the taxpayer chooses) of the taxpayer's foreign source taxable income.[29] For example, assume a corporation in year 1 utilizes $500,000 of net losses from foreign sources to reduce U.S. taxable income. In year 2 it realizes foreign source taxable income of $1 million. Under the special source rule in section 904(f), $500,000 of the corporation's foreign income would be treated as U.S. source income. As a result, the numerator of the section 904(a) fraction would be reduced and so would the amount of creditable foreign taxes. In the above example, assume that the U.S. corporation had $1 million of U.S. source taxable income in each of the two years. The deduction in year 1 produced a tax saving of approximately $250,000 (50% of $500,000). In year 2, the tentative U.S. tax would have been $1 million against which, absent the special rule, a maximum foreign tax credit of $500,000 ($1,000,000 × $1,000,000/$2,000,000) would have been available. Under the special rule in section 904(f), the maximum foreign tax credit in year 2 is reduced to $250,000 ($1,000,000 × $500,000/$2,000,000). Thus, the tax benefit granted by the U.S. in year 1 is 'recaptured' in year 2.

In addition, previously deducted losses will be recaptured if property used outside the U.S. is disposed of, regardless of whether the gain on the disposition would be taxed or not. Thus, if a taxpayer disposes of such property in a tax-free transaction, an amount of previously de-

29. A similar recapture rule had been introduced in 1975 applicable only to foreign oil related losses. This rule, in former sec. 907(f), is now incorporated in the broader provision in sec. 904(f) applicable to all foreign losses.

ducted losses equal to the full amount of the gain must be recaptured in the year of the disposition.[30]

6.2.6.4. Application of overall limitation to separate categories of income

Despite the nominal adoption of the overall limitation in section 904(a), a taxpayer is in fact required to compute as many as four separate 'overall' limitations: one for investment interest income, another for foreign source DISC dividend income, another for oil related income, and a final one for all other income. If foreign countries impose taxes on a U.S. corporation's business income higher than the 46 percent U.S. tax rate, the basic mechanism of section 904 contemplates that an excess foreign tax credit will be created to be utilized in the carryback or carryforward years when additional foreign source income taxed at less than 46 percent is generated. However, if it were possible to generate additional foreign source income currently which was only taxed at a low rate in the foreign country, the averaging operation of the overall limitation fraction would permit the crediting of the excess foreign taxes paid on the business income. Interest income, typically taxed at a low withholding rate, was often used to achieve this result.

For example, assume foreign countries impose a tax of 60 percent on $1 million of taxable business income of a U.S. corporation. The corporation also has $1 million of U.S. source income. In the absence of anything else, section 904 would limit the allowable foreign tax credit to $460,000 ($920,000 × $1,000,000/$2,000,000). Total taxes of $1,060,000 would be paid and the corporation would have a $140,000 excess foreign tax credit. Suppose that the U.S. corporation transfers short-term funds generating $250,000 in interest which is currently invested in the U.S. to a foreign country where the tax on interest is 15 percent. U.S. taxable income is reduced to $750,000, total foreign source income is increased to $1,250,000, and total foreign taxes paid thereon are $637,500 ($600,000 plus $37,500 on the interest income). The allowable foreign tax credit would then be $575,000 ($920,000 × $1,250,000/$2,000,000) (an increase of $115,000) and total U.S. and foreign taxes would be $982,500 (a decrease of $77,500).

30. Sec. 904(f)(3). See Mentz, The Effect of Net Operating Losses on the Foreign Tax Credit, 30 Tax Lawyer 309 (1977), for a discussion of the technical problems involved in applying sec. 904(f).

While this result is simply a function of the averaging effect of the overall limitation, because the source of interest income is so easily manipulated by taxpayers, sections 904(d)(1)(A) and (2) require that the overall limitation for foreign taxes on investment interest income[31] be computed separately from all other income. Thus, in the above example, the interest income would be isolated out in a separate computation and the U.S. would impose a tax of $115,000 on the investment income against which a credit of $37,500 would be allowed. The U.S. does not, therefore, have its tax on the interest income reduced by excess credits generated by other income.

For similar reasons, section 904(d)(1)(B) requires a separate section 904(a) computation with respect to DISC dividends which are treated as foreign source income. See 6.3.7.

In addition, section 907(b) requires that 'foreign oil related income' be subject to a separate section 904 limitation. 'Foreign oil related income' includes not only 'oil and gas extraction income', as discussed in 6.2.5.5., but also income from the processing and shipping of oil. In effect, the taxpayer must compute the limitation on oil and gas extraction income and the separate overall limitation on foreign oil related income and apply the lower of the two limitations.

After breaking out the above three categories of income – investment interest, DISC dividends, and oil related income – the limitation on foreign taxes attributable to the remaining taxable income is then computed under the general rule of section 904(a).

6.2.7. Foreign taxes imposed on international boycott income

As part of the Tax Reform Act of 1976, Congress enacted section 908 to require that the foreign tax credit allowable after applying the various limitations discussed in 6.2.5. and 6.2.6. must be reduced to the extent that the credit is attributable to income derived by the taxpayer from participating in or cooperating with an international boycott.[32] Any

31. The Code sections cited do not refer to 'investment' interest income as such. However, in general, interest income connected with a trade or business is not covered by the separate computation. See Treas. Reg. sec. 1.904-4 (which will require modification in light of the 1976 Act changes that shifted the separate computation for investment interest income from a per-country basis to an overall basis).

32. See U.S. Treasury Department Guidelines: Boycott Provisions (Section 999) of the Internal Revenue Code (Jan. 20, 1978), Part N (which also illustrates how the special boycott limitation is to be applied to foreign tax credit carryover and carryback situations).

credit disallowed as a result of section 908 may neither be carried back nor carried forward, but may be deducted in computing taxable income.[33]

The credit is reduced by an amount equal to the otherwise allowable foreign tax credit multiplied by the taxpayer's 'international boycott factor.' That factor is defined in section 999(c) as a fraction the numerator of which is the total operations conducted by the taxpayer with countries carrying out a boycott and the denominator of which is the taxpayer's total worldwide operations. The term 'operations' is an imprecise one, not utilized elsewhere in the Code. Its meaning is to be determined in Regulations to be issued by the Treasury.[34] However, if a taxpayer can establish that a specific amount of taxes is attributable to boycott operations, then the section 908 reduction can be determined by reference to that figure rather than by applying the international boycott factor.[35]

The Secretary of the Treasury is required to maintain and publish a list of countries which require participation in or cooperation with a boycott.[36] Any taxpayer that conducts operations in or with a country on the list must report that fact to the Treasury. Indeed, such a report is required even if a country is not on the list but the taxpayer knows or has reason to know that the country requires participation in or cooperation with a boycott as a condition of doing business in the country or with the government of, or any company or individual in, the country.[37]

An individual or a corporation is considered to have participated in or cooperated with an international boycott if there is an agreement by the taxpayer, as a condition of doing business within a country or with its government (or a company or a national thereof), (1) to refrain from doing business with or in a country (or with its government, companies or nationals) which is the object of the boycott; (2) to refrain from doing business with any U.S. person who engages in trade with those describ-

33. The availability of the deduction is, as in the case for any other deduction, governed by the rules of sections 861 and 862, discussed in Chapter 4. Only foreign taxes creditable under section 901 may be deducted; taxes creditable under section 902 which are disallowed as the result of the boycott limitation may not be deducted.

34. The method of computing the international boycott factor was prescribed in Temporary Treas. Reg. sec. 7.999-1 (1977). A definition of 'operations' is provided in Part B of the U.S. Treasury Department Guidelines, note 32, above.

35. Sec. 999(c)(2). See Part D of U.S. Treasury Department Guidelines, note 32, above.

36. The list is published quarterly.

37. Sec. 999(a). The taxpayer's reports must state not only whether it participated in or cooperated with a boycott, but also whether it was requested to do so. See Parts A and C of U.S. Treasury Department Guidelines, note 32, above.

ed in (1); (3) to refrain from doing business with any company whose ownership or management is made up of individuals of a particular nationality, race or religion, or to remove (or refrain from appointing) such persons to its board of directors; or (4) to refrain from employing individuals of a particular nationality, race or religion. In addition, the terms also cover agreements made, as a condition of selling a product to a country, to refrain from shipping or insuring that product on a carrier owned or operated by a person who does not participate in any of the actions specified in (1)–(4).[38]

If a taxpayer participates in or cooperates with an international boycott (as defined in the preceding paragraph) with respect to any operation in a country, then it is considered to have done so with respect to all operations in that country. The stigma, however, can be confined to a single operation within a country if the taxpayer can establish that there were separate and identifiable operations which had no connection with a boycott operation.[39]

Exceptions to the boycott definition are made for (1) operations that are sanctioned by the U.S. government; (2) compliance with a country's prohibition on importing goods into it, which were produced in a boycotted country; or (3) compliance with a country's prohibition that goods cannot be exported from it to a boycotted country.[40] Thus, for example, a company is not engaged in a proscribed boycott operation if it refuses to import into Saudi Arabia items produced in Israel if Saudi Arabia prohibits this action.

The language governing the statutory penalty for participating in or cooperating with an international boycott is broad and yet vague. To alleviate problems in acting so as to avoid the imposition of the tax penalty, taxpayers are entitled to receive advance rulings from the Treasury whether a particular operation constitutes a prohibited activity or not.[41]

38. Sec. 999(b)(3). See Parts I-M of U.S. Treasury Department Guidelines, note 32, above.

39. See sec. 999(b)(1) (last clause) and sec. 999(b)(2).

40. Sec. 999(b)(4). Limitations (2) and (3) in the text thus make the tax penalties applicable to participation in or cooperation with so-called 'secondary' or 'tertiary' boycotts. 'Primary' boycotts, which are sanctioned by international law, are not covered by the anti-boycott rules.

41. Sec. 999(d). Procedures to be followed in obtaining the advanced determination were issued in an Internal Revenue Service News Release, IR-1697 (Nov. 16, 1976), Commerce Clearing House, Standard Federal Tax Reporter, vol. 9, par. 6985 (1976), and Rev. Proc. 77-9, 1977-1 Cum. Bull. 542. For discussions of the boycott legislation, see Kaplan, Income Taxes and the Arab Boycott, 32 Tax Lawyer 313 (1979); Rubenfeld, Legal and Tax Implications of Participation in International Boycotts, 32 Tax Law Review 613 (1977).

The Export Administration Act of 1977 prohibited directly the participation in or cooperation with international boycotts. Substantial financial and criminal sanctions are imposed for violation of the law. While there is a considerable overlap with the tax rules described above, the Export Act does not cover some situations which the tax rules do. Whether the tax penalty in section 908 should be continued given the direct prohibitions and penalties imposed by the Export Act is a source of disagreement in the U.S.

6.2.8. A PERSPECTIVE ON THE FOREIGN TAX CREDIT MECHANISM

After examining the plethora of special limitations, overall limitations applied on the top of the special limitations, and further special limitations applied to the overall limitations to determine the allowable credit for foreign taxes paid or incurred, one can reasonably ask whether there is anything left of the fairly straightforward principle that was asserted in 6.1. to undergird the foreign tax credit system. If a country adopts the foreign tax credit as its fundamental mechanism for adjusting international tax burdens, why are all the limitations required? An identification of the broad problems to which the varied limitations are addressed may shed some light on this question.

The overall limitation on the credit itself represents a deviation from the principle of capital export neutrality which is one object of the credit mechanism. This deviation is employed solely to protect the revenues of the U.S. government. A pure credit mechanism would provide for full crediting of foreign taxes whatever the rate of foreign tax and refunds by the U.S. government where foreign taxes exceeded U.S. taxes. This, of course, puts the U.S. Treasury at the disposal of all foreign tax systems, a situation which neither the United States nor any other government has been willing to accept. The provisions for carryback and carryforward of excess credits represent a second best solution to mediate between the requirements of a pure credit mechanism and the fiscal concerns of the U.S. Treasury.

The application of the overall limitation is based on the general premise that foreign taxes are not to be traced to specific items of foreign income, but this principle is then subject to a number of exceptions. These exceptions are based on the special character of the types of foreign income involved. They fall into four broad categories:

(1) Types of income that can be easily manipulated by taxpayers from country to country, with a resulting increase in the allowable foreign tax credit. The special rules as to investment interest income

and the source rules for capital gain income respond to this problem and in effect deny the use of the basic averaging mechanism to such income.

(2) Types of income with respect to which the U.S. has granted preferential tax treatment. The special rules governing DISC dividends, mineral income subject to a percentage depletion deduction, and preferential rates for capital gains respond to this problem. The rules prevent the preferential tax treatment of such income by the U.S. from being used to increase the available foreign tax credit through impact of the preferences on the limitation mechanism.

(3) Types of income that are not subjected to the same tax rules abroad as are applied by the U.S. Failure to take these differences into account again can increase the allowable foreign tax credit at no increased U.S. tax cost. The separate limitation applicable to oil and gas income and the rule on recapture of foreign losses represent responses to this problem.

(4) Income earned in activities that run counter to foreign policy objectives of the U.S. The rule denying the foreign tax credit for boycott related income responds to this problem by imposing a tax penalty on such income.

Thus all of the special rules and limitations respond to what have been perceived as defects of various types in the operation of the credit when applied to the special cases of income involved. The complexities of the credit reflect the complexities of the underlying U.S. tax system and the international transactions with which the credit must deal.

6.3. The domestic international sales corporation (DISC)

6.3.1. Background

Under normally applicable U.S. tax principles, no special treatment is provided for income from export transactions. If, under the source rules discussed in Chapter 4, the income is from foreign sources and attracts a foreign tax, the foreign tax credit mechanism is available; if it is domestic source income, it is simply included in the tax base. In 1971, however, concern over the level of U.S. exports led Congress to create a tax subsidy for export income. It enacted the Domestic International Sales Corporation (DISC) provisions to provide a tax incentive for U.S. companies to conduct their overseas sales through domestic subsidiaries. It was thought that the incentive would encourage U.S. companies to keep their manufacturing operations in the U.S. and would offset subsidies for exports provided by other countries. The subsidy took the form of a deferral of U.S. tax on a portion of export income.

DISC proved to be a source of controversy almost from its inception. As a result of economic analyses that the revenue loss associated with DISC produced little or nothing in the way of increased exports[42], Congress in the Tax Reform Act of 1976 did cut back its scope significantly. A GATT panel in 1976 found that DISC violated the GATT provisions on export subsidies. The DISC provisions also appear rather clearly to constitute prohibited 'export subsidies' under the agreements reached in the Tokyo round of Multilateral Trade Negotiations.

The DISC provisions are quite complex. Accordingly, the following discussion represents a sharply abbreviated description of the rules. Special note is made of points of interaction between the DISC provisions and more fundamental U.S. international tax rules.

6.3.2. Basic operation of DISC

A DISC is not a taxable entity as such. Instead, the DISC income is taxed to its shareholder when distributed. However, a distribution is deemed to occur each year to the extent of the DISC's taxable income 'attributable to' its average base period export receipts (a 4 year moving average) plus 50 percent of the excess of its taxable income over that amount. For example, a shareholder of a DISC with $100 of current taxable income and $40 of taxable income attributable to adjusted base period export receipts, would be currently taxable on $70 [$40 + ½($100 – $40)]. The tax on the remaining $30 is deferred until an actual distribution occurs (or the DISC ceases to qualify as a DISC). The base period concept was introduced in 1976 to limit in general the benefits of tax deferral to those corporations that were increasing exports and to deny them to those whose export activities remained rather constant. This incremental approach also assists newly created DISCs since the 4 year base period includes years the DISC was not in existence. The 1976 legislation represented an attempt to make DISC a more efficient incentive for new and increased exports rather than serving merely as a windfall for companies who would have exported in the absence of a tax incentive.

42. See, e.g., Surrey, McDaniel and Pechman, (eds.), Federal Tax Reform for 1976 (1976), at pp. 93-99; U.S. Treasury Department, The Operation and Effect of the Domestic International Sales Corporation Legislation – 1976 Annual Report (April, 1978). For an explanation of how to operate a DISC (prior to the 1976 amendments), see U.S. Treasury Department, DISC: A Handbook for Exporters (1972).

In general, to qualify as a DISC, at least 95 percent of a corporation's assets must be related to export activities and 95 percent of its gross income must be derived from export sale or lease transactions and certain other export-related activities. Under the DISC rules, the gross income that qualifies will normally result from the sale of inventory items, manufactured or produced by a related corporation, which are to be used or consumed outside the U.S. In effect, the DISC rules really contemplate that the Disc will be little more than a paper corporation through which the export activities of its parent will be booked for tax purposes.[43] To facilitate this mode of operation, the restrictions of the section 482 intercompany pricing rules are drastically relaxed in order to permit a larger than normal profit to be allocated to the DISC (and hence to qualify for the tax deferral). When a DISC is sold or otherwise disposed of, or ceases to qualify, then the amounts previously deferred are recaptured and included in the income of the shareholders.

This relatively simple outline conceals an incredibly detailed statutory and regulatory structure. The more important features of that structure are discussed in the following material.

6.3.3. Requirements to qualify as a DISC

Section 991 relieves a DISC from any federal income tax liability if it meets the requirements of section 992(a). That section in turn imposes five conditions that must be fulfilled:

(1) The corporation must be a domestic U.S. corporation;

(2) At least 95 percent of its gross receipts must consist of 'qualified export receipts', i.e., those derived from export sales or lease transactions and certain export-related activities usually undertaken on behalf of a related corporation;[44]

(3) At least 95 percent of the assets of the corporation must consist of 'qualified export assets', i.e., property used in export-related activities;[45]

(4) The corporation must have a nominal capitalization of at least $2,500 consisting of one class of stock (thus emphasizing the paper nature of the corporation);

(5) The corporation has elected to be treated as a DISC.[46]

There is no restriction on a foreign corporation operating a DISC.

43. Rev. Rul. 72-166, 1972-1 Cum. Bull. 220 (only activities of qualified DISC were bookkeeping to identify DISC profits).

44. See sec. 993(a)(1), (c)(1); Treas. Reg. sec. 1.993-1.

45. See sec. 993(a)(2); Treas. Reg. sec. 1.993-2.

46. See sec. 992(b) and Treas. Reg. sec. 1.992-2, for the steps necessary to effect the →

6.3.4. PRODUCER'S LOAN

One of the types of assets included in the 'qualified export assets' (category 3 above) is the 'producer's loan'. A producer's loan is a loan made out of the tax-deferred funds of the DISC to the U.S. producer of the products sold or leased abroad by the DISC. Since normally the DISC's producer is its parent company, the producer's loan rule means that a U.S. parent of the DISC can receive a loan from its DISC and thus can have full use of the tax-deferred funds without losing the benefit of the deferral (compare the subpart F rule on earnings invested in U.S. property by a CFC, discussed in 7.5.2.). Various limitations are imposed on the loans, the most important of which is that the borrower must use the funds in its export-related production activities.[47]

6.3.5. MODIFICATION OF INTER-COMPANY PRICING RULES

As discussed in 8.3., below, section 482 generally requires that items of income and expense be allocated between related parties under an arms-length standard. Section 994 modifies this rule in the case of a sale by a parent to its DISC subsidiary.[48] Taxable income of the parent and the DISC is determined on the basis of a transfer price that allows the DISC to derive taxable income from a sale equal to the greater of:

(1) 4 percent of the qualified export receipts on the sale by the DISC plus 10 percent of the DISC's promotion expenses[49] attributable to the export sale;

(2) 50 percent of the combined taxable income of the DISC and its parent attributable to the qualified export receipts on the sale plus 10 percent of the DISC's promotion expenses on the export sale; or

(3) Taxable income computed by applying section 482 rules.

The first two allocations can be made regardless of the sale price

→
election. If a corporation that has elected DISC status fails to qualify in a particular year because it did not satisfy requirements (1) or (2) in the text, section 992(c) provides a method by which the DISC can make distributions to its shareholders and still retain its status as a qualified DISC. See Treas. Reg. sec. 1.992-3. Certain types of corporations, such as personal holding companies, banks, insurance companies and regulated investment companies (mutual funds) are ineligible for DISC benefits. Sec. 992(d).

47. Sec. 993(d); Treas. Reg. sec. 1.993-4. The interest derived from a producer's loan also constitutes an item of qualified export receipts to the DISC. Section 993(a)(1)(F).

48. The rules in sec. 994 actually apply to any sale by a related person to a DISC. The parent-subsidiary situation is the most common.

49. Sec. 994(c) and Treas. Reg. sec. 1.994-1(f) define export promotion expenses.

actually charged by the DISC for the property; the third must be based on the actual sale price.

The net result of the relaxation of section 482 is to reduce the tax rate on export profits from 46 percent to no more than 35 percent (in the case of the 50 percent of taxable income method) and possibly as low as 23 percent (under the 4 percent of qualified export receipts method).

Under Treasury Regulations, similar rules are applied to commissions, rental and other income of the DISC, i.e., where the DISC is acting as a commission agent or is subleasing export property. In addition, Treasury Regulations are authorized to permit marginal cost accounting for production expenses in computing the taxable income to which the 50 percent limitation described above is applied.[50]

6.3.6. Taxation of DISC shareholders

The earnings and profits of a DISC are in part taxed to the shareholder as deemed distributions; the tax on the balance is deferred and taxed upon actual distribution or upon the sale, disposition or disqualification of the DISC. The provisions are extremely detailed and are discussed here in some detail in order to indicate the general level of complexity present in the DISC legislation.

A DISC shareholder first must include in income currently the portion of the DISC's taxable income equal to the sum of:

(1) Interest on any producer's loan (6.3.4.) (thus cancelling out the interest deduction of the parent company on the loan);

(2) Gain from sales of certain nonqualified export assets;

(3) 'Recaptured' depreciation from the sale of certain depreciable property;

(4) 50 percent of the DISC's taxable income attributable to income from the sales of certain military property;

(5) Taxable income derived by the DISC attributable to participation in or cooperation with an international boycott (under the rules described in 6.2.7.); and

(6) The amount of any illegal bribe, kickback, or other payment paid by or on behalf of the DISC to an official, employee or agent of a foreign government (under the rules described in 7.8.).[51]

After these six categories of the DISC's taxable income are subtracted from its total taxable income, an additional portion of the taxable

50. Sec. 994(b); Treas. Reg. sec. 1.994-1(d).

51. The six categories of income are listed and defined in sec. 995(b)(1)(A)-(D), (b)(3).

income of the DISC is then taxed to the shareholders as a deemed distribution. This amount is the 'normal' level of the DISC's export income which is determined by the ratio of its current export receipts to its export receipts in a base period. Thus the tax deferral is limited (with some exceptions) to *increased* exports by the DISC. Technically, the amount currently taxable is the portion of current taxable income attributable to the DISC's 'base period export gross receipts'. The base period figure is determined by reference to the average of four years' export gross receipts beginning with 1972 (the four-year period then begins to move forward after 1979). An amount equal to 67 percent of this average figure is then considered to be the base period export gross receipts. For example, assume that for the applicable four-year period, a DISC's export gross receipts averaged $3000. Two-thirds (or 67 percent) of this amount is $2000 and any taxable income in the current year 'attributable to' this amount is taxed currently to the DISC shareholder as a dividend. The amount 'attributable to' export receipts is calculated by comparing current receipts to two-thirds of the base period average. Therefore, if in the current year, the DISC had taxable income (after reduction by the six categories listed above) of $600 and qualified export receipts of $3000, $400 would be taxed currently to the shareholder ($600 × $2000/$3000).[52]

After the above seven categories of deemed distributions have been computed, one-half of any remaining taxable income of the DISC is then also taxed currently to the shareholder. To continue the above example, this rule requires the shareholder to include in income an additional $100 [50% × ($600 – $400)].[53]

Finally, the shareholder (or, by this time, its exhausted accountant) must include in income the amount of foreign investments attributable to producer's loans.[54] This rule is designed to prevent the DISC parent from using tax deferred funds of the DISC to invest in foreign plants and equipment.

52. The text summarizes the rules adopted in the Tax Reform Act of 1976, set forth in sec. 995(b)(1)(E), (e). So-called 'small DISC's' are exempt from the incremental rule described in the text. If a DISC has taxable income of no more than $100,000, it qualifies for tax deferral on one-half of its taxable income regardless of whether it has increased exports or not. Sec. 995(f)(1). The exception from the incremental rules is gradually phased out between $100,000 and $150,000 of taxable income, so that when taxable income reaches the latter figure, the incremental rules are fully applicable. Sec. 995(f)(2).

53. Sec. 995(b)(1)(F). As this example shows, when the DISC does not increase its export receipts (i.e., when the base period amount of $3000 equals the current amount), the deferral is limited to 16.7% of its income.

54. Sec. 995(b)(1)(G); Treas. Reg. sec. 1.995-5.

The amounts on which taxes are deferred ($100 in the above example) are included in the income of the DISC shareholder when actually distributed.[55] If DISC stock is sold or otherwise disposed of (whether in a taxable or certain tax-free transactions) the remaining amount of income on which tax has been deferred is taxed to the shareholder.[56]

6.3.7. Interaction of DISC with other international tax rules

The DISC rules interact with other U.S. international tax rules in a number of respects. DISC dividends constitute foreign source income to the parent if they are attributable to qualified export receipts; in turn the DISC dividends qualify for the section 902 indirect credit; the overall limitation in section 904 must be applied separately to DISC income.[57] Other areas may be noted: the section 936 possessions credit (discussed in 6.4.2.5.) is not available to a DISC; DISC dividends to a foreign stockholder are treated as income effectively connected with the conduct of a U.S. trade or business through a permanent establishment (thus subjecting such income to taxation at full U.S. rates).[58]

6.4. Special rules applicable to foreign income

6.4.1. Treatment of income earned abroad

Prior to the Tax Reform Act of 1976, a U.S. citizen who worked in and was a resident of a foreign country could exclude, under section 911, $20,000 (or $25,000) of foreign source earned income from income

55. Sec. 996(a). Sec. 996 establishes an ordering procedure to determine whether actual distributions are from previsously taxed deemed distributions, tax deferred income, or other earnings and profits (which would generally arise from pre-DISC years of the corporation). Generally, distributions are considered to come out of previously taxed income first, then from tax-deferred income and finally from other earnings and profits. See sec. 996(b), (c) and (f). A DISC shareholder's basis in the DISC stock is increased by taxable deemed distributions and reduced by actual distributions out of previously taxed income. Sec. 996(e).
56. Sec. 995(c), 996(d). A similar recapture rule applies upon disqualification of a DISC, although the tax on accumulated tax-deferred income can be spread over a period of as much as 10 years in such a case. Sec. 995(b)(2).
57. Sec. 861(a)(2)(D); 901(d).
58. Sec. 996(g).

subject to U.S. tax. The 1976 Act reduced the section 911 exclusion to $15,000 and imposed some quite stringent limitations in response to problems which Congress perceived in connection with the exclusion.[59] Enormous pressure was placed on Congress, however, to ameliorate the effects of the 1976 Act changes, particularly by U.S. construction companies, oil companies and organizations of U.S. citizens resident abroad.[60]

Congress responded in the Revenue Act of 1978 by providing in section 913 a new special deduction for 'excess' living costs incurred by U.S. citizens or residents working abroad. The section 911 exclusion was retained for only a very limited category of employees, as discussed below.

To qualify for the section 913 deduction, the individual (1) must be a U.S. citizen[61] who is a bona fide resident of the foreign country for the entire taxable year,[62] or (2) a U.S. citizen or resident who is physically present in the foreign country for 17 months out of any 18 month period. The maximum deduction may not exceed the individual's foreign source 'earned income' for the year.[63]

59. The 1976 Act changes were described in the 1977 edition of this book at pages 89-90.

60. Although section 911 provided an exclusion for individuals, its benefits in part were realized by U.S. employers in the form of payment of lower salaries than would have been required in the absence of the exclusion. These employers asserted that the 1976 Act changes impaired their ability to compete abroad because of the higher costs they would incur if they compensated their employees for the increased taxes resulting from the 1976 changes. Self-employed individuals abroad also asserted that the interaction of inflation and fluctuating currency rates, now generally adverse to the dollar, also required special treatment in the U.S. income tax.

61. In addition, under a number of U.S. treaties, resident aliens were granted the benefit of the former section 911 exclusion (which was limited to citizens) under non-discrimination clauses. See Rev. Rul. 72-330, 1972-2 Cum. Bull. 444, amplified in Rev. Rul. 72-598, 1972-2 Cum. Bull. 451.

62. Temporary Treas. Reg. sec. 5b. 913-2(b), state that residence is to be determined on the basis of principles applicable to sec. 871 (see note 46 to Chapter 5).

63. Despite the breadth of the definition of earned income in sec. 911(b), there has been frequent controversy over whether an item is within the definition. See, e.g., Tobey v. Commissioner, 60 T.C. 227 (1973) (artist's receipts from sale of own paintings); Rev. Rul. 71-315, 1971-2 Cum. Bull. 271 (author's royalties); Rev. Rul. 66-56, 1966-1 Cum. Bull. 87 (interest income); Carey v. United States, 427 F.2d 763 (Ct.Cl. 1970) (partnership distributions).

The section 913 deduction is in effect allowed only against net foreign source earned income subject to tax since the limitation is measured by the individual's earned income reduced by any income that is excluded from tax under section 119 (employer-provided meals and lodging) and by any other deductions (other than the section 913 deduction itself) properly allocable to that income (using the allocation rules of Treas. Reg. sec. 1.861-8). The section 913 deduction so computed is taken from gross income, thus →

The section 913 deduction is equal to the sum of five separate components:

1. The 'qualified-cost-of-living differential' which, in general, is the amount by which the general cost of living in the individual's foreign tax home exceeds that of the U.S. metropolitan area with the highest cost of living.[64]

2. 'Qualified housing expenses' which, in general, represent the excess of the individual's reasonable housing expenses abroad for the year over an arbitrary 'base housing' allowance.[65]

→

permitting the taxpayer to obtain the benefit of the zero bracket amount (standard deduction) as well. In addition, because itemized personal deductions for medical expenses, charitable contributions, etc., are not allocable to earned income, they may be deducted in full against other taxable income. The allowable foreign tax credit is not reduced as a result of claiming the section 913 deduction, although the deduction is allocable entirely to foreign source income for purposes of computing the section 904 limitation. Treas. Reg. sec. 1.913-1(b).

Special rules are provided in sec. 913(j)(1)(A) for the treatment of deferred compensation.

Income from foreign sources does not include amounts paid by the U.S. government and hence is not covered by section 913. However, section 912 excludes from income a number of allowances paid to U.S. government employees. As to whether income is received from the U.S. government or one of its agencies, see, e.g., Johnson v. United States, 390 F.2d 715 (Ct.Cl. 1968); Rev. Rul. 67-87, 1967-1 Cum. Bull. 186.

64. Sec. 913(d); Treas. Reg. sec. 1.913-5. The Treasury publishes tables annually to determine the cost-of-living differential. The differential is based on reasonable daily living expenses (other than education and housing costs), taking into account family size and reflecting the costs of living incurred by a U.S. government employee earning $32,442 (at 1979 levels). For example, if the cost of living in the most expensive U.S. city for a family of four with the hypothetical salary is $20,000 and the cost of living for such a family in Copenhagen is $28,200, the $8,200 difference is the 'qualified-cost-of-living differential' component of the total section 913 deduction, regardless of the family's actual income or actual living costs.

65. Sec. 913(e). Housing expenses may not be 'lavish or extravagant'! Treas. Reg. sec. 1.913-6, provide guidelines to determine the costs which do and do not qualify as 'housing expenses'. The 'base housing amount' is equal to 20% of the excess of the individual's net worldwide earned income over the sum of the five amounts that constitute his section 913 components for the year (with the housing expenses included). Thus, for example, assume an individual's net earned income was $30,000, housing costs abroad were $10,000 and his four other section 913 components totalled $10,000. The 'qualified housing expense' component of his section 913 deduction would be $8,000 [$10,000 minus $2,000 (20% × ($30,000 – $20,000))]. The base amount is zero if, because of 'adverse living conditions', the individual's 'tax home', i.e., where he works, is in a hardship area and is separate from and in addition to a foreign household where his spouse and dependents live. 'Adverse living conditions' are defined as those which are dangerous, unhealthful or 'otherwise adverse'. See also Treas. Reg. sec. 1.913-3(b)(2). The excess costs of maintaining the second household also enter into the housing expense deduction. Sec. →

3. 'Qualified schooling expenses' which, in general, constitute the reasonable costs of elementary and secondary education of the individual's dependents in a U.S.-type school.[66]

4. 'Qualified home leave travel expenses' which, in general, include the reasonable costs of one round trip per year for the individual and his family from their foreign residence to the U.S.[67]

5. A 'qualified hardship area deduction' which, in general, is a special allowance for service in a post where extraordinarily difficult living conditions, notably unhealthful conditions, or excessive physical hardship prevail.[68]

The pre-1978 Act section 911 exclusion was retained in limited situations. A $20,000 annual exclusion is permitted for employees who reside in a 'camp'[69] which is located in a 'hardship area'[70] and who satisfy the residency tests under section 913, described above. An employee residing in a camp may elect either the benefits of the section 911 exclusion or the section 913 excess living costs deduction, but not both.[71]

→

913(e)(3), (i), (j)(1)(B)-(D). The definition of 'hardship area' is discussed in the text under component 5. of the section 913 deduction.

66. Sec. 913(f); Treas. Reg. sec. 1.913-7.

67. Sec. 913(g); Treas. Reg. sec. 1.913-8. Apparently the deduction is available if the taxpayer returns to the U.S. from one foreign location and departs from the U.S. to another foreign location as, for example, where the taxpayer has been reassigned by his employer.

68. Sec. 913(h); Treas. Reg. sec. 1.913-9. The allowance is a maximum $5,000 per year and is available for work in areas in which a U.S. government employee would qualify for a hardship post differential of 15% or more of salary.

69. A 'camp' is 'substandard lodging' which is (1) provided by the employer for the employer's convenience because the place of work is in a remote area where satisfactory housing is unavailable, (2) located as close as practicable to the place of work, and (3) a common living area, not open to the public, accomodating 10 or more employees. Sec. 911(c)(1)(B). The definition is obviously designed to provide the benefit of section 911 primarily to construction firms and oil companies. Treas. Reg. sec. 1.911-1 provide more detailed definitions of such terms as 'camp', 'substandard lodging', and 'remote areas.'

70. 'Hardship area' has the same meaning as in sec. 913(h), discussed above.

71. Sec. 911(l). An employee who elects the section 911 exclusion may not claim any deductions, except the moving expense deduction, nor any foreign tax credit, to the extent the deductions or credit are properly allocable to the excluded amount. Sec. 911(a). Treas. Reg. sec. 1.911-5, provide the methods of allocating deductions and the foreign tax credit to the excluded income. Under the Regulations, deductions related to earned income (under the tests of Treas. Reg. sec. 1.861-8) are allocated to excluded income (and thus disallowed) in the ratio excluded income bears to total qualifying earned income. Personal deductions, such as for medical expenses, charitable deductions, etc., are not subject to allocation and hence may be deducted in full. The foreign tax credit is allocated to excluded income (and hence disallowed) by multiplying the foreign taxes

→

The section 913 technique represents a more flexible subsidy mechanism than the former section 911 exclusion. Living conditions and costs vary widely from country to country and the several components of the section 913 deduction do attempt to reflect this fact. It is probable, however, that the 1978 Act will not be the final word on the U.S. tax treatment of U.S. citizens and residents working abroad.[72] Expatriate Americans can be expected to continue to urge complete exemption of foreign earnings; those concerned with tax policy may renew their efforts to repeal the existing special treatment.

6.4.2. Income derived from U.S. possessions

6.4.2.1. Income derived by individuals from possession other than Puerto Rico, the Virgin Islands and Guam

An individual U.S. citizen who is engaged in the active conduct of a trade or business in a U.S. possession (other than the Virgin Islands, Puerto Rico and Guam) may exclude, for U.S. income tax purposes, all income from sources outside the U.S. if for the 3-year period immediately preceding the close of the taxable year:

(1) 80 percent of the individual's total worldwide *gross* income was derived from sources within the possessions; and

(2) 50 percent of the individual's total worldwide *gross* income was derived from the trade or business.Section 931(a). The term 'trade or business' includes operating not only for the individual's own account, but also as an agent or employee of another (except that employees of the U.S. government are not covered by the exclusion).

→

paid by a fraction, the numerator of which is the amount excluded under section 911 (less related deductions) and the denominator of which is total earned income (less related deductions). Although the section 913 deduction is unavailable if the section 911 exclusion is adopted, the employee is entitled to exclude under section 119 the value of any meals and lodging furnished at the camp by the employer for the convenience of the employer. Sec. 911(c)(7).

72. The Treasury Department is required to submit to Congress a biennial report containing data on the scope, effects, costs, and administration of sections 911-913.
The Revenue Act of 1978 also liberalized other rules affecting U.S. citizens or residents working abroad. The changes included: (1) a longer time period within which to sell and reinvest in a principal residence on a tax-free basis, and (2) more generous limits on the allowable moving expense deduction where foreign moves are involved.

If the above tests are met, the individual is taxed in a manner similar to a nonresident alien who is not engaged in a trade or business in the U.S., i.e., he is taxed only on his U.S. source income.[73] Section 931(b), however, provides that amounts actually received by the individual in the U.S. are taxed as U.S. income, regardless of source.[74]

Where an individual has income that qualifies under section 931 and income from U.S. sources, deductions must be apportioned between the two types of income on the basis of the principles of sections 861-864.

Because section 931 grants an exclusion for *all* foreign source income of an individual U.S. citizen who meets its requirements, no foreign tax credit is allowed.[75]

The U.S. possessions covered by section 931 include the American Samoa, Wake Island, Midway Island and certain other islands listed in IRS Publication 570.

6.4.2.2. Puerto Rico

An individual who is a bona fide resident of Puerto Rico during the entire taxable year is exempt from U.S. tax on his Puerto Rico source income. Of course, the individual will be subject to Puerto Rico Tax.[76]

6.4.2.3. Virgin Islands

U.S. citizens permanently resident in the Virgin Islands are not requir-

73. Under sec. 932, citizens of U.S. possessions (other than Puerto Rico and Guam) who are not U.S. residents are taxed as nonresident alien individuals.

74. Thus, income earned by an individual in a U.S. possession did not qualify for the sec. 931 exclusion where his employer deposited it directly into the individual's U.S. bank account. Rev. Rul. 67-330, 1967-2 Cum. Bull. 260.

75. No sec. 911 exclusion is available either, and only one personal exemption is allowed. Prior to the 1978 legislative changes, section 931 was held to be elective, so that if an individual taxpayer derived a greater tax benefit by utilizing more personal exemptions, the former sec. 911 exclusion, and the allowable foreign tax credit, he could disregard section 931. Rev. Rul. 73-493, 1973-2 Cum. Bull. 294. Presumably the same rule will apply under amended section 911, although its conditions will rarely be met in the case of a U.S. citizen resident in a possession. By contrast, Treas. Reg. sec. 1.913-3(d), provide that the term 'foreign country' does not include a U.S. possession and hence the sec. 913 deduction would not be available to a U.S. citizen resident in a U.S. possession.

76. Deductions allocable to Puerto Rico source income may not be claimed against income taxable by the U.S. See, e.g., Rogue v. Commissioner, 65 T.C. 920 (1976) (moving expenses).

ed to file U.S. tax returns. Such persons satisfy their U.S. tax liability by paying Virgin Islands income taxes (which mirror the U.S. system) on their worldwide income.[77] Section 934 prevents the Virgin Islands from then granting tax rebates or other subsidies with respect to taxes attributable to U.S. source income. Exceptions are permitted for subsidies granted to U.S. corporations and individuals that derive the bulk of their income from within the Virgin Islands.

6.4.2.4. Guam

The Guam income tax system also mirrors that of the U.S., i.e., it adopts as its income tax laws those of the U.S. Section 935 integrates the two systems by providing that a tax return must be filed either in the U.S. or Guam, but not in both. Other than for the filing requirement, the U.S. and Guam generally are treated as a single tax jurisdiction. Thus, for example, no foreign tax credit is available in the one for taxes paid to the other.

6.4.2.5. Puerto Rico and possession tax credit

Prior to the Tax Reform Act of 1976, section 931 applied to exclude from U.S. tax the foreign source income (including income from U.S. possessions) earned by U.S. corporations and individuals if they met its requirements. The section 931 exclusion was applicable to corporations with business operations in any U.S. possession (other than the Virgin Islands). The primary possession affected, however, was Puerto Rico.

Prior to 1978, Puerto Rico, to attract investment, had granted tax holidays for corporate investment in the country. As a result, U.S. corporations could create a subsidiary operating in Puerto Rico which would pay little or no Puerto Rico tax. The subsidiary would then invest its Puerto Rican earnings in other countries and it would also be exempt on this foreign source income under section 931 so long as no dividends were repatriated to the U.S. parent. If the Puerto Rico subsidiary subsequently were liquidated, all its accumulated earnings could be repatriated to the U.S. tax-free.

Section 931 was intended as a subsidy to encourage U.S. corporations to invest in Puerto Rico. However, it was widely recognized that

77. See Rev. Rul. 60-291, 1960-2 Cum. Bull. 407.

the provision was seriously deficient in accomplishing its ultimate objective of providing jobs and capital for Puerto Rico.

In the Tax Reform Act of 1976, Congress removed domestic corporations from section 931 and in lieu thereof provided a new tax credit in section 936 for domestic corporations conducting a trade or business in a U.S. possession (other than the Virgin Islands).[78]

For taxable years beginning in 1976, a U.S. corporation that meets the 80%–50% tests like those in section 931 (see 6.4.2.1., above) is entitled to a credit against tax equal to the portion of the tax attributable to the corporation's (1) foreign source taxable income derived from the active conduct of a trade or business in a U.S. possession, and (2) qualified possession source investment income. In other words, a qualifying possessions corporation computes a tax at the 46% rate on its worldwide income and then takes a tax credit for 46% of its business and investment income from U.S. possessions.[79] The possessions tax credit is available even if no taxes were in fact paid by the corporation to any possession, and represents a kind of 'tax sparing' credit.

The section 936 credit is elective. For those corporations that utilize it, no foreign tax credit or deduction is allowed for taxes actually paid with respect to income exempt from U.S. tax which is taken into account in computing the section 936 credit.[80]

As in the case of section 931, income that is actually received by the possessions corporation within the U.S. is treated as U.S. source income and therefore does not generate a section 936 credit.

To correct one of the defects under section 931, the section 936 credit is available only with respect to investment income that is 'qualified possession source investment income'. In order to qualify, the income

78. For an analysis highly critical of section 936, see Surrey, McDaniel and Pechman (eds.), Federal Tax Reform in 1976 (1976) at p. 143. In 1978, Puerto Rico restructured its industrial incentives program to provide a declining partial exemption from tax instead of the complete tax holiday system previously employed. The effects of section 936 and the 1978 Puerto Rican changes are analyzed in U.S. Treas. Dept., The Operation and Effect of the Possessions Corporation System of Taxation: First Annual Report (June 1978). See also Griggs, Operating in Puerto Rico in the Section 936 Era, 32 Tax Law Review 239 (1977).

79. The credit is not allowed against certain taxes such as the minimum tax, the accumulated earnings tax, and the personal holding company tax. Sec. 936(a)(2).

80. Sec. 936(c), 901(g). On the other hand, if a distribution from a possessions corporation is fully taxable by the U.S., the foreign tax credit is allowed; thus, withholding taxes imposed on dividend distributions to individual U.S. shareholders would qualify for the foreign tax credit. Correspondingly, the income that generates a section 936 credit is to be excluded from both the numerator and denominator of the fraction in computing a corporation's overall limitation on its foreign tax credit under sec. 904. See sec. 904(b)(4).

must be (1) from sources within a U.S. possession in which the corporation conducts an active trade or business, and (2) the funds generating the investment income must themselves have been derived from the trade or business conducted in the possession.[81] The Congressional purpose was to try to confine the tax incentive to investment in U.S. possessions. Hence investment income derived by a possessions corporation from non-possessions sources will be taxed under normal U.S. rules and will not enjoy any favored status just because the corporation is operating a trade or business in a possession.

A corporation must elect to have section 936 apply to it.[82] Once it does, it cannot be a part of a consolidated return with other related taxpayers. Further, once the election is made it cannot be revoked for 10 years without the consent of the Internal Revenue Service.[83]

A dividends received deduction under section 243 is allowed with respect to dividends paid by a possessions corporation to its corporate shareholders.[84]

6.4.3. Western hemisphere trade corporations

Prior to the Tax Reform Act of 1976, the U.S. provided a 14 percentage point rate reduction for qualifying Western hemisphere trade corporations. The Act phased out this special rate reduction over four years and repealed it entirely for taxable years beginning after December 31, 1979.

6.4.4. China Trade Act corporations

Prior to the Tax Reform Act of 1976, the U.S. provided special tax benefits to so-called China Trade Act corporations. Generally, qualifying corporations and their shareholders were exempted from U.S.

81. Sec. 936(d)(2). See also Temporary Reg. sec. 7.936-1.
82. The credit is not available to a DISC or to any corporation that owns stock in a DISC. Sec. 936(f).
83. This provision was designed to end the practice under sec. 931 whereby corporations would elect in and out of sec. 931 on a yearly basis. For years in which the possessions corporation realized a loss, it would not elect sec. 931 and therefore could join a consolidated return to let its parent deduct its losses from income of the consolidated group. For years in which the possessions corporation realized taxable income it would elect to take the benefits of sec. 931.
84. Sec. 243(b)(1)(C).

income tax. The Act phased out these special exclusions over a three year period, repealing them entirely for taxable years beginning after December 31, 1977.

Chapter 7
Income taxation of foreign corporations controlled by U.S. persons

7.1. Background

Under the U.S. tax principles previously discussed, the income of a foreign corporation with U.S. shareholders is not taxed to the shareholder until repatriated, either in the form of a dividend or as a liquidation distribution. The appropriateness of the deferral of U.S. tax which these principles create was seriously questioned in 1962. Legislation was proposed which would have eliminated deferral for all U.S.-controlled foreign corporations and taxed the foreign profits directly to the U.S. shareholders on a current basis. After a lengthy and complex legislative process, the general elimination of deferral was rejected. However, deferral was curtailed through the so-called 'subpart F' provisions for foreign corporations engaged in certain 'tax haven' operations. In general, these provisions were directed at the use of foreign corporations which were used to accumulate certain types of income in a foreign 'base' company located in a jurisdiction with little or no tax. The types of income included passive investment income and income from dealings with related parties which were channeled through the base company. The 1962 legislation attempted to distinguish between 'legitimate' deferral of U.S. taxation in foreign operations and deferral resulting from a manipulation of U.S. tax rules. Accordingly, the lines drawn in reaching a compromise between those who favored complete elimination of deferral and those urging its retention are extremely detailed and complex. The following material will first examine the specific situations dealt with in subpart F and then consider the broader policy issues which are involved.

7.2. Basic operation of subpart F

A 'U.S. shareholder' that 'owns' 10 percent or more of the 'total combined voting power' of all classes of voting stock of a controlled foreign corporation (a 'CFC') must include in income each year its pro rata share of the CFC's undistributed '951(a)(1) income' (authors' term).

A CFC is a foreign corporation in which more than 50 percent of the total combined voting power of all classes of voting stock is owned by 10% or greater U.S. shareholders on any day during the taxable year of the CFC. The '951(a)(1) income' is taxed to the U.S. shareholder in the year earned by the corporation; when it is subsequently distributed as a dividend, no further tax is imposed. A foreign tax credit is granted to the U.S. corporate shareholder for the taxes it is deemed to have paid on the '951(a)(1) income' (and, of course, the U.S. shareholder includes the amount of the deemed foreign tax credit in income also). The basis of the U.S. shareholder's stock in the CFC is increased by the amount of any '951(a)(1) income' that is taxed by subpart F and decreased by subsequent distributions of previously taxed '951(a)(1) income'.

Within this deceptively simple statutory framework lie a host of definitions, exceptions, limitations and qualifications.

7.3. Tax treatment of U.S. shareholder

A U.S. shareholder is any U.S. citizen, resident, partnership, corporation, estate or trust.[1] If the shareholder owns directly or is treated as owning ('constructive ownership') at least 10 percent of the total combined voting power[2] of all classes of stock entitled to vote in a CFC, the shareholder is taxed on his pro rata share[3] of the CFC's undistributed '951(a)(1) income'.[4] Constructive ownership of the stock of a CFC can result if a U.S. person is a stockholder, partner, or beneficiary of a

1. Sec. 951(b), 7701(a)(30). Sec. 957(d) modifies the definition in the case of corporations organized in U.S. possessions. For a shareholder that is taxed on the income of a CFC under sec. 1247, 8.1.2.7., below, or under the foreign personal holding company rules, 8.4.3., below, sec. 951(c)-(d) provides coordination with the sec. 951 rules.
2. As to what constitutes 'voting power', see Treas. Reg. sec. 1.951-1(g)(2).
3. Sec. 951(a)(2). For examples of the computations of pro rata shares, see Treas. Reg. sec. 1.954-1(b).
4. The constitutionality of sec. 951 has been upheld in Garlock, Inc. v. Commissioner, 489 F. 2d 197 (2d Cir. 1973); Estate of Whitlock v. Commissioner, 494 F.2d 1297 (10th Cir. 1974); Dougherty v. Commissioner, 60 T.C. 917 (1973).
Prior to 1975, U.S. shareholders could avoid being taxed under sec. 951 by electing to distribute certain minimum dividends under sec. 963. Sec. 963 was repealed in 1975, effective for taxable years beginning in 1976.

corporation, partnership, trust or estate that owns stock in a CFC.[5] Generally speaking, constructive ownership of CFC stock is determined by applying the attribution rules of section 318 although some modifications are made.[6] While the attribution rules may push a U.S. person above the 10 percent stock ownership level, he is only taxed on his pro rata share of '951(a)(1) income' based on the stock he owns directly (or which is attributed to him from a foreign entity).

7.4. Definition of a CFC

A CFC is a foreign corporation in which *more than* 50 percent of the total combined voting power of all classes of stock entitled to vote is owned by 10% or greater U.S. shareholders.[7] Thus CFC status may be avoided if there are 11 unrelated U.S. shareholders who own ratably 100 percent of the voting stock of a foreign corporation or if one or more U.S. shareholders own exactly 50 percent of the voting stock of a foreign corporation, the balance being owned by foreign shareholders. A foreign corporation is a CFC if the more-than-50 percent test is met on any one day during the taxable year.[8]

7.5. Income taxable to U.S. shareholders

A U.S. shareholder of a CFC must include in income his pro rata share of the sum of the CFC's:

(1) Subpart F income;

5. Sec. 958(a).
6. Sec. 958(b); Treas. Reg. sec. 1.958-2. See Alexander, Controlled Foreign Corporations and Constructive Ownership, 18 Tax Law Review 531 (1963). In general, under sec. 318, a person is considered to be the owner of stock owned by close relatives (spouse, children, etc.), by his 50% controlled corporation, or by a partnership or trust of which he is a partner or beneficiary. For purposes of subpart F, the percentage of stock ownership deemed to be controlling is reduced from 50% to 10%.
7. Sec. 957(a). The 50 percent figure is reduced to 25 percent in the case of certain insurance subsidiaries. Sec. 957(b). Nor does it include stock in certain U.S. possessions corporations as defined in sec. 957(c).
8. For examples holding that the more than 50 percent test was met although nominal stock ownership by U.S. persons was 50 percent or less, see Rev. Rul. 70-426, 1970-2 Cum. Bull. 157; Garlock, Inc. v. Commissioner, *supra* note 4; Weiskopf Estate v. Commissioner, 64 T.C. 78 (1975); Koehring Co. v. United States, 583 F.2d 313 (7th Cir. 1978). But compare CCA, Inc. v. Commissioner, 64 T.C. 137 (1975) (Acq), holding the control test not satisfied where the U.S. shareholders owned exactly 50 percent of the stock and the foreign shareholders possessed real powers.

(2) Previously excluded subpart F income withdrawn from investment in less developed countries for the year;[9]

(3) Previously excluded subpart F income withdrawn from foreign base company shipping operations for the year;[10] and

(4) Increase in earnings invested in U.S. property for the year.

7.5.1. SUBPART F INCOME

The first major category of income currently taxable to a U.S. shareholder is his pro rata share of the CFC's 'subpart F income'. Subpart F income, as defined in section 952,[11] consists of two principal categories of income:

(1) That derived from insurance of U.S. risks;[12] and

(2) Foreign base company income.[13]

(See also 7.8., below, for two special categories of subpart F income). Even if income is within one of the two categories, it does not constitute subpart F income if it is effectively connected with the conduct of a U.S. trade or business of the CFC (unless by treaty the income is excluded from tax or taxed at a reduced rate).[14]

9. Prior to 1975, income which would ordinarily have been subject to current taxation was exempted from the subpart F provisions if it was invested in certain qualified investments in less developed country corporations. When the income was withdrawn from investment, it then became subject to tax. This exception to the application of subpart F was repealed in 1976.

10. Shipping income is treated as subpart F income but is not currently taxed if it is invested in shipping operations. Upon withdrawal of the income from investment, it then becomes taxable under sec. 951. See sec. 955, effective for taxable years beginning after 1975, and Proposed Treas. Reg. sec. 1.955A-1 to 4 (1976), for the rules employed to determine the time and extent of the withdrawal.

11. A CFC's subpart F income cannot exceed its earnings and profits as defined in sec. 964(a). Generally a CFC's earnings and profits are computed in the same manner as those of a U.S. corporation. See Treas. Reg. sec. 1.964-1. See also Weiss, Earnings and Profits and the Determination of the Foreign Tax Credit, 43 Taxes 849 (1965). Nor does subpart F income include earnings and profits that are attributable to foreign income that is blocked from repatriation by, for example, currency regulations of the foreign country. Treas. Reg. sec. 1.964-2. In general, U.S. tax rules apply to determine the gross income and taxable income of a CFC. Treas. Reg. sec. 1.952-2. Foreign currency fluctuations can affect the amount of a corporation's earnings and profits for subpart F purposes; see Henrey, Tax Consequences of Foreign Exchange Gains and Losses Within the Corporate Family, 37 New York University Institute on Federal Taxation sec. 20.00 (1979).

12. Sec. 952(a)(1). This category of subpart F income is defined in detail in sec. 953 and the Regulations thereunder.

13. Sec. 952(a)(2).

14. Sec. 952(b).

Subpart F income which is distributed currently to the U.S. shareholders technically retains its character as subpart F income, and is taxed as such, despite its actual distribution.[15]

The term 'foreign base company income' (FBCI) is defined in great detail in section 954 and the Regulations issued thereunder. The basic arrangement sought to be brought within these rules is one in which a U.S. parent creates a foreign subsidiary in a country that imposes little or no tax. The parent sells products to the subsidiary which then makes the sale to the ultimate customer. The various 'sale' prices can be manipulated so that most of the profit winds up in the subsidiary in the non-tax country, thus avoiding both U.S. and foreign tax. The same kind of arrangement can be structured involving the provision of services for a related party. The rules focus on sales or services provided outside the country of incorporation of the CFC since it is in those cases that the CFC is being used as a 'base' company. Another type of situation at which the subpart F rules are aimed is the use of the foreign corporation as a holding company to accumulate passive investment income.

FBCI includes four categories of income:

(1) Foreign personal holding company income (as defined in section 553, discussed in 8.4.3., below). Basically this income consists of passive investment income such as dividends, interest, rents and royalties. The FBCI rules are stricter than the foreign personal holding company rules in some respects,[16] but looser in others.[17]

(2) Foreign base company sales income, which consists of income from property purchased from or sold to a related party if the property is manufactured and sold for use outside the CFC's country of incorporation.[18]

(3) Foreign base company services income, which is income derived

15. Treas. Reg. sec. 1.959-1(b). However, under sec. 959 amounts distributed which were previously taxed under sec. 951(a) are not included in the income of the U.S. shareholder when received.

16. All qualified rents are included in FBCI regardless of the percentage of gross income they represent. See also 8.4.2.2.2.

17. Excluded from FBCI are rents and royalties from unrelated parties received in the active conduct of a trade or business, passive income from related persons operating in the CFC's country, or dividends, interest and securities gain received by certain banks and insurance companies. See Treas. Reg. Sec. 1.954-1(e).

18. In some instances a branch of the CFC may be treated as if it were a subsidiary, and hence a related person, so that the subpart F rules come into play. See Treas. Reg. sec. 1.954-3.

from performing services outside the CFC's country of incorporation for or on behalf of a related person.[19]

(4) Foreign base company shipping income, which is income derived from the use of aircraft or vessels in foreign commerce, outside the CFC's country of incorporation.[20]

In each category of income, the amount of FBCI is reduced by the deductions properly allocable thereto.[21]

The statute provides certain exceptions for income that otherwise would constitute FBCI:[22]

(1) If the FBCI of a CFC is less than 10 percent of its total gross income, then the CFC shall be considered to have no FBCI. (Conversely, if the FBCI exceeds 70 percent of the CFC's gross income, then all of its gross income is considered FBCI).[23]

(2) FBCI does not include any item of income if the taxpayer can establish that neither the creation or organization of the CFC nor effecting through the CFC the transaction giving rise to the income had as a 'significant purpose' the 'substantial' reduction of income taxes.[24]

(3) FBCI does not include foreign base company shipping income that is reinvested in increased qualified foreign base company shipping operations.[25]

7.5.2. Increase in earnings invested in U.S. property

The second major category of CFC income that section 951(a)(1)

19. See Treas. Reg. sec. 1.954-4.
20. See sec. 954(f), sec. 954(b)(7), and Proposed Treas. Reg. sec. 1.954-6, 7 (1976). For the order of computation of the four categories, see Proposed Treas. Reg. sec. 1.952-3 (1976).
21. Sec. 954(b)(5).
22. In addition to the exceptions listed in the text, sec. 970-972 provide that a CFC that is a qualified Export Trade Corporation (ETC) can reduce FBCI by the portion of the FBCI that is 'export trade income'. In very general terms an ETC is a corporation engaged in selling abroad products that were manufactured, produced, grown or extracted in the U.S. The tax deferral lasts so long as the income is invested is qualified export trade assets. See sec. 951(a)(1)(A)(ii). The ETC provisions were in effect supplanted by the enactment of the DISC provisions in 1971, discussed in 6.3., and apply only to foreign corporations which qualified as ETCs before that date.
23. Sec. 954(b)(3).
24. Sec. 954(b)(4); Treas. Reg. sec. 1.954-1(b)(4). See Rev. Proc. 76-25, 1976-1 Cum. Bull. 349, for a check list of information to be submitted by a taxpayer who seeks an advance ruling from the Internal Revenue Service that an item falls within the exception.
25. Sec. 954(b)(2); see note 10.

subjects to current taxation to the U.S. shareholders is any increase in the earnings of the CFC invested in U.S. property. Even if a CFC had no 'subpart F income', it would be possible for it to avoid U.S. taxation on its income but still make that income available to its U.S. shareholders. For example, the CFC could loan its earnings to the U.S. parent. There would be no U.S. tax since the tax applies only to repatriated dividends; but the U.S. parent would have the use of the funds in just the manner that would have been produced had a dividend in fact been paid. Accordingly, the special rules treat any increase in a CFC's earnings that are invested in U.S. property for the year as if a dividend in that amount had been paid to the U.S. shareholder and tax that amount currently. The 'increase' taxed is the excess of the CFC's earnings invested in U.S. property at the end of the taxable year over the amount invested at the beginning of the year.[26]

U.S. 'property' is defined to include the following types of property:

(1) Tangible property located in the U.S. (excluding certain oil and gas drilling rigs, certain transportation property and property intended for export from the U.S.);[27]

(2) Stock of a related U.S. corporation (i.e., the corporation invested in is itself a shareholder of the CFC, or U.S. shareholders of the CFC own 25 percent or more of the voting stock of the corporation in which the investment is made);[28]

(3) Obligations of a U.S. person (excluding debt of an unrelated corporation as defined in (2), money, bank deposits, obligations of the U.S. government) and obligations arising in the ordinary course of trade or business;[29]

(4) The right to use patents, copyrights, secret processes, etc.

26. Sec. 956(a)(2); Treas. Reg. sec. 1.956-1(c).

27. Sec. 956(b)(1)(A); (b)(2)(B), (D), and (G).

28. Sec. 956(b)(1); (b)(2)(F). Changes made in 1976 now allow investment in the stock of unrelated U.S. corporations; previously stock in any U.S. corporation was treated as 'U.S. property'.

29. Sec. 956(b)(1)(C); (b)(2)(A) and (C). For the operation of sec. 956 where indirect transactions were treated as acquisitions of an obligation of a U.S. person, see Greenfield v. Commissioner, 60 T.C. 425 (1973), affirmed, 506 F.2d 972 (5th Cir. 1975); Rev. Rul. 76-125, 1976-1 Cum. Bull. 204. Sec. 956(c) provides that a CFC will be considered to hold an obligation if it is a 'pledgor or guarantor' of the obligation. Ludwig v. Commissioner, 68 T.C. 979 (1977), held that a CFC was not to be treated as the guarantor of a loan made to a shareholder who had pledged his stock in the CFC as security for the loan. See, however, Treas. Reg. sec. 1.956-1(e)(2), 1.956-2(c). For computations of 'increased' investment, see Rev. Rul. 74-436, 1974-2 Cum. Bull. 214. See also Lederman, U.S. Taxation of U.S. Portfolio Investments of Controlled Foreign Corporations, 31 Tax Lawyer 399 (1978).

Section 959(a) coordinates the rules on increases of investment in U.S. property with the basic subpart F rules to prevent the same item of income from being taxed twice.

7.6. Foreign tax credit

Section 960 provides a foreign tax credit for income taxed to a U.S. shareholder under the subpart F rules. For corporations, the rules in general correspond to those of section 902 (6.2.4., above). The deemed foreign tax credit under section 960 is available for taxes paid by subsidiaries as low as the third tier.[30] Section 78 applies the gross-up requirement to foreign tax credits allowed under section 960.[31]

Individual U.S. shareholders can obtain the benefits of the section 960 credit by electing to be taxed at corporation rates on their income taxable under subpart F.[32]

7.7. Adjustments to basis

Generally the basis in CFC stock is increased by the amount of income included under section 951 (as if the dividend had been paid and then recontributed to the CFC) and reduced under section 959 by amounts received that constitute previously taxed earnings (basis having previously been increased at the time the tax was imposed). For individuals who elect to be taxed at corporate rates, the basis adjustments are the same except that the amount of increase or reduction is only of the tax itself.[33]

If the amount of previously taxed earnings received in a year exceeds basis, the excess is taxed as a capital gain.[34]

7.8. Denial of deferral benefits for boycott income and foreign bribes

The Tax Reform Act of 1976 added two new categories to the subpart F

30. The intricate computations necessary under sec. 960 are illustrated in Treas. Reg. sec. 1.960-1, 2.
31. See Treas. Reg. sec. 1.960-3.
32. Sec. 962.
33. Sec. 961(a), (b)(1).
34. Sec. 961(b)(2).

income described in 7.5.1., above. Under section 952(a)(3), CFC earnings and profits attributable to participation in or cooperation with an international boycott are treated as subpart F income and are currently taxable to a U.S. shareholder of the CFC. The rules discussed in 6.2.7. apply to determine the amount of a CFC's undistributed earnings and profits that are subject to current taxation under this rule.

Section 952(a)(4) includes in a CFC's subpart F income an amount equal to the sum of illegal bribes, kickbacks and other payments (as defined in section 162(c)) that are paid by or on behalf of a foreign corporation directly or indirectly to any offical, employee or agent of a foreign government. In addition, in computing the earnings and profits of a CFC, no reduction is allowed for such payments. Note that the amount of income that is taxable to the U.S. shareholder under section 952(a)(4) is not the income produced as a result of the bribe, but the amount of the bribe itself. The inclusion of these two items in subpart F income obviously rests on policy bases quite different from those discussed in 7.5., above. The factors behind the inclusion of boycott income were discussed in 6.2.7., above. Congressional concern over revelations that U.S. corporations, and their foreign subsidiaries, had been engaged in extensive bribing of foreign officials prompted the action with respect to illegal payments. The Foreign Corrupt Practices Act of 1977 imposes criminal sanctions for illegal payments to foreign government officials. The criminal sanctions are obviously much more important than the income tax limitations, but the coverage of the two sets of laws is not coextensive. Accordingly, the tax rules must continue to be taken into account.

7.9. Legislative proposals regarding controlled foreign corporations

In recent years, considerable sentiment has developed in the U.S. Congress to apply the subpart F rules of current taxation of the income of controlled foreign subsidiaries to *all* U.S. controlled foreign subsidiaries. Thus, under these proposals, the income of controlled foreign subsidiaries, regardless of its type, would be taxed directly to the U.S. shareholders in the year earned, whether repatriated or not. Current shareholder taxation of the income of controlled foreign subsidiaries would constitute a departure from the practice in other countries and it is important to understand why the movement in the United States is in this direction.

As discussed in 6.2., the foreign tax credit is the basic mechanism adopted by the U.S. to effect the proper application of its tax rules when U.S. citizens or corporations derive income from other countries. One basic purpose of the credit is to achieve tax neutrality (so-called 'capital export neutrality') in decisions by U.S. taxpayers whether to invest in the U.S. or abroad. For example, a U.S. corporation that decides to expand into a new line of operations can do so through a U.S. branch or division, a wholly owned U.S. subsidiary, a foreign branch, or a foreign subsidiary. The U.S. tax system is neutral among the first three choices: a single U.S. tax will be imposed on the profits of the operation if conducted through a U.S. division or subsidiary (either because of the consolidated return rules or because of the dividends received deduction), and a single U.S. tax will be imposed on the profits of the foreign branch. In all these cases, a foreign tax credit will be allowed for the foreign taxes paid. These tax results occur whether the new operation actually remits its profits to its parent or retains them. Thus in all these situations, the foreign tax credit device generally insures that the U.S. taxpayer's investment decision will not be influenced by taxes and the decision to invest at home or abroad can be based solely on economic considerations.[35]

If a foreign subsidiary is used, however, the situation changes. The U.S. tax on the foreign earnings is only imposed when the earnings are repatriated to the U.S. At that time, they are included in income, and under the 'deemed paid' credit provisions, a credit is given for the foreign taxes paid. Thus the foreign taxes are always creditable, but the U.S. tax is *deferred* through the use of a foreign subsidiary until the profits are brought home. If the foreign tax rate is lower than the U.S. rate, this deferral of tax gives a higher after-tax rate of return to operations undertaken through a foreign subsidiary than that available to the other forms of operation discussed above.

The tax deferral for operations conducted through foreign subsid-

35. As discussed in 6.2.2., capital export neutrality would theoretically require that the U.S. grant a foreign tax credit even where the foreign tax rate exceeds the U.S. tax rate. The U.S., however, has been unwilling to extend the credit this far. Thus foreign taxes in excess of the United States rate represent an additional cost of doing business for foreign investment and to this extent the capital export neutrality standard is not followed. In addition, of course, there are a number of explicit deviations from capital export neutrality in the form of various tax preferences granted solely to domestic investment, the most significant of which is the investment tax credit discussed at 2.2.3. The point here is that, given the general principle of capital export neutrality, foreign earnings of U.S. controlled subsidiaries should be taxed currently as a structural matter; it is then an independent descision as to whether tax (or direct) subsidies for investment should be extended to foreign investment.

iaries can be viewed as a subsidy granted by the United States government to enable its corporations more effectively to compete abroad with businesses controlled by foreign companies from countries that employ the exemption mechanism as their basic method of international tax accommodation. (See 6.1.) Such corporations will only be taxed in the country of operation. U.S. companies successfully argued in 1962 that they must be able to defer the U.S. taxes on their foreign operations until repatriation in order to compete effectively with corporations operating out of an exemption country. This deferral of tax is aimed at achieving 'capital import (or competitive) neutrality' in the foreign market.[36]

The current rules which allow deferral in effect sacrifice capital export neutrality in the interest of capital import neutrality in the case of controlled foreign subsidiaries. The tax deferral allowed to the foreign subsidiaries thus functions as a subsidy device operated through the tax system, when measured against the standard of capital export neutrality. The subpart F provisions, which eliminate deferral in certain situations, function as a part of this subsidy program. Their role is to limit deferral to those activities in which competitive neutrality is truly a factor. That is, in very general terms, the income and activities that are excluded from subpart F are those that the U.S. wishes to include in its tax subsidy program. These primarily include the income of CFCs which is generated in the country in which the CFC is actually located. In these situations the subsidy helps the CFC compete with foreign companies operating in the same country in which the CFC is conducting its business operation. But, if the CFC buys from its parent in one country and sells to a related corporation in another country, no competitive purpose is achieved by granting a subsidy for the CFC operation; it is simply a conduit and the real competitive situation is in the third country. Similarly, no competitive purpose is achieved if the U.S. grants its subsidy to a CFC that is merely a holding company. Thus the subpart F rules can be seen as defining the limits of the current

36. The standard of capital import neutrality raises a number of questions. In the first place, achievement of the goal requires that only the country of operation tax the profits earned abroad. This would only be the case if all countries adopted a pure exemption system for the relief of international double taxation, which is presently not the case. Thus, in practice the goal of capital import neutrality is not attainable even by those countries that have adopted the exemption system. In addition, from an economic point of view, it is unclear whether failure to grant deferral on the difference between the U.S. and the foreign tax in fact would have an adverse impact on the U.S. corporations' competitive position abroad. If not, capital import neutrality is not an objective worth pursuing in a country's tax system.

U.S. tax subsidy program. Beyond the subpart F situations, however, many in and out of government have increasingly come to question the appropriateness of *any* deferral or tax subsidy for controlled foreign corporations.

The same sort of questions have been raised about the tax subsidy program that would be raised about a similar direct subsidy program for investment abroad. For example, when there is a capital shortage in the U.S., should the U.S. provide a subsidy which can be availed of only by maintaining capital abroad? Should the U.S. subsidize investments which create jobs abroad when it is experiencing a high unemployment rate? Is the subsidy an efficient mechanism (under cost-benefit analyses) even if the U.S. decides to subsidize its corporations that desire to operate abroad?

In the course of its consideration of the Tax Reform Act of 1976, a number of members of the U.S. Senate answered these questions in the negative and an amendment to apply subpart F rules to all U.S. controlled foreign corporations was narrowly defeated. The complete termination of tax deferral was proposed by President Carter as part of his 1978 Tax Program. While the President's proposals were not adopted, it is likely that there will be continuing pressure in the U.S. for complete elimination of deferral of tax on U.S. controlled foreign subsidiaries.

One widely discussed form of terminating tax deferral for CFCs would permit a U.S. parent to consolidate the earnings and profits of all of its foreign subsidiaries, regardless of where located. U.S. tax due would then be based only on the net surplus, if any, for the year of all earnings and profits from foreign operations. No loss deduction would be permitted if a consolidated foreign earnings and profits deficit resulted for the year. The President's 1978 Tax Program would have terminated deferral by including in the income of the U.S. shareholders their pro rata share of the gross income and deductions of the CFC. As a result, foreign losses could currently offset U.S. source income. Under either approach, a foreign tax credit would be allowed as under present subpart F rules. It is also likely that termination of tax deferral for CFCs would occur gradually over a period of five or ten years. There has been some discussion of a system that would allow the U.S. parent corporation to include the taxable income (or loss) of its 80% controlled foreign subsidiaries in its consolidated tax return, thus permitting current utilization of losses from foreign operations against the parent's U.S. income.

Chapter 8
Special provisions affecting international transactions

Apart from the rules establishing the basic patterns of taxation of foreign persons and foreign income discussed in Chapters 3 through 7, there are a number of other provisions which bear on the treatment of international transactions. Some of them are rules which are applicable only when there is an international element in the situation, e.g., a reorganization involving a foreign corporation. In other cases, special problems arise where rules normally covering domestic taxation are extended to the international area. A number of these provisions will be discussed in the following material. They include the special requirements concerning foreign corporations involved in tax-free transactions; intercompany pricing problems; the provisions dealing with accumulations of corporate income; and the treatment of trusts. When necessary the normally applicable domestic rules are discussed and then the international aspects considered.

8.1. Foreign corporations

8.1.1. Section 367: tax-free transactions

8.1.1.1. Background

As discussed briefly in 2.2.5., under U.S. law a number of transactions involving the formation and reorganization of corporations are tax-free to the shareholders and the corporations involved. In qualifying transactions, immediate recognition of gain (or loss) is deferred and the taxpayer is taxed only when the stock or other property received in the transaction is disposed of at some subsequent date. Similarly, gain (or loss) on assets transferred by the corporation in such transactions is deferred until the assets are disposed of in a taxable transaction by the acquiring corporation. If it were possible to utilize one of the tax-free techniques to transfer appreciated property beyond the U.S. taxing jurisdiction to a foreign corporation, U.S. tax on the potential gain would be completely avoided. (On the other hand, taxpayers would always recognize losses.) To deal with this problem, the U.S. revenue laws since 1932 have provided that certain transfers involving foreign corporations will not be accorded tax-free treatment unless the taxpayer obtains a ruling from the Internal Revenue Service that the transaction is not part of a plan having as one of its principal purposes the avoidance of federal income taxes (a 'section 367 ruling)'. Prior to 1976, a section 367 ruling was required *before* any transaction was undertaken, but changes adopted in the Tax Reform Act of 1976 eliminated this requirement.

8.1.1.2. Procedures for obtaining a ruling

Section 367, as amended in 1976, distinguishes between two types of transfers involving foreign corporations. First, for transfers involving property moving from the U.S. to the foreign corporation ('outbound' transfers), the taxpayer must obtain a section 367 ruling within 183 days after the beginning of the transfer. For other transactions which are covered by the section but which do not involve the transfer of property from the U.S. (for example, the reorganization of two foreign corporations controlled by a U.S. parent), the section requires the fiscal authorities to promulgate Regulations setting forth the principles under which non-outbound transactions involving foreign corporations will be given tax-free treatment. The Regulations, issued in late 1977, have brought greater clarity and certainty to an area which up to 1976 had been a matter of substantial administrative discretion.[1] With respect to outbound transfers which still require a ruling, the 1976 changes provide for judicial review of the Internal Revenue Service action in granting or denying a ruling.[2]

1. Temporary Treas. Reg. sec. 7.367(a)-(c). For a discussion of the Temporary Regulations, see New York State Bar Association Tax Section, Report on the Proposed Regulations Under Section 367, 34 Tax Law Review 79 (1978); Kingson, The Theory and Practice of Section 367, 37 New York University Institute on Federal Taxation, sec. 22.00 (1979).
2. In Dittler Bros., Inc. v. Commissioner, 72 T.C. 896 (1979), the first case involving a judicial review of a section 367 ruling under the 1976 legislation, the Tax Court held that the standard of review was whether the decision of the fiscal authorities was supported by 'substantial evidence'; see also note 6, below. Rev. Proc. 77-5, 1977-1 Cum. Bull. 536, sets forth the procedural requirements for obtaining judicial review of a section 367 ruling action by the Internal Revenue Service.

8.1.1.3. Transactions covered

Under section 367, a number of transactions which would otherwise be tax-free under various provisions of the Internal Revenue Code lose their tax-free status if the transactions involve a foreign corporation and the provisions of section 367 are not followed. Technically, section 367 achieves this result by providing that a foreign corporation 'shall not be considered to be a corporation' for purposes of the various sections providing for nonrecognition of gain on corporate formation or reorganization transactions unless the section is complied with.

Section 367 only covers transactions to the extent a gain is involved. The taxpayer may not take affirmative advantage of section 367, for example, by failing to obtain a section 367 ruling so that the transaction would be taxable and a resulting increase in basis would be obtained for its assets.[3] The transactions in which a section 367 ruling is required or to which the section 367 Regulations are applicable are described below.

8.1.1.3.1. Formation of corporation

Under section 351, no gain or loss is recognized in a transaction in which property is transferred to a corporation in exchange for stock of the corporation if, after the transfer, the transferor owns at least 80% of the voting stock of the corporation. Section 367 must be complied with for section 351 to apply to the formation of a foreign corporation. On the other hand, where a foreign corporation is the transferor of property in connection with the formation of a *U.S.* corporation, section 367 is not applicable since, under section 351, nonrecognition does not depend on the status of the transferor as a corporation.

8.1.1.3.2. Reorganizations

In general, the Internal Revenue Code permits certain corporate reorganizations to proceed on a tax-free basis both to the shareholders and the corporations involved. Under the basic statutory patterns, six different types of tax-free reorganizations are permitted. They are:

Type (*A*): A merger or consolidation in compliance with state law, as

3. Rev. Rul. 64-177, 1964-1 Cum. Bull. 141.

where Corporation X is merged into Corporation Y or Corporations X and Y consolidate into Corporation Z.

Type (B): The acquisition by one corporation of an 80% interest in the voting stock of another corporation solely in exchange for the voting stock of the acquiring corporation. The shareholders of the acquired corporation thus become shareholders of the acquiring corporation.

Type (C): The acquisition by one corporation of substantially all the assets of another corporation in exchange for the voting stock of the acquiring corporation. The acquired corporation which receives the stock would generally distribute the stock to its shareholders in liquidation and they would then become shareholders of the acquiring corporation.[4]

Type (D): The creation of a new corporation to which are transferred some or all of the parent's assets with the shares of the new corporation distributed to the parent's shareholders.

Type (E): A change in the capital structure of an existing corporation, for example, the exchange of common stock for a new class of stock.

Type (F): A mere change in the identity, form or place of organization of the corporation.

In all of these transactions, section 361 provides that the corporation transferring its assets or shares does not recognize gain or loss and section 354 provides similar nonrecognition treatment for shareholders exchanging their shares in connection with the reorganization transaction. However, if a foreign corporation is a party to the reorganization, section 367 denies nonrecognition treatment unless the requirements of that section are fulfilled.

8.1.1.3.3. Liquidations

Under section 332, the liquidation of a subsidiary by a corporate parent

4. The type A, B, and C reorganizations thus provide a variety of techniques for undertaking corporate acquisitions on a tax-free basis. The provisions and their judicial interpretations are enormously complex, but the basic principle behind the sections is that if the shareholders of the acquired corporation continue their investment in the form of stock in the acquiring corporation, the transaction should not be subject to current taxation. On the technical level, the reorganization forms described in the text can also be undertaken through the use of subsidiaries of the acquiring corporation. Sec. 368(a)(2)(D) and sec. 368(a)(2)(E) set forth certain additional requirements when subsidiaries are used as the acquiring vehicle but, in general, the principles remain the same.

owning at least 80% of the voting stock of the subsidiary is tax-free to the parent corporation. Here again section 367 is applicable if a foreign corporation is involved in the liquidation.

8.1.1.4. 'Toll charge' approach

In granting rulings under section 367, the Internal Revenue Service has developed a so-called 'toll charge' approach to the problems of dealing with nonrecognition transactions involving foreign corporations. Basically a favorable ruling will be granted only if the taxpayer agrees to pay a certain 'charge' in connection with the transaction. For example, suppose a U.S. corporation wishes to transfer assets of its business to a foreign corporation in a transaction which would normally be tax-free under section 351. Since the transfer involves an outbound transfer to a foreign corporation, a ruling under section 367 is required for tax-free treatment to apply. Under the administrative guidelines developed under section 367,[5] a favorable ruling will be granted if the foreign corporation uses the property transferred to it in the active conduct of its trade or business and meets certain other tests. However, a favorable ruling will not be issued to the extent that inventory or stock or securities are transferred to the foreign corporation (these types of property are easily sold and, therefore, the gain could escape U.S. taxation). If assets of this latter type are involved in the transfer, the U.S. corporation must pay a 'toll charge' by including in its taxable income the appreciation attributable to the 'tainted' inventory or securities. Having paid this charge, the remainder of the transaction will be treated on a tax-free basis.[6]

5. Rev. Proc. 68-23, 1968-1 Cum. Bull. 821, sets forth the general principles under which favorable rulings will be issued. Additional requirements are set forth in other Revenue Rulings. See, e.g., Rev. Rul. 78-201, 1978-1 Cum. Bull. 91 (where a foreign branch had been operating at a loss for several years and it was desired to transfer the branch operations to a foreign subsidiary corporation in a section 351 transaction, favorable treatment under section 367 was conditioned on the taxpayer's including in income an amount equal to the previously deducted losses).

6. Rev. Proc. 68-23 also sets forth the circumstances under which the transfer of intangible assets such as patents or know-how may be made tax-free to a foreign corporation under sec. 351. In Dittler Bros., Inc. v. Commissioner, 72 T.C. 896 (1979), the taxpayer challenged the Internal Revenue Service's refusal to grant a favorable ruling on the transfer of manufacturing know-how to a foreign corporation. The court held, contrary to the Service, that the know-how would be used in the active conduct of a trade or business carried on by the foreign corporation; thus the foreign corporation was an operating company and the section 367 ruling should have been granted.

Similarly, suppose a U.S. corporate parent wished to liquidate its foreign subsidiary. For the transaction to be tax-free, the parent under pre-1976 Act law would have been required to obtain a section 367 ruling that the transaction did not involve a tax avoidance purpose. As a 'toll charge' for the ruling, the parent would be required to include in its income as a dividend the earnings and profits of the subsidiary corporation. Thus, the foreign earnings on which the U.S. tax had been deferred would not escape taxation in the otherwise tax-free liquidation. After the 1976 Act changes, no ruling is required in this situation but the Regulations issued under section 367 for non-outbound transfers continue the 'toll charge' approach by requiring the earnings of the liquidated subsidiary to be included in the parent's income as a dividend as a condition for the other aspects of the liquidation to be treated on a tax-free basis.[7] Section 367 thus insures that U.S. tax jurisdiction cannot be avoided by transferring appreciated assets, or earnings on which tax has been deferred, beyond its reach.

8.1.2. Section 1248: Disposition of Stock in a Controlled Foreign Corporation

8.1.2.1. Background

With the introduction in 1962 of the subpart F provisions discussed in Chapter 7, it was no longer possible to achieve deferral of U.S. tax on foreign base company income. However, for non-base company income, the deferral privilege continued without limitation. Having deferred U.S. taxation when the income was being earned by the foreign corporation, several avenues were open to the U.S. shareholder to avoid ordinary income treatment on the foreign earnings when they were repatriated to the U.S. For example, the shareholder could simply sell the stock of the foreign corporation and thus realize the increase in

7. Temporary Treas. Reg. sec. 7.367(b)-5(b). Similarly, the Temporary Regulations provide that a reorganization transaction involving foreign corporations with U.S. shareholders will retain its tax-free character only if the U.S. shareholders consent to treat as taxable dividends the foreign profits on which U.S. tax has been deferred. See Temporary Treas. Reg. sec. 7.367(b)-9(f). In some circumstances, while no toll charge is imposed, the taxpayer is still required to file certain information with the Internal Revenue Service; this notice requirement is applicable not only to U.S. taxpayers, but also to foreign taxpayers who are otherwise engaged in a U.S. trade or business. Temporary Treas. Reg. sec. 7.367(b)-1(c).

value of the stock at capital gain rates. Alternatively, the shareholder could, in certain circumstances, liquidate the corporation and likewise convert the foreign earnings into a capital gain. Section 1248, enacted in conjunction with the subpart F provisions, was intended to deal with this problem. Under section 1248, gain on the disposition of stock in a controlled foreign corporation which otherwise would be treated as capital gain must be reported as ordinary income to the extent of the foreign corporation's earnings and profits accumulated after 1962.

8.1.2.2. Scope of coverage

Section 1248 applies to any sale or taxable exchange by a U.S. person of stock in a controlled foreign corporation and to any corporate distribution to such person for which capital gain treatment is provided.[8] The foreign corporation must be a controlled foreign corporation as defined in the subpart F provisions and the U.S. person selling or exchanging the stock must own at least a 10% interest in the voting stock of the corporation. For section 1248 to apply, the corporation need not be a controlled foreign corporation at the time of the sale or other disposition as long as it was a controlled foreign corporation at any time during the five year period preceding the sale.

8.1.2.3. Calculation of tax

Under section 1248, the gain recognized on the sale or exchange of stock in the controlled foreign corporation is included 'as a dividend' in the income of the selling U.S. shareholder to the extent of the earnings and profits of the foreign corporation accumulated after December 31, 1962 during the period that the stock sold was held by the selling shareholder.

The following simple example illustrates the operation of section 1248. Suppose a U.S. individual shareholder owns all of the stock in a controlled foreign corporation and has a basis of 50 for his stock. During the period in which he is a shareholder, the corporation earns 130 and pays foreign taxes of 30. The stock is then sold for 175. The U.S. taxpayer's gain on the transaction would be 125 (175-50) of which 100 would be treated as ordinary income and 25 as capital gain. The 30

8. That is, liquidations covered by sec. 331 and redemption distributions which are given capital gain treatment under sec. 302.

of foreign taxes paid would not be available as a credit since individual U.S. shareholders receive no deemed paid credit under section 902. However, if the selling shareholder had been a U.S. corporation, a deemed paid credit for the 30 of foreign taxes would have been available.[9]

In calculating the earnings and profits of the foreign corporation, the Regulations under section 964 of subpart F are applied.[10] In addition, there are some special rules applicable only to section 1248 which operate to exclude from dividend treatment earnings and profits accumulated while the foreign corporation qualified as a less developed country corporation under pre-1976 Act law.[11]

Earnings and profits for purposes of section 1248 also exclude any items of income of the foreign corporation which were themselves subject to U.S. taxation as effectively connected income of the foreign corporation. However, under section 1248(h) the burden of proof in establishing the amount of earnings and profits is on the taxpayer and, if he cannot establish the amount of earning and profits, the entire gain on the sale is taxed as a dividend.

The section 1248 rules are coordinated with the subpart F principles by excluding from the earnings and profits subject to section 1248 any earnings and profits previously included in the U.S. taxpayer's income under subpart F.[12]

Section 1248 was modified in 1976 to apply to certain corporate transactions which previously had not been covered by the section.[13]

8.1.2.4. Limitation for individuals

Section 1248 contains a limitation on the tax imposed on individuals who dispose of stock in a controlled foreign corporation in a transaction subject to section 1248. Very generally, the U.S. individual share-

9. Treas. Reg. sec. 1.1248-1(d).
10. Treas. Reg. sec. 1.1248-2(d).
11. Sec. 1248(d)(3); see 7.2.
12. Sec. 1248(d)(1).
13. Under pre-1976 Act law, techniques were available by which a domestic corporation which held stock in a controlled foreign corporation could dispose of that stock either in liquidation or as a dividend distribution to its shareholders and thereby avoid the tax under sec. 1248 on the earnings of the foreign corporation. The Tax Reform Act of 1976 closed these avenues of avoiding the impact of sec. 1248 and required the domestic corporation, in effect to treat the dividend or liquidating distribution as a sale or exchange to which sec. 1248 is applicable.

holder's tax liability is limited to the liability he would have incurred if (1) the foreign corporation had been taxed as a domestic corporation with an allowance for the foreign tax credit for foreign corporate taxes paid and (2) the shareholder was taxed at capital gains rates on the liquidation of the corporation. For example, suppose an individual is in the 70% marginal bracket and disposes of stock in a transaction in which 100 of the gain on the stock would be treated as a dividend under section 1248, thus generating a tax liability of 70. If the corporate level tax which would have been paid by the foreign corporation had it been a U.S. corporation was 20, after taking the foreign tax credit into account, and the capital gain tax which the U.S. taxpayer would have paid on the disposition of the stock, absent section 1248, would have been 28, the total tax burden under section 1248(b) would be limited to 48 rather than 70.[14]

8.1.2.5. Effect of taxation under section 1248 on earnings and profits

While section 1248 treats the post-1962 earnings and profits of the foreign corporation as a dividend in the hands of the U.S. shareholder on the disposition of the CFC stock, it is the position of the Internal Revenue Service that the earnings and profits of the controlled foreign corporation are not reduced by the amount included as a dividend by the U.S. shareholder.[15] Thus, even though the selling shareholder would recognize ordinary income on the portion of his gain attributable to the accumulated earnings and profits of the controlled foreign corporation, a dividend subsequently paid to the purchaser of the stock could, under section 316, result in a second dividend tax to the purchaser on the same earnings and profits component. As a related matter, it is unclear whether the purchaser in the above example may take a foreign tax credit for the underlying corporate taxes paid by the foreign subsidiary, where the selling shareholder was also entitled to a credit for those taxes under section 1248.

14. The theory behind the limitation in sec. 1248(b) is that the U.S. shareholder should not be worse off than if he had undertaken his foreign activities through a domestic corporation. In that situation the foreign tax credit would have been available at the corporate level and capital gain rates would have been applicable to the liquidating distribution by the corporation. Sec. 1248(d) achieves this result by hypothetically constructing the tax which the foreign corporation would have paid had it been a domestic corporation and then limiting the individual shareholder's tax to that hypothetical tax plus the hypothetical capital gain tax which would have been paid on the liquidation.
15. Rev. Rul. 71-388, 1971-2 Cum. Bull. 314.

8.1.2.6. Comparison of repatriation techniques

While the general thrust of U.S. tax rules is to require the taxation as ordinary income of all repatriated foreign earnings, the pattern of rules used to achieve this result is extremely complicated and contains certain inconsistencies. In the first place, section 1248 only applies to post-1962 earnings and profits. Thus earnings and profits accumulated before 1963 can still be returned at capital gain rates. In addition, section 1248 only applies to the extent that there is a gain on the sale or liquidation of the foreign corporation. Under section 332, no gain or loss is recognized by a corporate parent on the liquidation of a subsidiary which is 80% or more controlled by the parent. Where the subsidiary is a foreign corporation, however, this nonrecognition treatment in turn depends on compliance with section 367. The Regulations under that section require as a toll charge the inclusion of *all* accumulated profits as a dividend, with a corresponding foreign tax credit for foreign corporate taxes paid. Thus, the treatment of repatriated foreign earnings depends on a large number of variables including the status of the shareholder, the period during which the profits were accumulated, and the availability of the foreign tax credit. The following table summarizes these rules:

AMOUNTS TREATED AS ORDINARY INCOME ON REPATRIATION

	Method of Repatriation		
Status of Shareholder	Ordinary Dividend	§ 1248	§§ 332/367
Individual	all	post-1962 e & p	not applicable
Corporate, under 80% ownership	all[1]	post-1962 e & p[1]	not applicable
Corporate, 80% or more ownership	all[1]	post-1962 e & p[1]	all e & p[1,2]

1. Indirect foreign tax credit available for foreign corporate taxes paid by subsidiary.
2. Temporary Treas. Reg. sec. 7.367(b)-5(b).

8.1.2.7. Foreign investment companies

Both the subpart F provisions and section 1248 are focused primarily on closely held foreign corporations. Thus both provisions only apply to U.S. shareholders with a 10% or larger voting interest in the foreign corporation. The provisions do not reach a relatively widely held foreign corporation and, prior to 1962, foreign investment corporations were formed which enabled U.S. taxpayers to accumulate income abroad with no current U.S. tax and subsequently to realize those earnings at capital gain rates on the sale of the stock in the foreign investment company. Sections 1246 and 1247, enacted in conjunction with section 1248 and the subpart F provisions, are aimed at this problem.

Under section 1246, gain on the disposition of stock in a foreign investment company[16] is treated as ordinary income to the extent of the shareholder's ratable share in the foreign investment company's post-1962 earnings and profits. This treatment is the same as that given closely held controlled foreign corporations under section 1248. Section 1247 allows the foreign investment company to elect in effect to be treated as a mutual fund with its earnings and capital gains passed through directly to its U.S. shareholders. If the section 1247 election is made, the ordinary income treatment provided for in section 1246 on the disposition of the investment company stock is not applicable.

Thus, in general, after the 1962 legislation it is not possible to defer U.S. taxation on the profits of a foreign corporation and then repatriate those profits at capital gain rates, whether the investment vehicle is a closely held corporation subject to subpart F and section 1248 or a widely held investment company covered by sections 1246 and 1247.[17]

16. Sec. 1246(b) defines a foreign investment company as (1) a foreign corporation which is registered under the Investment Company Act of 1940, i.e., a mutual fund, or (2) a corporation (a) which is engaged primarily in the business of investing, reinvesting or trading in securities and (b) more than 50% of the voting stock of which is held by U.S. persons.

17. With careful planning of the stockholding it is still possible to avoid subpart F and the foreign investment company provisions, e.g., by having exactly 50% of the voting power owned by non-U.S. persons. However, in such cases the foreign corporation will not be controlled by U.S. shareholders and thus the question is really whether, as a policy matter, the United States wishes to eliminate deferral of tax on foreign corporations in such situations. See 7.9.

8.2. Section 1491: excise tax on transfers to foreign entities

Section 1491 imposes a 35% excise tax on the appreciation inherent in any property which is transferred by U.S. persons or corporations to a foreign trust, a foreign partnership, or as a contribution to capital of a foreign corporation. The original version of section 1491 was enacted at the same time as section 367 and, like that section, was intended to prevent tax avoidance through the tax-free transfer of appreciated property to an entity outside the U.S. taxing jurisdiction. The section originally applied only to the transfer of appreciated stock or securities, but was expanded in 1976 to include all transfers of appreciated property to foreign organizations and trusts.

As in section 367, the excise tax can be avoided if it is established to the satisfaction of the fiscal authorities that the transfer is not in pursuance of a plan having a tax avoidance purpose.

The 35% rate roughly approximates the highest marginal rate on capital gains realized by individual taxpayers. Since the purpose of section 1491 is to prevent the tax-free transfer of appreciated property for sale outside the U.S. taxing jurisdiction, the section should have no application if the taxpayer agrees to include the appreciation element in income. Accordingly, section 1057 provides the taxpayer with an election to treat the transfer to the foreign organization or trust as a taxable sale of the property at its fair market value. As a result, the taxpayer will pay an income tax on the appreciation rather than being subject to the 35% excise tax rate.

The section is coordinated with section 367 so that a transfer to a corporation which is covered by section 367 does not fall within section 1491.

The section 1491 tax is payable at the time of the transfer, but can be abated or refunded if, after the transfer, the taxpayer can establish that the transfer did not have a tax avoidance purpose.

The broadened scope of section 1491 after the 1976 changes will have a substantial impact on foreign joint venture operations with U.S. partners. Transfers by U.S. partners of appreciated property to such partnerships are subjected to section 1491 even though the U.S. partners remain taxable in the U.S. on their share of income from the foreign partnership.

8.3. Section 482: intercompany pricing rules

8.3.1. Background

Section 482 authorizes the fiscal authorities to allocate gross income, deductions, and credits between related taxpayers to the extent necessary to prevent evasion of taxes or clearly to reflect the income of related taxpayers.[18] The section has a very broad scope. It applies to domestic as well as international transactions and does not require a finding of a tax avoidance purpose on the part of the parties involved for a reallocation of income to be undertaken. Detailed Regulations have been issued under the section which are based on the principle that transactions between related parties should take place on an arm's length basis.[19]

The section performs two related but distinct functions in the U.S. tax system. In the first place, it prevents a shifting of income or deductions between related taxpayers in order to take advantage of differentials in rate brackets, whether in the domestic or international context. In the international setting, however, the section plays an additional role. Even if intercompany transactions result in no overall reduction in tax burden on the controlled group when U.S. and foreign taxes are taken into account, it is still necessary that the U.S. protect its appropriate share of tax revenues in international transactions. Thus the arm's length standard of section 482 is invoked to allocate income to the U.S. even where there has been no reduction in overall tax burden on the group because of the non-arm's length intercompany pricing practices in the group.

The following discussion views the operation of section 482 primarily from the perspective of a U.S. parent with a foreign subsidiary. But it must be kept in mind that the section is equally applicable to the converse situation, i.e., a foreign parent with a U.S. subsidiary.

18. A version of sec. 482 has appeared in the United States internal revenue provisions since 1921.

19. The arm's length standard is not contained in the statute itself which speaks only of the need clearly to reflect the income of related parties. However, the Regulations, which were first issued in their present detailed form in 1968, interpret the statutory requirement that income be clearly reflected in terms of the necessity of arm's length dealings between related parties. Treas. Reg. sec. 1.482-1(b)(6). The Regulations in general are in accord with prior case law.

8.3.2. Scope of coverage

The allocation of income and deductions under section 482 is only available to the fiscal authorities; the section may not be invoked by the taxpayer.[20] The section applies in any case where two taxpayers are 'owned or controlled directly or indirectly by the same interests'. The Regulations interpret the 'controlled' requirement quite broadly and look to the realities of the situation and not to the presence of formal legal control.[21]

There was initially some question whether the section could be used to *create* income as well as simply allocate income between related parties. But the court decisions in general have upheld the authority of the Commissioner of Internal Revenue to create income in transactions between related parties. For example, in the case of interest free loans between parent and subsidiary, the Commissioner has successfully imposed an arm's length interest charge under section 482.[22]

Section 482 operates to allocate properly income and deductions between related taxpayers. After this allocation is made, section 861 and the Regulations thereunder then are employed to determine the source of the income and deductions so allocated. See 4.4.

8.3.3. Specific transactions

8.3.3.1. Loans

Loans between related parties must be made at an arm's length interest rate. In general, the interest rate prevailing at the situs of the lender or creditor is the standard. However, if the loan represents the proceeds of a borrowing by the lender undertaken at the situs of the related party-borrower, that rate may be used.[23]

The Regulations also provide a range of 'safe haven' rates within which the actual rate of interest will not be challenged.[24] If the rate of

20. Treas. Reg. sec. 1.482-1(b)(3).
21. Treas. Reg. sec. 1.482-1(a)(3).
22. B. Forman and Co. v. Commissioner, 453 F.2d 1144 (2d Cir. 1972); Kahler Corp. v. Commissioner, 486 F.2d 1 (8th Cir. 1973); Fitzgerald Motor Co. v. Commissioner, 508 F.2d 1096 (5th Cir. 1975).
23. Treas. Reg. sec. 1.482-2(a).
24. Treas. Reg. sec. 1.482-2(a)(iv). The 'safe haven' rules only apply if the creditor is not regularly engaged in the business of making loans or advances. The fiscal authorities may change the safe haven rates discussed in the text from time to time. For example, Proposed Treas. Reg. sec. 1.482-2(a)(2)(iii) (1980), would provide an 11-13% range of rates which, if adopted, would be effective August 29, 1980.

interest actually charged is at least 6% but not greater than 8%, that interest charge will be treated as arm's lenght. If no interest is charged, or if the rate is less than 6% or in excess of 8%, then 7% will be charged unless the taxpayer can establish that an arm's length charge would have been different.

8.3.3.2. Services

An arm's length charge for services undertaken for or on behalf of a related party is deemed to equal the costs or deductions incurred with respect to such services by the related party rendering the services. Thus the Regulations do not in general require that a profit be made on the charge for services between related parties.

If the services are an 'integral part' of the business activity of the providing party, however, then the arm's length charge must be the amount which would have been charged for the same or similar services to an independent party; in other words, some sort of profit factor must be included.[25]

In general, a charge for services need not be made if the probable benefits to the related members are remote or indirect.[26]

8.3.3.3. Tangible property

Where tangible property is leased between related parties (the lessor not being in the trade or business of leasing such property), the arm's length charge required by the Regulations is based on the amount of direct and indirect expenses (including depreciation) incurred with respect to the property plus a percentage of the property's depreciable basis.[27] Like the charge with respect to services, the arm's length charge for renting tangible property does not require the lessor to realize a profit.

25. Treas. Reg. sec. 1.482-2(b)(3). For a case in which the taxpayer was able to establish an arm's length charge for services based on services performed for unrelated third parties, despite the fact that the income from unrelated parties was only a small percentage of the taxpayer's total income, see U.S. Steel Corp. v. Commissioner, 617 F.2d 942 (2d Cir. 1980).
26. Treas. Reg. sec. 1.482-2(b)(2). The line between services benefiting the related party and general supervisory services is often hard to draw. See, e.g., Young and Rubicam, Inc. v. United States, 410 F.2d 1233 (Ct. Cl. 1969).
27. Treas. Reg. sec. 1.482-2(c)(2).

If the lessor or lessee is in the business of leasing such property the above cost related rule does not apply and a comparable independent transaction standard is used.

8.3.3.4. Intangible property

Unlike the cost related standards used in transactions involving services and tangible property, the Regulations with respect to transfer or use of intangible property look first to comparable transactions with unrelated companies. If such transactions are not present, then all relevant factors (such as prevailing rate in the industry, offers of competing transferors, etc.) are used in determining the appropriate arm's length charge.[28]

The Regulations have special rules for so-called 'cost sharing' arrangements between related parties which provide for the sharing of costs and risks in developing intangible property in return for a specified interest in the property. When such cost sharing arrangements are present, no charge need be made between related parties for intangible property developed under the agreement.[29]

8.3.3.5. Sales

In sales of goods between related parties, the Regulations define an arm's length price as the price an unrelated party would have paid under the same circumstances for the property involved. The Regulations set forth three pricing methods to be used in determining the arm's length price. They are, in order of preference, the comparable uncontrolled price method, the resale price method, and the cost plus method.[30]

8.3.3.5.1. Comparable uncontrolled price method

Under the comparable uncontrolled price method, the price is determined on the basis of 'uncontrolled sales' made to buyers which are not members of the same controlled group. Such comparable sales include sales made by a member of the group to an unrelated party and com-

28. Treas. Reg. sec. 1.482-2(d)(2).
29. Treas. Reg. sec. 1.482-2(d)(4).
30. Treas. Reg. sec. 1.482-2(e)(1).

parable sales of the same product made between parties which are not members of the controlled group and are unrelated. In determining the basis for comparability, differences in the properties of the product sold and the circumstances surrounding the sale are taken into account.[31]

8.3.3.5.2. Resale price method

If there are no comparable sales, the Regulations then specify that the resale price method is to be used. The resale price method is applicable where the buyer does not add significant value to the product, i.e., is simply a distributor.[32] The method in effect works back from the sales price of the product to unrelated parties outside the group and determines an appropriate mark-up percentage for sales between the related parties. Thus, for example, if the property is sold outside the group by the distributor subsidiary in an uncontrolled sale for a price of 100 and the appropriate percentage mark-up is 20%, the arm's length price for the sale within the group from the manufacturing parent to the distributor subsidiary would be 80 (100 minus 20% × 100). The appropriate mark-up percentage is determined by examining similar transactions or if necessary on an industry-wide basis.[33]

8.3.3.5.3. Cost plus method

The cost plus method is used by the Regulations in those situations in which there are no comparable unrelated sales and the retail sales method is not appropriate because the functions performed by the seller are more than simple distribution, i.e., involve the addition of substantial elements of value to the product. Under the cost plus method, the costs of the company selling to the related party are determined under normal accounting concepts and then an appropriate gross profit percentage is applied.[34]

8.3.3.5.4. Other methods

In addition to the three methods described above, the Regulations provide for the use of 'some appropriate method' of pricing where none

31. Treas. Reg. sec. 1.482-2(e)(2)(ii).
32. Treas. Reg. sec. 1.482-2(e)(3)(ii).
33. Treas. Reg. sec. 1.482-2(e)(3)(vii). The taxpayer attempting to justify intercompany pricing by using the resale price method must establish the appropriate mark-up percentage on the basis of unrelated party transactions. For a case in which the taxpayer was unable to establish the appropriate mark-up, see DuPont v. United States, 608 F.2d 445 (Ct.Cl. 1979).
34. Treas. Reg. sec. 1.482-2(e)(4). For an application of the cost plus method, see Eli Lilly and Co. v. United States, 372 F.2d 990 (Ct. Cl. 1967).

of the described methods can reasonably be applied under the facts and circumstances of the particular case.[35] Such 'other methods' would include an allocation of the overall profit earned by the group on the particular transaction, a calculation of an appropriate rate of return on the taxpayer's investment, or some combination of these factors. In a study of section 482 adjustments made in 1968 and 1969 some 40% of all intercompany sales pricing adjustments were made on the basis of some 'other' method.[36]

8.3.4. Other aspects of section 482 allocations

8.3.4.1. Set-offs

The Regulations provide that in making allocations under section 482, the fiscal authorities shall consider the effect of any other non-arm's length transactions between the parties in the taxable year in question. The Regulations give the example of a situation in which one party performs services without an arm's length charge for a related party which in turn sells products to the first party at a discount.[37] The value of the services received without charge would be off-set against the allocation which otherwise would be made under section 482 as to the discount.

8.3.4.2. Correlative adjustments

The Regulations require that where the fiscal authorities make an adjustment to the income of one member of a group under section 482 a corresponding adjustment (correlative adjustment) must be made in the income or deductions of the related party.[38] For example, in an interest free loan situation, imputation of income to the lending party results in a corresponding interest deduction to the borrowing party. In a purely

35. Treas. Reg. sec. 1.482-2(e)(1)(iii).
36. Treasury Department News Release, January 8, 1973, Commerce Clearing House, Standard Federal Tax Reporter, vol. 7, par 6419 (1973). See also The Conference Board, Tax Allocations and International Business (1972); Taxation of Intercompany Transactions in Selected Countries in Europe and USA (Kluwer, 1979).
37. Treas. Reg. sec. 1.482-1(d)(3).
38. Treas. Reg. sec. 1.482-1(d)(2).

domestic context, this could result in a reduction of income tax liability for the related party or perhaps in an increased net operating loss carryover.

In the international context, where the related party is not subject to U.S. tax jurisdiction, no such direct correlative adjustment can be made. However, if it later becomes necessary to determine the income of the related party, for example, in connection with the foreign tax credit, the earnings and profits of the related party will be computed as if the correlative adjustment had been made.

8.3.4.3. Adjustment of accounts after section 482 allocation

When a section 482 allocation has been made, the income of one of the related parties will be increased. However, the actual funds representing that allocation will still remain with the other party. If no special rules were applicable, when those funds were subsequently transferred to the related party, for example, as a dividend distribution, an additional tax would be incurred. To solve this problem the Internal Revenue Service has issued administrative guidelines which provide that the taxpayer to whom income is allocated under section 482 may receive a dividend payment from the related party in the year in which the allocation has been made which it can exclude from its U.S. income.[39] If such a dividend is not paid, the taxpayer has the alternative of setting up an account receivable on its books reflecting the amount of the section 482 adjustment which can then be paid over to it by the related party with no further tax consequences. These relief procedures, however, apply only in the case that the arrangements or

39. Rev. Proc. 65-17, 1965-1 Cum. Bull. 833. For a case involving the utilization of Rev. Proc. 65-17 to repatriate income allocated to the U.S. domestic parent under section 482, see Schering Corp. v. Commissioner, 69 T.C. 579 (1978).
It should be noted that a section 482 allocation can have effects beyond simply increasing the income of one related taxpayer and decreasing the income of another. For example, suppose there are business transactions between two subsidiary corporations of the same parent corporation. If the dealings between the two subsidiary corporations are found not to have been at arm's length, income from one corporation will be allocated to the other corporation. However, the actual funds representing the income will remain with the corporation from which the income was allocated. In such a case, the Internal Revenue Service may take the position that the excess funds were first distributed as a dividend by one subsidiary to the parent corporation and then contributed to the capital of the second subsidiary. For an example of this type of 'triangular' dividend see Rev. Rul. 78-83, 1978-1 Cum. Bull. 79.

transactions giving rise to the section 482 allocation did not have as one of their principal purposes the avoidance of federal income tax.

8.3.5. International aspects

8.3.5.1. Treaties

Most U.S. income tax treaties contain an article which allows the U.S. to determine the income of persons subject to its taxing jurisdiction on the basis of an arm's length principle in any situation in which arrangements or conditions in transactions between related parties do not conform to the arm's length standard.[40] In general, the tests applied under section 482 are also relevant under the treaties. Under recent treaties, where a reallocation of income has been made by one country, the other country agrees to make corresponding adjustments to the extent that it agrees with such a redetermination of income. To the extent that the other country does not agree with the redetermination, the two countries endeavor to reach a compromise under the general mutual agreement procedures contained in the treaty.[41] If no such compromise can be reached, the taxpayer is faced with possible international double taxation as a result of the countries' disagreement on the proper allocation of the income or deductions in question.

8.3.5.2. Foreign tax credit

Under the U.S. foreign tax credit provision discussed in 6.2., the amount of foreign tax credit available is determined in part by the U.S. taxpayer's foreign source income. Thus a section 482 allocation which has the effect of increasing the U.S. taxpayer's U.S. source income and correspondingly decreasing the income of a foreign related party can have an effect on the available foreign tax credit. For example, suppose

40. See, e.g., the U.S. treaties with France, Art. 8, and Germany, Art. IV; Model Income Tax Treaty of May 18, 1976, Art. 9.

41. See Model Income Tax Treaty, Art. 9(2). For a discussion of the mutual agreement procedure, see 10.11.1. The procedures to be followed under a treaty where section 482 allocations are involved are set out in Rev. Proc. 70-18, 1970-2 Cum. Bull. 493. See also Surrey, United Nations Group of Experts and the Guidelines for Tax Treaties Between Developed and Developing Countries, 19 Harvard International Law Journal 1 (1978).

a U.S. parent corporation receives a dividend from its foreign subsidiary and claims the deemed paid foreign tax credit under section 902 for the taxes paid by the subsidiary. In a subsequent year, a section 482 adjustment is made allocating income, which was reported initially by the foreign subsidiary, to the U.S. parent corporation. Under the correlative adjustment principle, the foreign subsidiary's income will be reduced correspondingly and the foreign tax credit calculation, which under section 902 is based in part on the subsidiary's income in the year in question, will be changed.[42] To claim the foreign tax credit for the foreign taxes imposed on the items of income allocated under section 482 from a foreign subsidiary to the U.S. parent, the taxpayer must establish that the foreign subsidiary has exhausted its administrative remedies in seeking a refund of the foreign taxes paid on the income so reallocated.[43]

Otherwise, it is presumed that the foreign taxes paid were in fact a contribution to the foreign government not qualifying for the foreign tax credit. In addition, if the allocation under section 482 is made in connection with a foreign subsidiary in a country with which the U.S. has an income tax treaty, the parent must demonstrate that it exhausted its rights under the competent authority provision of the treaty.

Thus the U.S. insures that, if at all possible, the increase in revenue under the section 482 allocation will not simply be offset by an increased foreign tax credit resulting from a failure to adjust the taxes paid in the foreign country to reflect the section 482 adjustment.

8.3.5.3. Blocked income

If a payment between related parties is prevented because of currency or other restrictions under the laws of a foreign country and a section 482 allocation is made, the taxpayer may defer the reporting of the section 482 allocation under the general method for accounting for income subject to currency restrictions. The taxpayer is not forced to pay current tax on an income allocation which it in fact cannot receive because of the currency restrictions.[44]

42. Rev. Rul. 74-158, 1974-1 Cum. Bull. 182. See generally, Surrey, Reflections on the Allocation of Income and Expenses Among National Jurisdictions, 10 Law and Policy in International Business 409 (1978).
43. Rev. Rul. 76-508, 1976-2 Cum. Bull. 225; Rev. Rul. 80-231, I.R.B. 1980-34, 14.
44. Treas. Reg. sec. 1.482-1(d)(6).

8.4. Corporate accumulations to avoid shareholder tax

8.4.1. Accumulated earnings tax

8.4.1.1. Background

As discussed in Chapter 2, the U.S. has a classical form of corporation tax system in which corporate earnings are taxed both at the corporate level and in the hands of individual shareholders when they are distributed as dividends. As a result, the total tax burden can be minimized by retaining profits in the corporation for as long as possible before subjecting them to the second tax at the shareholder level. In order to discourage such accumulations, sections 531–537 impose an 'accumulated earnings tax' on certain corporate retentions. The tax is applied to every corporation 'formed or availed of for the purpose of avoiding the income tax with respect to its shareholders . . . by permitting earnings and profits to accumulate instead of being divided or distributed'. The tax is imposed at a rate of 27 1/2% of the first $100,000 of accumulations and 38 1/2% of the excess over $100,000. The accumulated earnings tax does not apply to personal holding companies or foreign personal holding companies, discussed in 8.4.2. and 8.4.3., as other Code sections deal expressly with the methods of tax avoidance involved in the use of such companies.

8.4.1.2. Proscribed purpose

Under section 532, it is not sufficient for imposition of the penalty tax that the corporation have accumulated profits; those profits must have been accumulated with the purpose of avoiding the income tax on the shareholders. However, to eliminate the need for a subjective inquiry into the corporation's purpose for the accumulation, section 533 provides that the purpose of avoiding the tax is to be determined by whether earnings and profits have been permitted to accumulate 'beyond the reasonable needs of the business'. If accumulations beyond reasonable business needs have taken place, the proscribed purpose is presumptively present unless the corporation can by a preponderance of the evidence prove the contrary.[45]

45. In United States v. Donruss Co., 393 U.S. 297 (1969), the Supreme Court held that, in →

8.4.1.3. Reasonable needs of the business

The determination of the reasonable needs of business involves a complex factual inquiry into all aspects of the corporation's business. The Regulations set forth a number of factors which can be taken into account.[46] These include the need to expand business or replace existing equipment; to acquire a related business enterprise; to provide for the retirement of indebtedness; and to provide for necessary working capital.[47] On the other hand, the following factors point in the direction of improper accumulation: investments in unrelated property or securities, especially if those investments are liquid; loans to individual shareholders; loans to corporations related to or controlled by the controlling shareholders of the corporation.[48]

8.4.1.4. Calculation of the tax

Assuming that the proscribed purpose of accumulation to avoid tax at the shareholder level is present, the accumulated earnings tax is imposed on 'accumulated taxable income'. Accumulated taxable income is arrived at by making certain adjustments to 'normal' taxable income to establish the corporation's true dividend paying capacity. For example, in this computation a deduction is allowed for federal and foreign income taxes which have been paid by the corporation.[49] On the other hand, taxable income is increased by the amount of the intercorporate dividends received deduction since that deduction represents funds which are available for distribution.

→

order to rebut the presumption in sec. 533, the taxpayer must establish that tax avoidance was not 'one of the purposes' for the accumulation of the earnings beyond the reasonable needs of the business. It is not sufficient for the taxpayer to establish that tax avoidance was not the 'dominant, controlling or compelling' reason for the accumulation. Thus, though the statute makes a finding of proscribed purpose the crucial event for tax purposes, the reasonableness of the accumulation will be determinative of the issue of purpose in practically all cases.

46. Treas. Reg. sec. 1.537-2. The statute itself recognizes that accumulation justifications can include the needs of the business in the future, i.e., 'anticipated needs', as well as certain other specific situations.

47. There is a great deal of case material on the method by which the appropriate level of working capital is to be determined. In general a formula taking into account the cyclical nature of the corporation's business is used. Bardahl Manufacturing Corp. v. Commissioner, 24 T.C.M. 1030 (1965).

48. Treas. Reg. sec. 1.537-2(c).

49. Treas. Reg. sec. 1.535-2(a).

Section 535(c) allows a credit against accumulated earnings for an amount equal to the greater of $150,000 or such part of the earnings and profits as were retained for the reasonable needs of the business. As a result, all corporations are in effect allowed to accumulate at least $150,000 of earnings before the accumulated earnings tax can become a problem.[50]

8.4.1.5. International aspects

8.4.1.5.1. Foreign corporations

8.4.1.5.1.1. STATUS OF SHAREHOLDERS. Section 531 does not deal explicitly with the question of the coverage of foreign corporations. The Regulations, however, provide that the section is applicable to any foreign corporation which has income derived from U.S. sources if any of the shareholders of the corporation are subject to U.S. income tax on the distributions of the corporation. This can be the case either because the shareholders are subject to world wide U.S. taxing jurisdiction as residents or citizens or because they are non-resident alien individuals subject to tax under section 871.[51]

The situation is relatively clear for U.S. shareholders in foreign corporations. It is somewhat more complicated with respect to foreign corporations whose only shareholders are nonresident alien individuals. Under section 861(a)(2)(B), dividends paid by a *foreign* corporation are not treated as U.S. source income unless 50 percent or more of the foreign corporation's income is effectively connected with a U.S. trade or business.[52] Because of this source rule, any dividends paid by a foreign corporation without substantial U.S. business income would be treated as foreign source income in the hands of a nonresident alien individual shareholder and would not be subject to U.S. tax. As a result, for corporations in this position, section 531 would not be applicable since there has been no avoidance of U.S. taxation by failing to make dividend distributions. Similarly, even if the foreign corporation does have substantial U.S. effectively connected income, many

50. Special rules apply in the case of a holding or investment company. Note that the concept of the 'reasonable needs of the business' plays a role both in determining the liability for the accumulated earnings tax and establishing the amount of accumulated earnings subject to tax. As a result, almost all issues in the accumulated earnings tax area turn in one way or another on the establishment of the reasonable needs of the business.

51. Treas. Reg. sec. 1.532-1(c).

52. See 4.2.2.

U.S. income tax treaties exempt dividends received by nonresident aliens from foreign corporations organized in the treaty country.[53] In these cases as well, section 531 would not be applicable since there could be no U.S. tax avoidance present.

8.4.1.5.1.2. COMPUTATION OF TAX. Assuming the foreign corporation is subject to the accumulated earnings tax because of the taxable status of its shareholders, some difficult and unanswered questions are still involved concerning the computation of the tax. In the first place, it is not clear whether the earnings and profits referred to in section 531 are limited to earnings and profits from U.S. sources or include the foreign corporation's worldwide earnings and profits. A similar question exists with respect to the appropriate 'reasonable needs of the business'. Should these needs include the worldwide needs of the foreign corporation or only its U.S. needs? The absence of any decided cases on these fundamental points may indicate that the Internal Revenue Service does not actively pursue the accumulated earnings tax issues with foreign corporations.

8.4.1.5.2. Foreign shareholders of U.S. corporations

If a U.S. corporation with foreign shareholders is involved, there is no question as to the relevant earnings and profits and business needs of the corporation. However, since nonresident shareholders are in general taxed at a 30 percent rate on dividends in comparison with the maximum 70 percent rate for U.S. individual shareholders, it would appear less likely that corporations with foreign shareholders would retain earnings to avoid the tax at the shareholder level.[54] This argument has even more applicability in situations in which tax treaties would reduce the rate of tax on the dividends. On the other hand, such an argument would be more difficult in the case of a foreign corporation which had both U.S. and foreign shareholders since presumably a finding of the proscribed purpose with respect to one group of shareholders would be sufficient for the accumulated earnings tax to apply to all.

53. See, e.g., Income Tax Convention Between the United States and Germany, Art. XIV.

54. The tax impact which dividend distributions would have had on the shareholders is generally included in the presentation of an accumulated earnings tax case by the government. See, e.g., Magic Mart, Inc. v. Commissioner, 51 T.C. 775 (1969).

Proposed Treas. Reg. sec. 1.532-1, 1.533-1, and 1.535-1 (1980), address a number of the issues and questions raised in the text.

8.4.2. Personal holding company tax

8.4.2.1. Background

While the accumulated earnings tax deals with the problem of accumulations at the corporate level in general, the U.S., since 1934, has had a special set of provisions dealing with accumulations by personal holding companies, i.e., so-called 'incorporated pocketbooks'. Under the personal holding company provisions, a penalty tax of 70 percent (the highest marginal individual rate) is imposed on the 'undistributed personal holding company income' (basically passive investment-type income) of a corporation which qualifies as a personal holding company. Unlike the accumulated earnings tax, the personal holding company provisions apply if certain objective conditions are met; there is no resort to criteria such as the need for the accumulations or the purpose of the accumulation.

8.4.2.2. Scope of coverage

8.4.2.2.1. Shareholding requirement

The personal holding company provisions are aimed at closely held corporations which, in terms of the statute, means that five or fewer individuals must own more than 50 percent of the stock of the corporation. Stock ownership is determined in the light of complex attribution rules, which are similar to, though not identical with, the attribution rules applicable under subpart F.[55] The stock ownership requirement is phrased in terms of the value of the outstanding stock of the corporation and does not turn on voting control.

8.4.2.2.2. Character of the income

Since the statute is aimed at closely held corporations which are in effect being used as investment vehicles, the provisions are applicable to the investment-type income realized by the corporation. The rules are extremely complex but, in general terms, a corporation is a personal holding company if 60 percent or more of its gross income[56] is 'personal

55. Sec. 544.

56. The statute is phrased in terms of 'adjusted ordinary gross income'. This special statutory concept was introduced in 1964 to prevent corporations with high gross income but low net income (for example, from rental real estate) from avoiding the personal holding company provisions.

holding company income'. Personal holding company income includes dividends, interest, income from personal services performed by a substantial shareholder, royalties of certain types, and rental income.[57]

The personal holding company provisions do not apply to banks, life insurance companies and lending and finance companies which, though they may receive income of the type in general covered by the personal holding company rules, are typically engaged in an active business and thus do not represent the problem to which the provisions were aimed.[58]

8.4.2.3. Calculation of the tax

If the corporation falls within the definitional scope of the personal holding company provisions, it is subject to a 70 percent tax on its undistributed personal holding company income. This tax is in addition to the normal federal income tax imposed on the corporation. The tax base to which the 70 percent penalty rate is applied begins with the corporation's taxable income but, as in the case of the accumulated earnings tax, a number of adjustments are made in order to arrive at the amount which has in fact been economically retained by the corporation. Thus a deduction is allowed for dividends paid, for federal income taxes paid and for charitable contributions in excess of the applicable limitation.[59] On the other hand, the corporation must add back to the tax base for personal holding company tax purposes the dividends received deduction; personal holding company income therefore can exceed taxable income in certain situations.

Since the purpose of the penalty tax is to force distributions by the corporation, a special procedure is available by which the corporation can pay a so-called 'deficiency dividend' for the year in which a determination as to personal holding company liability has been made.[60] The

57. Each of the various categories of income involve detailed definitional provisions intended to separate out purely investment income from business income. For example, with respect to rental income, a corporation which has substantial rental income in relation to its other forms of personal holding company income can avoid personal holding company status if it distributes these latter amounts and retains only the rental income. Sec. 543(a)(2). Similarly, copyright royalties in general are treated as personal holding company income, but there are exceptions in the case of publishers and others for whom such royalties represent business income.
58. Sec. 542(c).
59. Sec. 545(b).
60. Sec. 547.

deficiency dividend can be deducted at the corporate level and will eliminate the personal holding company tax liability (but not the liability for interest or other penalties in connection with the personal holding company tax). The shareholders will then include the deficiency dividend in income.

8.4.2.4. International aspects

The personal holding company provisions apply to foreign as well as to domestic corporations. However, there are a number of special rules for foreign corporations which are determined to be personal holding companies.

8.4.2.4.1. Foreign corporations as personal holding companies

While a foreign corporation may be subject to the personal holding company provisions, in general under section 882(b) its gross income includes only income from U.S. sources. The exposure of the foreign corporation to the personal holding company tax is thus automatically limited to its U.S. source investment-type income.

Even in the case when U.S. source income is present, a foreign corporation is exempted from the personal holding company provisions if *all* of its stock is owned by nonresident alien individuals.[61] If the foreign corporation has *any* U.S. shareholders this exception is not available, but a general *de minimus* rule may still be applicable. If the U.S. ownership is less than 10 percent of the value of the outstanding stock of the foreign corporation, then only that percentage of the corporation's undistributed personal holding company income is subject to the personal holding company tax.[62] This rule in effect limits the impact of the penalty tax to the U.S. shareholders' proportionate interest in the corporation. However, if the U.S. interests in the corporation exceed the 10 percent floor, the limitation does not apply and the personal holding company tax is fully applicable.

61. Sec. 542(c)(7). The exemption applies if all of the stock of the foreign corporation outstanding during the last half of the taxable year is owned directly or indirectly by nonresident alien individuals. The exception does not apply, however, where the foreign corporation has personal holding company income from personal services performed by shareholders.
62. Sec. 545(a).

8.4.2.4.2. Foreign shareholders in U.S. corporations

There are no special rules applicable to foreign shareholders in U.S. personal holding companies. Thus, regardless of the level of foreign ownership or the source of the U.S. corporation's income, the personal holding company tax provisions are applicable.

8.4.3. Foreign personal holding companies

8.4.3.1. Terminology

As seen in 8.4.2.4.1., foreign corporations can be subject to the personal holding company provisions of sections 541-547. In addition, another set of provisions, sections 551-558, apply to foreign personal holding companies. Thus a foreign corporation can be:

(1) subject to the personal holding company provisions;
(2) subject to the foreign personal holding company provisions; or
(3) subject to both sets of provisions.

In case (3), section 542(c)(5) provides that the foreign personal holding company provisions control and thus a foreign corporation which falls within both sets of provisions will be treated as a foreign personal holding company. In the following material the term 'foreign personal holding company' will only be used to describe those corporations which fall under sections 551-558 and does not cover foreign corporations which are personal holding companies under sections 541-547.

8.4.3.2. Background

While the penalty tax on accumulations imposed by the personal holding company provisions applies to foreign corporations, Congress in 1937 added a separate set of provisions dealing with foreign personal holding companies as such. Under the foreign personal holding company rules, rather than imposing a penalty tax on the foreign corporation, the U.S. shareholder in the foreign personal holding company is taxed directly on the undistributed income. The foreign personal holding company provisions were thus the forerunner of the subpart F provisions enacted in 1962 for controlled foreign corporations in general.

8.4.3.3. Scope of coverage

8.4.3.3.1. Shareholding requirements

For a foreign corporation to be classified as a foreign personal holding company, more than 50 percent in value of its outstanding stock must be owned directly or indirectly by not more than five U.S. individual citizens or residents.[63] The statute refers to the U.S. shareholders whose stock ownership is taken into account in establishing foreign personal holding company status as the 'United States group'. In determining whether the stock ownership requirements are met, complex attribution rules apply.[64]

8.4.3.3.2. Character of the income

In order to be classified initially as a foreign personal holding company, at least 60 percent of the foreign corporation's gross income must be foreign personal holding company income, as defined.[65] Once the foreign corporation has been classified as a foreign personal holding company, the percentage requirement drops to 50 percent for subsequent years, subject to some qualifications. In determining the foreign corporation's gross income for purposes of the classification test, the gross income is computed as if the foreign corporation were a domestic corporation, i.e., income from foreign sources as well as U.S. sources is included.[66] This provision is necessary to prevent U.S. shareholders from sheltering foreign source income in a foreign personal holding company.

Foreign personal holding company income includes most kinds of passive investment-type income and is similar in scope, though not identical, to the personal holding company definition.[67] In addition to including dividends, interest, royalties, rents, etc. as foreign personal

63. Sec. 552(a)(2).
64. Sec. 554. The rules are similar in scope, though not in detail, to the constructive ownership rules applicable under subpart F in sec. 958. A special problem in the foreign personal holding company area involves the attribution of stock of nonresidents to U.S. shareholders in determining the status of the corporation as a foreign personal holding company. While the statute would appear to require such attribution, the Tax Court in Estate of Miller v. Commissioner, 43 T.C. 760 (1965), refused to apply the rules in a situation in which the U.S. shareholder to whom the stock was attributed had no direct interest in the foreign corporation and the effect of the attribution rules was to make the minority U.S. shareholders subject to the foreign personal holding company tax.
65. Sec. 552(a)(1).
66. Sec. 555(a).
67. See 8.4.2.2.2.

holding company income, gains from the sale or exchange of stock or securities and gains on commodity transactions are also covered.[68]

Foreign personal holding company income also includes the undistributed foreign personal holding company income of any subsidiary foreign personal holding company in which the first foreign personal holding company is a shareholder. The income attributed to the parent foreign personal holding company is then taken into account in calculating the latter's income for purposes of the 60 percent gross income test.[69]

8.4.3.4. Calculation of the tax

Assuming that the shareholding and income requirements are met, the U.S. shareholders[70] must include currently in their income the undistributed foreign personal holding company income of the foreign corporation. As in the case of the accumulated earnings tax and the personal holding company tax, the calculation of the amount subject to tax begins with the foreign corporation's taxable income with adjustments downward for taxes paid, charitable contributions, etc. and adjustments upward for certain deductions such as the dividends received deduction. The U.S. shareholder includes in income the amount which he would have received had the foreign personal holding company distributed its undistributed foreign personal company income as a dividend on the last day of its taxable year. Thus under the literal language of the statute, if the U.S. shareholder acquired the stock on the last day of the corporation's taxable year he would be subject to tax on his share of the undistributed foreign personal holding company income for the entire year.[71]

68. Sec. 553(a)(2)-(3).
69. Sec. 555(b). This technique of attributing the income of the subsidiary to the foreign parent corporation is to be contrasted to the so-called 'hopscotch' principle used in subpart F provisions under which the income of the foreign subsidiary is attributed through the chain of foreign ownership directly to the U.S. shareholder. See sec. 951(a).
70. For purposes of the foreign personal holding company provisions, the U.S. shareholder subject to tax must *actually* own the shares of the foreign corporation. The rules of constructive ownership apply only to determine whether or not the foreign corporation is to be treated as a foreign personal holding company. This approach is to be contrasted with the subpart F approach under which, in certain circumstances, the U.S. shareholder may be subject to tax even though it does not own directly any shares of stock in the controlled foreign corporation. See sec. 958(a).
71. Several courts have refused to apply this rule where the U.S. shareholder was a nonresident alien for some portion of the tax year in question. See Marsman v. Com- →

Where the U.S. shareholder is taxed on the undistributed foreign personal holding company income of the foreign corporation, appropriate adjustments are made in the foreign corporation's earnings and profits and in the U.S. shareholder's basis in the shares of the foreign corporation.[72]

8.4.4. Relationship of provisions dealing with corporations used to avoid shareholder tax

As the previous material indicates, the U.S. tax system contains a number of overlapping provisions which deal in one way or another with the problem of avoidance of tax at the shareholder level by having a corporation accumulate income. The provisions have been introduced at various times in the development of the tax laws with little attention to the coordination of the provisions. The different sets of rules abound with technical distinctions. For example, under the foreign personal holding company rules, U.S. ownership is tested in terms of the value of the U.S. stock interest which can be taken into account. On the other hand, in the controlled foreign corporation provisions, the test is in terms of voting power and only U.S. interests of 10 percent or more are considered. The definition of the type of income reached by the provisions also varies for controlled foreign corporations, foreign personal holding companies, and personal holding companies. The methods of taxation are likewise different. In the personal holding company provisions, a penalty tax is applied to the corporation. In the foreign personal holding company area, the U.S. shareholders who actually own stock are taxed directly, and in the controlled foreign corporation sections U.S. shareholders are in some cases taxed even where the stock ownership is indirect.

In addition to the above mentioned provisions, section 1248 (discussed in 8.1.2.) operates to tax as ordinary income gain on the disposition of the stock of a controlled foreign corporation, thus inserting still another layer of statutory complexity. The table on page 162 summarizes in a general way some aspects of the interrelation between the various provisions.

→

missioner, 205 F.2d 335 (4th Cir. 1953); Gutierrez v. Commissioner, 53 T.C. 394, aff'd per curiam, 72-1 USTC ¶ 9121 (D.C. Cir. 1971). Sec. 551(b) itself provides for an allocation if the U.S. group is not in control at the end of the corporation's taxable year.

72. Sec. 551(d)-(e).

SUMMARY OF UNITED STATES TREATMENT OF ACCUMULATIONS

	Status of Shareholder	Nature of Income	Taxation	Relation to Other Provisions
1. Controlled Foreign Corporation (CFC)	U.S. share-holders own more than 50%	base company income	constructive dividend to U.S. shareholders	If FPHCo., CFC does not apply to base company income
2. Personal Holding Company (PH Co.)	5 or fewer individuals[1] own more than 50%	passive income (not capital gain)	70% penalty[2] tax on corpor-ation	If FPHCo., PHCo. does not apply; see 4
3. Foreign Personal Holding Company (FPHCo.)	5 or fewer *U.S.* individ-uals[3] own more than 50%	passive income (includes capital gain)	constructive dividend to U.S. share-holders	see 4
4. Accumulated Earning Tax (AET)	no limitation (not applicable to PHCo. or FPHCo.)	accumulation of any kind beyond reason-able needs of business[4]	27.5%–38.5% on accumula-tions in excess of $150,000	If PHCo. or FPHCo., AET does not apply

1. The tax applies to both foreign and domestic corporations regardless of nationality of shareholders. However, a foreign corporation wholly owned by nonresident alien individuals is not in general subject to the personal holding company tax.
2. In the case of foreign corporations, the tax applies only to U.S. source income.
3. Foreign personal holding company provisions do not tax foreign shareholders since they only attribute constructive dividends to U.S. shareholders.
4. Foreign corporations can be subject to the accumulated earnings tax if any of their shareholders would be subject to U.S. income taxation on the distribution from the foreign corporation. Other aspects of the accumulated earning tax as applied to foreign corporations are uncertain.

8.5. Foreign trusts

8.5.1. Background

Under U.S. tax principles, trusts are in general not treated as separate entities. Thus, in the case of a simple trust that distributes all of its trust income currently, the trust pays no income tax and the beneficiary includes the distributed amount in his own income. In more complex trusts which accumulate all or part of the trust income, the trust does pay tax on the income in the year accumulated. However, when the accumulated income is distributed, the beneficiaries, under a prescribed procedure, must include the accumulated income (plus the taxes paid thereon) in their own income, compute tax thereon based on a three-year average of the taxes that they would have paid had the income in fact been distributed currently, and then receive credit for the taxes previously paid by the trust with respect to the accumulated income. This is the so-called 'throwback rule' that applies to distributions of accumulated income.[73]

In some cases, the grantor of a trust retains such extensive controls or powers over the trust that he is considered to remain the owner of the trust property for income tax purposes. Under the 'grantor trust' rules, the creator of the trust is taxable on the trust income each year, and in effect makes a gift of the trust income to the beneficiary who in fact receives it.[74]

If a trust derives capital gain income, the trust itself pays the tax thereon unless such gains are specifically allocated to an income beneficiary by the trust instrument. In the case of grantor trusts, capital gains derived by the trust generally are taxed to the grantor.[75]

Where a trust has derived income on which taxes have been paid to a foreign country, the foreign tax credit is allocated between the trust and the beneficiaries by first allocating the credit to the income received by the beneficiaries.[76]

73. The rules described in the text are contained in sec. 641-667 of the Code. The U.S. tax treatment of trusts, which can be quite complex in its technical detail, is described in Surrey, Warren, McDaniel and Ault, Federal Income Taxation, vol. 1., pp. 1288-1332 (1972) and 1979 Supplement.

74. See sec. 671-677. The grantor trust rules are described in greater detail in Surrey, Warren, McDaniel and Ault, above, vol. 1., pp. 1332-1359, and 1979 Supplement.

75. In addition, a grantor of a trust is taxable on gain realized by the trust where the grantor transfers appreciated property to the trust and the trust sells the property within two years after the transfer to the trust. Sec. 644.

76. Sec. 642(a)(1).

Generally speaking, a 'foreign trust' is defined to mean a trust whose foreign source income is not subject to U.S. tax under the rules prescribed for nonresident alien individuals.[77] Whether a trust is in a status comparable to a nonresident alien individual, so that its foreign source income is not subject to tax, is determined by reference to a variety of factors such as the residence of the trustee, physical location of the trust assets, the country under whose laws the trust was created, etc.[78]

In most respects, the basic rules governing taxation of U.S. trusts apply to foreign trusts. Significant financial advantages could be obtained, however, by proper planning. For example, prior to 1976, a U.S. grantor could create a foreign trust to accumulate income for the children or grandchildren, locating the trust in a country that imposed no tax on the trust entity. The trust funds would be invested in a country which imposed a low rate of tax on dividends and interest paid to foreign investors. The trust income would thus be accumulated free of any income tax. Although the U.S. would impose a tax on the accumulated income when distributed (under the 'throwback rule') the beneficiary in effect received the benefit of an interest-free loan in the amount of the taxes that would have been paid had the trust income been distributed currently. The Tax Reform Act of 1976 included provisions to reduce this benefit.[79]

8.5.2. Grantor trusts

The 1976 legislation added section 679 which subjects to the grantor trust rules a U.S. grantor who transfers property to a foreign trust that has *a* U.S. beneficiary. As a result, the U.S. grantor will be taxed currently on all income earned by the trust, whether distributed or accumulated, that is attributable to the property he transfered to the trust.

Section 679 applies to all grantors who are U.S. 'persons', thus including individuals, corporations, partnerships, trusts, and estates. The section does not apply to (1) testamentary trusts, (2) certain qualified retirement benefit trusts, or (3) property transfered to the trust in a sale or exchange where the transferor has recognized the gain in full at the time of the transfer for income tax purposes.[80]

77. Sec. 7701(a)(31).

78. See, e.g., Rev. Rul. 60-181, 1960-1 Cum. Bull. 257.

79. In addition, the 1976 Act imposed more stringent rules on transfers of appreciated property to foreign trusts and other entities as discussed in 8.2.

80. Recognition of gain on a deferred basis is permitted for a transaction that qualifies for installment reporting of the gain under sec. 453 of the Code.

Section 679 covers indirect as well as direct transfers by U.S. persons. Thus, if a U.S. individual transfers property to a foreign entity which in turn transfers property to a trust with a U.S. beneficiary, the U.S. individual will generally be treated as the grantor of the trust under section 679.[81]

A foreign trust is treated as having a U.S. beneficiary unless (1) under the terms of the trust no part of the trust income can be paid to or accumulated for the benefit of a U.S. person, *and* (2) if the trust were to terminate during the taxable year, no part of the income or corpus of the trust could be paid to or for the benefit of a U.S. person. Attribution rules are also applied so that a U.S. beneficiary is present if amounts are paid to or accumulated for the benefit of a foreign corporation controlled by U.S. shareholders (50%), a foreign partnership with a U.S. partner, or another foreign trust with a U.S. beneficiary.[82]

At the time a U.S. person transfers property to a foreign trust it may have no U.S. beneficiary. However, if a U.S. person subsequently becomes a beneficiary of the trust, section 679 is triggered. In such a case, the U.S. grantor is then treated as the owner of the trust and is taxable on the income attributable to the property originally transfered. Moreover, the trust may have accumulated income which would be taxable to the new U.S. beneficiary if distributed. The grantor must include this accumulated income (attributable to the property he transferred) in his own income in the taxable year a U.S. person becomes a beneficiary, unless the trust distributed all accumulated income before the end of the prior taxable year.[83]

8.5.3. Accumulation Trusts

The Tax Reform Act of 1976 also modified the rules governing foreign trusts that accumulate income. In cases where the grantor trust rules do not apply, e.g., testamentary trusts or trusts created by foreign grantors, section 668 imposes an interest charge on the tax deferral resulting from the accumulation of the income.[84] The interest rate is 6 percent (nondeductible) per each year the income has been accumulat-

81. Only if the initial transferor can establish that the ultimate transfer to the trust was unrelated to his initial transfer can he escape classification as a grantor of the trust. For other examples of indirect transfers, see Senate Finance Committee Report, Tax Reform Act of 1976, S. Rep. No. 94-938, 94th Cong., 2d Sess. 219 (1976).

82. Sec. 679(c).

83. Sec. 679(b).

84. The provision is effective for taxable years beginning after December 31, 1976.

ed applied to the tax paid by the beneficiary on the accumulated distribution (net of the credits for foreign taxes paid by the trust). For example, if a foreign trust accumulates income earned in 1977 for 8 years, the interest charge upon distribution is 48% of the amount of tax imposed on the beneficiary as the result of the accumulation distribution.[85] The interest charge is added to the tax, but the total amount due cannot exceed the amount actually distributed by the trust to the beneficiary.

Other 1976 revisions in the rules governing accumulation trusts (not governed by the grantor trust rules) include (1) application of the three-year throwback rule that applies to trust beneficiaries generally;[86] (2) application of the multiple trust rules to foreign trusts;[87] and (3) taxation of all accumulated capital gains income distributed from a foreign trust as ordinary income.[88]

85. Where an accumulation distribution represents amounts accumulated in more than one year, the interest charge is based on the average period of accumulation.

86. Prior to the Tax Reform Act of 1976, the tax on an accumulation distribution was computed either on an 'exact method' or on a 'short cut' method. Under the 'exact method,' the trust beneficiary recomputed his tax for the years in which the accumulation occurred as if the trust income had in fact been distributed. This additional tax (less the taxes paid by the trust) was then payable in the year of distribution. Under the 'short cut' method, the beneficiary computed the average amount accumulated by the trust during the years of accumulation, included the average in income for his 3 preceding taxable years, and then multiplied the average additional tax for those years by the number of years during which the accumulations took place. The amount so computed (less the taxes paid by the trust) was the additional tax due in the year of the distribution. Under either method, refunds of excess taxes paid by the trust were allowed. The 1976 Act repealed the 'exact method' and modified the 'short cut' method. The 3-year period was changed to 3 years out of the preceding 5 years (excluding the highest and lowest income years), and all refunds were eliminated. For *foreign trusts*, income accumulated prior to the beneficiary's attaining age 21 is subject to the throwback rule (although it is not in the case of domestic trusts). Sec. 665(b).

87. Sec. 667(c) provides that a beneficiary who receives distributions from two or more trusts which represent accumulations during the same taxable years cannot receive credit for the taxes paid beyond those paid by the first two trusts.

88. Sec. 643(a)(6). Previously this rule had applied only to foreign trusts created by U.S. persons. The 1976 Act did repeal the capital gain throwback rule in former sec. 669. But the rule in sec. 643(a)(6) means that accumulated capital gains that are distributed will be treated as ordinary income and then be subject to tax under the throwback rule described in note 86.

Chapter 9
Income tax treaties

9.1. Background

The U.S. has entered into numerous bilateral income tax conventions and a few estate tax conventions. The focus of the following material will be on the extent to which the tax treaty provisions modify the otherwise applicable U.S. tax rules discussed in the preceding chapters. Two points must be kept in mind at the outset, however. First, each of the individual treaties represents a separate and independent source of law. Hence a particular question may be regulated one way in Treaty A, another way in Treaty B and not dealt with at all in Treaty C. Second, since the treaties are not uniform, it is difficult to use the interpretation of one treaty as precedent in a case arising under another treaty.

The U.S. in 1977 published a Model Income Tax Treaty which will be used as the basis for its future treaty negotiations. As more and more treaties become based on this model, presumably some greater uniformity of treaty interpretation practice will develop.[1]

9.2. Treaty objectives and techniques

U.S. tax treaties, like those of all countries, deal with the problems which result when two or more countries assert taxing jurisdiction over the same persons or transactions. Since this problem is dealt with unilaterally by most countries either in the form of a foreign tax credit

1. Model Income Tax Treaty of May 17, 1977. The influence of the Model Treaty on the 1980 revised treaty between the United States and the United Kingdom is clearly evident. In addition, the U.S. is a member of the Organization for Economic Cooperation and Development (OECD) which has also prepared a draft model income tax convention. That convention has also influenced U.S. treaty practice. Moreover, the United Nations Draft Model Double Taxation Convention Between Developed and Developing Countries apparently has begun to influence U.S. tax treaty negotiations with developing countries.

or an exemption for foreign source income, the treaties by and large operate to refine and adapt these techniques for avoiding international double taxation to the specifics of the tax relationships between the two countries involved.

From the U.S. point of view several basic techniques are used in the treaties. First, a reduction in or exemption from the foreign tax otherwise applicable to U.S. taxpayers is negotiated with the treaty partner on a reciprocal basis. This usually involves the country of source ceding taxing jurisdiction to the country of residence. Second, the treaties attempt a clarification and modification of otherwise applicable principles involved in the application of the U.S. foreign tax credit to insure that, to the extent possible, the provision achieves its objective of eliminating tax barriers to foreign investment by U.S. residents. In addition, the treaty partner generally obligates itself to grant to its citizens or residents some form of tax relief from double taxation (foreign tax credit or exemption) on investment in the U.S. This provison reduces or removes double tax barriers to investment in the U.S. by treaty country residents. Finally, the treaties attempt to coordinate the administration of the tax laws of the two countries. This involves various procedures for consultation on outstanding tax issues and provisions for the exchange of information.

9.3. Status of treaties

Under general principles of U.S. law, international treaties and legislative enactments are of equal force. As a result, where treaties and legislative provisions conflict, the later in time prevails.[2]

Two special statutory provisions bear on these general principles in the tax area. First, section 894(a) provides that income exempt under a treaty obligation of the U.S. remains exempt under the Internal Revenue Code despite any Code provisions to the contrary. Second, section 7852(d) states that no provision of the Code shall be applied where it is contrary to any treaty obligation of the U.S. in effect on August 16, 1954. While this provision would give precedence to pre-1954 treaty obligations over subsequently enacted legislation, it itself of course is a legislative enactment and can be made inapplicable in particular situations.[3] In addition, section 7852(d) is expressly ap-

2. Whitney v. Robertson, 124 U.S. 190 (1888); Cook v. United States, 288 U.S. 102 (1933).

3. The Foreign Investment in Real Property Tax Act of 1980 contained a specific section →

plicable only to treaty obligations in effect prior to August 16, 1954 and has no relevance for subsequently enacted treaties. However, if a legislative enactment is to override a treaty, Congress must clearly so indicate.

9.4. Qualifications for treaty benefits

9.4.1. Persons covered

The various benefits contained in U.S. tax treaties are generally provided to 'residents', both natural and juridical, of the countries involved. Thus nationals of a third country can benefit from U.S. treaties provided that they qualify as residents of one of the contracting countries.[4] Some treaties provide a special definition of residence but in most cases, as is generally the practice with undefined treaty terms, reference is made to the law of the country involved to determine whether the particular individual or organization claiming treaty benefits qualifies as a resident.[5]

Most U.S. treaties contain a so-called 'savings clause' which allows the U.S. to continue to tax its citizens and residents without regard to any provision of the treaty. For example, Article 22(4)(a) of the French treaty provides: 'The United States may tax its citizens and residents as if the present Convention had not come into effect'.[6] As a result of the savings clause, even though a particular treaty article may, by its terms, appear to assign exclusive taxing jurisdiction of a particular type of income to the country of source, the savings clause would operate to deny that benefit to a U.S. citizen or resident.

On the other hand, the treaties generally provide that they may not operate to the detriment of the taxpayers covered by the treaty. Thus, Article XVIII(2) of the German treaty states: 'The provisions of the

→

exempting the Act from the application of sections 894(a) and 7552(d), making the Act controlling over inconsistent treaty provisions after January 1, 1985.

4. In addition, third country nationals can generally benefit from the treaty provision which exempts dividends and interest paid by corporations organized in a treaty country from the 'second level' withholding tax imposed on dividends from foreign corporations with substantial U.S. source income. See, e.g., Germany, Article XIV [All citations to treaties are to U.S. income tax treaties if not otherwise indicated].

5. For a case involving the question of residence for purposes of the Swiss treaty in which a Swiss administrative determination as to residence was not followed by a U.S. court, see Johansson v. United States, 336 F. 2d 809 (5th Cir. 1964).

6. For text footnote 6 see p. 170.

present convention shall not be construed to restrict in any manner any exemption, deduction, credit or other allowance now or hereafter accorded by the laws of [the U.S.] in the determination of the tax imposed by [the U.S.]'. Accordingly, the benefits of a provision of the Internal Revenue Code cannot be limited by a more restrictive treaty provision, even if the treaty provision is later in time and thus would otherwise be controlling.

9.4.2. Taxes covered

The U.S. treaties generally cover Federal income taxes but are not extended to state and municipal levies.[7]

9.5. Treatment of business income

9.5.1. In general

As discussed in Chapter 5, a nonresident alien or foreign corporation is generally taxed on his business income from U.S. sources at the usual U.S. tax rates. Technically, the tax is imposed on all income which is effectively connected with the foreign taxpayer's U.S. trade or business. This Code treatment of business income is modified by U.S. treaties. In general, the treaties provide that a foreign taxpayer will not

6. There are often some minor exceptions contained in the savings clauses. For example, the French treaty itself provides that the savings clause does not affect certain benefits concerning the taxation of social security payments expressly contained in the treaty. In addition, any treaty changes in the foreign tax credit rules as regards U.S. citizens and residents are generally an implicit exception to the savings clause since otherwise the changes would serve no purpose.

7. The original version of the 1980 revised treaty with the United Kingdom did not deal directly with state taxation but did have a provision to prevent the assertion of state taxing jurisdiction based on the so-called 'unitary' method of allocating a portion of worldwide profits to the company's operation that is located in the state. Under the original treaty provision, a state could only tax on the basis of a method that confined its jurisdiction to the particular operation located within the state. The proposed provision proved controversial and led to a reservation on the part of the U.S. Senate with respect to the provision in its consideration of the treaty. The treaty was ultimately ratified without the provision.
In general the 'nondiscrimination' articles in U.S. treaties do extend to state taxes. See 9.10.

be taxed on business income from sources within the U.S. unless that income is attributable to a *permanent establishment* located in the U.S. If no permanent establishment is present, business income which would otherwise be subject to U.S. tax is exempt under the treaty.

Conversely, a U.S. taxpayer who realizes business income in a foreign country with which the U.S. has a treaty will be taxed in that country only if the income is attributable to a permanent establishment located there. While the foreign taxes attributable to the foreign business profits would generally qualify for the foreign tax credit, the exemption is nonetheless important to the U.S. taxpayer. In the first place, it frees him from the burdens of filing and paying foreign taxes which he would then subsequently credit. More important, it allows him to avoid any problems of the possible nonapplication of the foreign tax credit. For example, suppose the foreign country's concept of source of income differed from that of the U.S. The income could be subject to foreign taxation but not qualify as foreign source income for purposes of the foreign tax credit provisions. The exemption for business income absent a permanent establishment avoids these problems.

Article 6(1) of the French treaty is typical of the reciprocal exemption contained in U.S. treaties:

'Industrial or commercial profits of a resident of one of the Contracting States shall be taxable only in that State unless such resident is engaged in industrial or commercial activity in the other Contracting State through a permanent establishment situated therein. If such a resident is so engaged, tax may be imposed by such other state on the industrial or commercial profits of such a resident but only on so much of them as are attributable to the permanent establishment.'

9.5.2. Permanent establishment

The definitions of permanent establishment in the various U.S. treaties are similar in outline but differ substantially in detail. In general, a permanent establishment may take the form of an office or other fixed place of business or a resident agent of the taxpayer with authority to enter into contractual relationships or who fills orders from a stock of goods located in the foreign country. Beyond these two general principles, many treaties enumerate in detail the types of activities which will or will not constitute a permanent establishment. For example, the German treaty specifically provides that the maintenance of a fixed place of business for the purpose of advertising, supplying information, or undertaking certain types of scientific or other research activities which do not involve the providing of services to third parties will not constitute a permanent establishment.[8] The treaty with Ireland, on the other hand, does not contain any such specific exceptions.

Most treaties provide that a domestic subsidiary corporation of the foreign taxpayer will not 'of itself' be treated as a permanent establishment. The permanent establishment of a partnership is attributed to the partners.

9.5.3. INDUSTRIAL OR COMMERCIAL PROFITS

The permanent establishment exemption applies in general only to business income of the foreign taxpayer. The treaty term is 'industrial or commercial profits' and is defined with various degrees of specificity in the treaties.[9] Some of the classification issues are discussed at 9.6.2.

9.5.4. 'ATTRIBUTABLE TO'

The industrial or commercial profits which may be taxed because of the presence of a permanent establishment are generally limited to those which are 'attributable to' the permanent establishment. In general, U.S. treaties treat the permanent establishment as if it were an independent entity engaged in arm's length dealings with third parties and the home office, rather than allocating the worldwide income of the enterprise on some formula basis.[10] Many treaties contain an article, such as Article 6(3) of the French treaty, which specifically allows as a deduction a portion of general executive and administrative expenses incurred with respect to the branch operation. These provisions are in response to the position of a number of countries which do not allow a deduction for branch expenses not directly incurred in the branch country.

8. Germany, Article II(1)(c)(cc).

9. See, e.g., Germany, Article III(1); Netherlands, Article III(5).

10. While U.S. treaties, in general, appear to adopt the 'direct' method of determining the profits of a foreign branch, the Internal Revenue Service has nonetheless taken the position that the 'indirect' or formulary method of Treas. Reg. sec. 1.861-8 (discussed in 4.3. and 4.4.) is nonetheless the appropriate method for determining branch profits. Rev. Rul. 78-423, 1978-2 Cum. Bull. 194, stated that the 'direct' method set out in the treaties is only to be used as an anti-tax avoidance provision in correcting the dealings between branch and home office. The basic method of income computation, however, remains the indirect method. The position taken by the Ruling seems questionable. For a discussion see Kaplan, United States: Taxing Foreign Firms by Formula, Tax Management International Journal, 79-9, 3 (1979).

9.6. Treatment of investment income

9.6.1. In general

As discussed in Chapter 5, investment-type income of a foreign taxpayer from U.S. sources is taxed at a flat 30% rate on the gross amount of the income. If the income is effectively connected with a U.S. trade or business, it is treated as business income and subject to normal rates on a net basis.

U.S. treaties generally modify these rules by providing for a reciprocal reduction of rates (often to zero) for investment-type income. Typically the rates on dividends are reduced to 15%, with a 5% rate applicable in the case of dividends paid by a U.S. subsidiary to a foreign parent company. Interest income is generally exempt or subject to a 5% rate. Royalties of various types are also usually exempt.

Prior to 1966, under the so-called 'force of attraction' principle, the U.S. taxed all investment-type income at ordinary rates if the taxpayer was engaged in a U.S. trade or business. Correspondingly, tax treaties entered into prior to 1966 generally did not extend the normally applicable treaty exemption or reduction to such income where the foreign taxpayer had a permanent establishment in the U.S., regardless of whether the investment-type income was in fact attributable to the permanent establishment.

To conform the treaty rules to the amended domestic legislation, the Foreign Investors Tax Act of 1966 enacted section 894(b) which provides that where a foreign taxpayer has investment-type income which is not effectively connected with a U.S. trade or business, the foreign taxpayer will be deemed not to have a permanent establishment within the U.S. for purposes of applying any treaty exemptions or reductions. Thus, non-effectively connected investment-type income can qualify for the reduced treaty rates of taxation despite the existence of a permanent establishment.

9.6.2. Classification problems

While the line between industrial or commercial profits (to which the permanent establishment rule applies) and investment income (taxable at reduced rates) is generally clear, there are some difficult borderline situations. Consider, for example, the case of a commercial bank. Its income consists principally of interest which normally is treated as investment income. On the other hand, interest in the hands of a bank clearly represents business income. A similar problem exists with respect to leasing and rental activities, e.g., film rentals of a distribution company.

The classification issues are resolved differently in the various treaties. For example, Article 6(6) of the French treaty specifically includes rents or royalties from motion picture films as industrial or commercial profits. On the other hand, Article VIII(3)(a) of the German treaty treats motion picture rents or royalties under the royalty article. The treatment of bank interest is likewise not consistent among the treaties.

9.6.3. Real property

Under the Internal Revenue Code, the treatment of income from real property depends initially on whether or not the foreign taxpayer's real estate activities within the U.S. constitute a trade or business. If a trade or business is present, then the income is subject to tax at normal rates on a net basis. However, if the taxpayer is not engaged in a trade or business, as would generally be the case in certain net lease transactions, the rental income is treated as investment income subject to the 30% withholding tax on the gross amount of the rentals. Under sections 871(d) and 882(d), however, the foreign taxpayer may elect to have the income from real property (including gain on dispositions) treated as income which is effectively connected with a U.S. trade or business and thus subject to normal tax rates on a net basis. (See 5.3.) The election once made may not be revoked without special permission of the fiscal authorities.

A number of U.S. tax treaties contain a similar election provision which differs somewhat in scope from the Code election. Most importantly, the election may be made on a year by year basis.[11]

11. As a result, prior to the 1980 legislation discussed in 5.3.3., the foreign taxpayer could avoid a U.S. capital gain tax on real property by selling the property in a year in which the election to be taxed on a net basis had not been made. The 1980 Act foreclosed this tax avoidance strategy by treating such gains as effectively connected with the conduct of a U.S. trade or business. U.S. tax treaties typically reserve to the U.S. the right to tax the gains derived from U.S. real estate. Accordingly, the Act did not conflict with such treaty provisions. If the U.S. real estate were held in a U.S. corporation and the stock were disposed of, a treaty provision exempting capital gains realized by residents of the treaty partner will continue to apply until January 1, 1985; thereafter the legislation taxing such gain will control. See notes 3 and 15.

9.7. Treatment of personal services income

9.7.1. Employees

Under the Code, a nonresident alien employee of a foreign employer is not subject to U.S. tax on compensation for labor or personal services performed in the U.S. if the nonresident is not present within the U.S. for more than 90 days in the taxable year *and* the compensation does not exceed $3,000. This exemption is liberalized in a number of U.S. treaties. For example, in the treaty with Germany, the time limit is extended to 183 days and there is no dollar limitation on the compensation which can be received without tax. However, the compensation must be 'borne by' the German employer and not by its permanent establishment within the U.S.[12]

9.7.2. Independent personal services

If a nonresident alien individual performs independent personal services in the U.S., e.g., as a lawyer, under normally applicable Code principles he would be engaged in a U.S. trade or business and would be subject to tax at normal rates. However, a number of treaties exempt such income from U.S. taxation under varying conditions. For example, the treaty with Japan exempts income derived from independent personal services if the nonresident alien individual is not present within the U.S. for a period in excess of 183 days and does not have a 'fixed base' in the U.S. for the purposes of performing his services. This exemption does not apply, however, to services of athletes or entertainers where special rules apply.[13] The scope of the exemption for independent personal services varies substantially from treaty to treaty.

9.7.3. Compensation for personal services as business income

As in the situations discussed in 9.6.2., there are some overlap problems concerning the treaty articles dealing with business profits

12. Germany, Article X(2). A number of treaties also contain special rules dealing with the taxation of students, professors, and others in special employment categories.
13. Japan, Article 17.

and those dealing with personal services. Here again the resolution of the question differs from treaty to treaty. Under the German treaty, Article III(5), the term 'industrial or commercial profits' expressly includes 'income derived by an enterprise from the furnishing of services of employees or other personnel'. Thus, such income would be taxed to the German enterprise only if it had a permanent establishment in the U.S. However, the Article specifically excludes services covered by Article X dealing with personal services provided in the U.S. by an employee of the German firm. Thus, the taxation of the employee himself would depend, not on the presence of a permanent establishment, but on the length of his stay in the U.S.[14]

9.8. Capital gains

Under normal Code rules, capital gains which are not effectively connected with the foreign taxpayer's trade or business generally are exempt when realized by a foreign corporation and are taxable to a nonresident alien individual at a 30% rate if he is present in the country at least 183 days during the year. These rules usually are not modified by treaty though there are some important exceptions.[15]

14. Under the general rules outlined above, it would thus be possible to avoid U.S. taxation completely in some situations by performing personal services for a foreign employer not having a permanent establishment within the U.S. For example, suppose a nonresident alien entertainer forms a corporation which contracts to provide his services in the U.S. The foreign corporation does not have a permanent establishment in the U.S. and the fees are paid directly to the corporation which in turn pays a salary to the foreign individual. The corporation, having no permanent establishment, would be exempt on its business income and the individual could qualify under the employee exemption.
The Internal Revenue Service has issued two important Rulings dealing with the applicable treaty benefits in such circumstances. The basic thrust of the Rulings is to limit exemption benefits to the situations in which the foreign corporation is an independent entity providing such services generally and is not simply a conduit for passing the U.S. source income through to the foreign individual taxpayer. The problem originally came up in the context of the United Kingdom treaty and Article 17 of that treaty deals specifically with the case. See Rev. Rul 74–330, 1974-2 Cum. Bull. 278; Rev. Rul. 74–331, 1974-2 Cum. Bull. 281.

15. For example, Article IXA of the German treaty exempts from U.S. tax all capital gains realized by a German resident from assets which have been held for more than six months. The capital gains articles generally do not apply to gains from real estate which are subject to a special pattern of taxation. See 9.6.3.

9.9. Foreign tax credit aspects

In accordance with the overall purpose of tax treaties to reduce international double taxation, the U.S. in its treaties commits itself, with varying degrees of specificity, to grant its citizens and residents a foreign tax credit for the foreign income taxes paid to treaty countries. Correspondingly, the U.S. insists that its treaty partners likewise provide some mechanism to their nationals for the relief of double taxation, by either granting a credit for U.S. taxes or exempting income from U.S. sources.

In addition, some U.S. treaties clarify the operation of the foreign tax credit with respect to the taxes of the treaty partner. For example, Articles 10 and 23 of the United Kingdom treaty set out specific rules for dealing with the United Kingdom's 'integrated' corporation tax.

Sometimes the treaties modify source rules which would otherwise prevent the crediting of foreign taxes on items of income which, under normal U.S. concepts, would be deemed to be from U.S. sources.[16]

9.10. Nondiscrimination

U.S. treaties typically contain a 'nondiscrimination' article. For example, Article XVIII(3) of the German treaty provides: 'The citizens of one of the contracting States shall not, while resident in the other contracting State, be subject therein to other or more burdensome taxes than are the citizens of such other contracting State residing in its territory'. The nondiscrimination clause in the German treaty is, as is usually the case, extended to state and municipal taxes.

There is little authority on the question of what constitutes discrimination against foreign taxpayers for purposes of the equal treatment or

16. See, e.g., Japan, Article 6; Rev. Rul. 79–28, 1979-1 Cum. Bull. 457 (for purposes of the section 901 tax credit, income of a U.S. citizen residing in Japan from services performed within the U.S. in employment as a flight attendant on international flights of a Japanese airline was considered foreign source income by virtue of Article 6(6) of the Japan Treaty; the source rules of the Treaty took precedence over the usual source rules of the Internal Revenue Code). The 1979 Third Protocol to the French Treaty likewise modifies the usually applicable U.S. source rules to accomodate the fact that both the U.S. and France subject the income of U.S. citizens residing in France to worldwide tax liability. Under the Protocol, the U.S. allows the U.S. citizen resident in France to credit certain French taxes payable on U.S. source investment income and, correspondingly, recharacterizes the income as French source income for purposes of the foreign tax credit limitation. France Treaty, Article 23(3).

nondiscrimination clauses.[17] The Model Treaty expressly provides that the U.S. need not grant to the foreign taxpayer in the U.S. 'any personal allowances, reliefs and reductions for taxation purposes on account of civil status or family responsibilities which it grants to its own residents'. (Article 24(3)). One possible area of application for the nondiscrimination clause is the 'similar credit' requirement of section 901(c) which denies alien residents a foreign tax credit where their country of nationality does not grant a similar credit.[18]

The 1980 legislation, subjecting to tax the gains on U.S. real property interests disposed of by foreign investors, raises issues under the nondiscrimination clauses of U.S. treaties. For example, as discussed in 5.3.3., under section 897, foreign corporations which dispose of U.S. real property interests by means of dividend distributions or pursuant to redemptions or liquidation are subject to tax on the accrued gain in the property. U.S. corporations would not be subject to tax on comparable distributions. In an attempt to avoid treaty nondiscrimination problems, the statute provides that any foreign corporation with a U.S. permanent establishment may elect, for purposes of section 897 and the reporting requirements, to be treated as if it were a U.S. corporation. This election would mean that the gain realized by foreign shareholders on the disposition of the corporation's shares could be subject to U.S. tax, but would allow the corporation to avoid the special provisions requiring recognition of gain at the corporate level.

Whether the statutory election will be sufficient to prelude foreign taxpayers' claims under nondiscrimination clauses may ultimately have to be resolved by the courts. The 1980 legislation also provides a 20% minimum tax rate for gains realized on dispositions of U.S. real property interests by nonresident aliens. The minimum tax rate for U.S. individuals is 10%. Again, a possible violation of treaty nondiscrimination clauses may be involved.

The U.S. has a number of Treaties of Friendship, Commerce and Navigation containing nondiscrimination clauses which may also have application in the tax area.

17. An instance in which the nondiscrimination clause of a treaty was found to override the otherwise applicable provisions of the Internal Revenue Code involved section 911(a)(2) prior to its amendment in 1976. That section had limited the exclusion of income earned abroad to U.S. citizens. Rev. Rul. 72–330, 1972-2 Cum. Bull. 444, and Rev. Rul. 72–598, 1972-2 Cum. Bull. 451, held that residents of treaty countries were entitled to the benefits of section 911 by virtue of the treaty nondiscrimination clauses. On the question of nondiscrimination generally, see O'Brien, The Nondiscrimination Article in Tax Treaties, 10 Law and Policy in International Business 545 (1978).
18. See Owens, *The Foreign Tax Credit* 480 (1961). See 6.2.5.2.

9.11. Administrative provisions

9.11.1. COMPETENT AUTHORITY PROVISIONS

U.S. treaties generally contain a so-called 'competent authority' provision. It provides a mechanism whereby the taxpayer can insure that his rights under the treaty are respected by the country involved. In order to invoke the competent authority provision, the taxpayer must in general establish 'that the action of the tax authority of the contracting state has resulted or will result in double taxation contrary to the provisions of the [treaty]'. In such a case, the taxpayer presents his case to the state of which he is a citizen or resident and if the state agrees that the claim is worthy of consideration, the 'competent authority' of the state endeavors to reach some agreement with the other country in order to avoid double taxation.[19]

By far the most important functions of the competent authority provisions are to deal with cases involving the attribution of industrial or commercial profits to a permanent establishment and the allocation of income between related taxpayers. The Internal Revenue Service has issued detailed guidelines as to how U.S. taxpayers can invoke the competent authority procedure in income allocation cases.[20]

Some of the more recent treaties provide that the taxpayer may obtain relief under the competent authority provisions even where the statute of limitations or other procedural barriers would normally bar relief.[21]

9.11.2. EXCHANGE OF INFORMATION

The U.S. generally obligates itself to exchange information with its treaty partner in order to carry out the provisions of the treaty and to prevent tax fraud. The U.S. routinely supplies its treaty partners with information returns concerning reduced rates of withholding tax or exemption as to items of income covered by the treaty. The Tax Reform

19. The general procedures for applying for competent authority relief are set forth in Rev. Proc. 77–16, 1977-1 Cum. Bull. 573.

20. Rev. Proc. 70–18, 1970-2 Cum. Bull. 493. It has been reported that as of 1973 some 151 allocation cases had been received by the Internal Revenue Service under Rev. Proc. 70–18.

21. See, e.g., Model Income Tax Treaty, Article 25(2).

Act of 1976 specifically authorized the U.S. to disclose to a competent authority of a foreign government tax return information to the extent provided for in the treaty.[22]

In a 1975 decision concerning the Canadian treaty it was held that the exchange of information procedures could be used to obtain information which was solely necessary to assist the Canadian tax authorities in their investigation and had no bearing on U.S. tax liability.[23]

22. Sec. 6103(k)(4).

23. United States v. A. L. Burbank & Co. Ltd, 525 F. 2d 9 (2d Cir. 1975).

Chapter 10
Wealth transfer taxation

10.1. The U.S. wealth transfer tax system: general description

10.1.1. Background

Prior to the Tax Reform Act of 1976, the U.S. employed a dual transfer tax system. One set of rates, rules, exemptions and exclusions applied to transfers during lifetime and were taxed under the gift tax; a separate set of rates, exemptions, and rules applied to transfers at death, and were taxed under the estate tax.

The Tax Reform Act of 1976 moved the U.S. closer to a unified transfer tax. A single unified rate of tax was adopted to apply to transfers at death and during life. Thus, the rate of tax imposed on a transfer will not be affected by whether the transfer is made at death or during life. In addition, a single unified tax credit was adopted in lieu of the prior double set of exemptions (one applicable to the gift tax and one applicable to the estate tax). Under this unified credit, an individual may transfer (after 1981) wealth in the total amount of $175,625 free of tax. Although the exemption level and rates were thus unified in the 1976 Act, the estate and gift taxes were maintained as separate technical structures. And, in some important instances, the substantive rules do differ depending on whether the transfer is during life or at death.

In addition, the 1976 Act introduced a third transfer tax – the generation-skipping tax. This tax is designed to insure that property transferred in trust will be subject to a transfer tax that is structured to approximate the transfer taxes that would have been paid had the property passed directly from generation to generation in the normal pattern. The generation-skipping tax is, in terms of its technical structure, a third transfer tax. However, the tax imposed is determined by reference to the unified transfer tax rates and the unified transfer tax credit applicable to transfers subject to the gift and estate tax rules.

10.1.2. THE ESTATE TAX

Section 2001 provides that a tax is imposed at progressive rates (from 18 to 70%) on the transfer at death of the *taxable estate* of every citizen or resident of the U.S. The taxable estate is equal to the gross estate less certain allowable deductions. The *gross estate* includes the value of all property interests owned by the decedent at the date of the death. Most typical of these are such items as bank accounts, real estate, and securities. The gross estate is not limited, however, to the value of assets which are physically in the decedent's actual or constructive possession. It includes the value of any interest in property which the decedent had at the time of death, such as a general power of appointment. In addition, there also is included in the gross estate the value of transfers made by the decedent during his lifetime, which, under the Code, are treated as substitutes for testamentary dispositions (e.g., a transfer to a revocable trust). The gross estate therefore may exceed greatly the actual wealth which the decedent had in physical possession immediately before his death.[1]

The permissible *deductions* from the gross estate include funeral and administration expenses, claims against the estate, uncompensated casualty losses arising during the settlement of the estate, transfers to or for charitable organizations, a marital deduction for certain bequests to the surviving spouse, and a limited deduction for transfers to orphans.[2]

A few special exclusions from the gross estate are provided for non-tax policy reasons. Among these are annuities received from qualified retirement plans that are given special income tax concessions.[3]

After the taxable estate has been thus determined, a *tentative estate tax* is computed by applying the tax rates set forth in section 2001 to the *sum of* the taxable estate plus the *adjusted taxable gifts* of the decedent (that is, taxable gifts made by the decedent after December 31, 1976 minus any gifts which are included in the estate of the decedent) and subtracting from this amount the gift tax payable on account of the decedent's gifts made after 1976.

The final estate tax payable is then determined by subtracting from the tentative estate tax the *credits against tax* which include (1) a unified credit against the estate tax, equal to $47,000 (when fully implemented in 1981) which in effect provides exemption from estate

1. Items included in the gross estate are defined in sec. 2033-2043.
2. Sec. 2053-2057.
3. Sec. 2039(c), (e).

tax for estates up to $175,625; (2) a credit for certain state death taxes; (3) a credit for foreign death taxes; (4) a credit for certain transfer taxes paid on prior transfers of property; (5) and a credit for gift taxes paid with respect to property transferred prior to 1977 and included in the gross estate.[4] The subtraction of these tax credits from the tentative estate tax constitutes the final step in the determination of the estate tax payable.

10.1.3. The gift tax

The tax on any gift made by a donor is determined by adding the amount of the taxable gift to prior taxable gifts and imposing the specified progressive gift tax rates (18 to 70%). The rates applicable to the gift tax are the same as those applicable to transfers at death under the estate tax.

The tax base for the gift tax is *taxable gifts*. This term means the *total gifts* made during the calendar quarter minus allowable *exclusions and deductions*. The allowable exclusions and deductions include (1) a $3,000 per donee annual exclusion; (2) a deduction for charitable contributions; (3) a marital deduction for gifts between spouses; (4) an exclusion for gifts made by married persons to third parties that in effect splits the gifts between the spouses.

The gift tax is then computed by applying the unified transfer tax rates to the taxable gifts. The unified transfer tax credit applicable to the estate tax ($47,000 after 1981) is applied to the gift tax due. To the extent the unified transfer tax credit is utilized by a donor during lifetime, it is in effect reduced for purposes of computing the estate tax.[5]

10.1.4. The generation-skipping tax

The Tax Reform Act of 1976 imposed for the first time a transfer tax on certain generation-skipping transfers which had been subject neither to estate nor gift tax in the skipped generation. Thus, a transfer in trust from A to B (A's child) for life, remainder to C (A's grandchild) is not subject to *estate tax* in B's estate upon B's death. However, the generation-skipping tax would apply to impose a tax on the property received by C at B's death. The amount of the tax is calculated by

4. Sec. 2010-2016.
5. Sec. 2501-2524.

reference to the tax rates applicable to B's estate taxes and, subject to several exceptions, approximates the amount which would have been payable had the property subject to the tax passed outright from generation to generation.

In very general terms, the generation-skipping tax is imposed on any generation-skipping transfer (more technically a 'taxable distribution' or a 'taxable termination') from a 'generation-skipping trust' (or a trust equivalent). A *generation-skipping trust* is one which has beneficiaries in more than one generation younger than that of the grantor of the trust. A *taxable distribution* results upon the distribution of property from a generation-skipping trust to a beneficiary who is more than one generation younger than the grantor of the trust while a member of the intervening generation is still alive. A *taxable termination* generally occurs at the time a present interest or power in a generation-skipping trust which is held by an individual who is in a generation younger than the grantor dies (B in the above example). There are several exceptions to the generation-skipping tax. First, the tax is not imposed on outright transfers that skip generations. Second, there is a cumulative exclusion for the first $250,000 of otherwise taxable generation-skipping transfers made to grandchildren of the grantor of the trust. One $250,000 exclusion is available for each child of the grantor. Third, distributions from or terminations of generation-skipping trusts which were irrevocable on April 30, 1976 are not subject to the tax.

The taxed imposed on a generation-skipping transfer is determined by reference to the transfer tax bracket of the deemed transferor, i.e., the intervening skipped generation. Generally, this person will be the parent of the ultimate distributee of the property. The tax is not payable by the deemed transferor or his estate. Instead, the tax is usually to be paid out of the property distributed by, or out of the corpus of, the generation-skipping trust. In general, a generation-skipping transfer attributable to a deemed transferor is not included in his transfer tax base for purposes of computing either his estate or his gift tax.[6]

10.2. Jurisdictional principles

As in the case of the income tax, the U.S. tax jurisdiction with respect to transfers at death or by gift is likewise global in reach. Thus, under section 2031, the value of the gross estate is determined by including the value of all property owned by the decedent 'wherever situated'.

6. Sec. 2601-2622.

Again, the basis of the tax is U.S. citizenship (or residency in the case of aliens). Likewise, the gift tax applies to all lifetime donative transfers by U.S. citizens or residents regardless of where the property is located. The same is true of the generation-skipping tax added in 1976.

Special-rules are provided for nonresident aliens. As in the case of the income tax, the scope of the U.S. jurisdiction is determined on a geographical basis. Thus, the estate tax, the gift tax, and the generation-skipping tax in general apply to nonresident aliens only with respect to property which is 'situated within the United States'. Moreover, the rates of tax imposed on transfers by nonresident aliens are in general lower than those applicable to U.S. citizens.

The U.S. has also entered into a relatively few bilateral tax treaties governing estate and gift taxation. And, as in the case of the income tax, certain special provisions are included to prevent avoidance of U.S. wealth transfer taxes.

10.3. Estate tax: international aspects

10.3.1. Background

Legislative actions in 1966 and 1976 produced substantial changes in the taxation of transfers at death by U.S. citizens, resident aliens and nonresident aliens.

Prior to passage of the Foreign Investors Tax Act of 1966, the U.S. imposed higher effective rates of tax on foreign decedents transferring U.S. property than on its own citizens. This situation was perceived as a deterrent to foreign investment in the U.S. Accordingly, the 1966 Act completely revised the system of taxing death transfers of U.S. property by nonresidents who were not U.S. citizens. The basic principle adopted was that the effective rate of estate tax paid by nonresident alien decedents would reflect the effective rate of tax imposed on a U.S. citizen transferring a like amount of property at death (assuming that the U.S. decedent's estate utilized the marital deduction that permits approximately one-half of the decedent's estate to pass tax-free to a surviving spouse). Correspondingly, as discussed in 10.4., anti-tax avoidance rules were likewise adopted in 1966 lest the revised transfer tax rules make it attractive for U.S. citizens to become 'foreigners' for U.S. estate tax purposes.[7]

7. See Hellmuth and Oldman (eds.), Tax Policy and Tax Reform: 1961-1969, Selected Speeches and Testimony of Stanley S. Surrey (1973) pp. 394–395. Assistant Secretary of →

As discussed above, the Tax Reform Act of 1976 effected fundamental revisions in the U.S. transfer tax system. These quite basic changes in the U.S. transfer tax system in turn required changes in the taxation of nonresident aliens in order to maintain the pattern of taxation developed in the 1966 Act.

10.3.2. General pattern of estate taxation

The U.S. estate tax is a tax on the 'transfer' of property. In the case of U.S. citizens and resident aliens, the U.S. asserts worldwide jurisdiction, imposing the tax on the transfer of all property 'wherever situated'.[8] International double taxation is alleviated through the mechanism of the foreign tax credit and/or by death tax conventions.

In the case of nonresident individuals who are not U.S. citizens, the estate tax is imposed only on the transfer of property 'situated in the United States'.[9] As noted above, special rates of tax are then imposed to correlate the tax burden on such transfers with that borne by estates of U.S. decedents.

10.3.3. Situs rules

The 'situs' rules developed to apply the estate tax in an international context perform a function similiar to the 'source' rules in the income tax (discussed in Chapter 4). Whether property is 'situated' within the U.S. or in a foreign country determines the amount of the allowable foreign tax credit for U.S. citizens and resident aliens and, for nonresident aliens, whether the U.S. estate tax will apply at all. The estate tax statutory provisions and Regulations follow the approach of the income tax rules by specifying the circumstances when particular types of property will be situated within or without the U.S. The level of detail is, however, much less than in the income tax. In each case, the situs rule may be modified by treaty.

→

the Treasury Gerald L. Parsky, in 1976, expressed concern in testimony before the Subcommittee on Foreign Commerce and Tourism of the Senate Commerce Committee that even the post-1966 Act estate tax rules operated as a deterrent to foreign portfolio investment in U.S. stocks, securities and obligations, encouraged the use of tax-haven personal holding companies by nonresident aliens as their investment vehicle in the U.S., encouraged the growth of offshore financial institutions, and were easily circumvented by those foreign investors with proper advice.

8. Sec. 2031.

9. Sec. 2106.

10.3.3.1. Property situated within the U.S.

The following property is considered situated within the U.S.:

(1) Real estate located in the U.S.[10]

(2) Tangible personal property located in the U.S.[11] (except for certain works of art as noted in 10.3.3.2).

(3) Shares of stock issued by a corporation organized under the laws of the U.S.[12]

(4) Transfers of property (a) within three years of death (§2035), (b) in which the transferor retained an interest for life (§2036), (c) taking effect at death (§2037), or (d) which were revocable by the transferor (§2038), if the property was situated in the U.S. either at the time of the original transfer *or* at the decedent's death.[13]

(5) Debt obligations issued by a U.S. 'person'[14] or by the U.S. government or a state or local government (except as noted in 10.3.3.2.).[15]

(6) Certain deposits with a U.S. branch of a foreign corporation if the branch is engaged in the commercial banking business.[16]

10.3.3.2. Property situated outside the U.S.

The following property is considered situated without the U.S.:

(1) Real estate located outside the U.S.[17]

(2) Tangible personal property located outside the U.S.[18]

(3) Works of art owned by a nonresident alien that are at the time of death on loan or exhibition in the U.S.[19]

(4) Shares of stock in a corporation organized and incorporated under the laws of a foreign country.[20]

10. Treas. Reg. sec. 20.2104-1(a)(1).
11. Treas. Reg. sec. 20.2104-1(a)(2).
12. Sec. 2104(a).
13. Sec. 2104(b). See Estate of Swan v. Commissioner, 247 F.2d 144 (2d Cir. 1957) (revocable inter vivos trust property was situated within the U.S. where cash and securities were deposited with New York trust companies).
14. A 'person' includes an individual, a trust, estate, partnership, association, company or corporation. Sec. 7701(a)(1).
15. Sec. 2104(c).
16. Sec. 2104(c).
17. Treas. Reg. sec. 20.2105-1(a)(1).
18. Treas. Reg. sec. 20.2105-1(a)(2).
19. Sec. 2105(d).
20. Treas. Reg. sec. 20.2105-1(f).

(5) Proceeds of insurance on the life of a nonresident alien.[21]

(6) Debt obligations issued by a U.S. corporation if the interest thereon was treated as foreign source income to the nonresident alien holder of the obligation under section 861(a)(1)(B), (G), or (H) (discussed in 4.2.1.).[22]

(7) Deposits with a U.S. financial institution if the interest thereon constituted income to the nonresident alien decedent that was not effectively connected with the conduct of a U.S. trade or business.[23]

(8) Deposits with a foreign branch of a U.S. commercial bank.[24]

10.3.4. U.S. Taxation of citizens and resident aliens

U.S. citizens and resident aliens who die owning property situated in another country are subject to full U.S. estate taxation under the rules and at the rates described in 10.1.2. Foreign tax credits for death taxes imposed by foreign countries on the property situated outside the U.S. are allowable under the rules discussed in 10.3.6.

10.3.5. U.S. Taxation of nonresident aliens

The U.S. estate tax imposed on the transfer of property by a nonresident alien begins with a determination of the value of that part of the decedent's *gross estate*[25] which, under the rules described in 10.3.3.1., at the time of death, is situated within the U.S.[26]

From the gross estate situated within the U.S. are subtracted the portion of debts, expenses of administration, claims against the estate, mortgages, funeral expenses, and losses suffered by the estate that is allocable to the U.S.[27] In addition, a deduction for transfers to qual-

21. Sec. 2105(a).

22. Sec. 2104(c).

23. Sec. 2105(b). The amounts must be on deposit with a 'bank'. See Estate of Ogarrio v. Commissioner, 337 F.2d 108 (D.C. Cir. 1964) (amounts on deposit with a U.S. stock brokerage firm were situated within the U.S.); Rev. Rul. 69-596, 1969-2 Cum. Bull. 179 (same result where amounts were deposited with a fiduciary). Amounts held in a safe deposit box are not on 'deposit' and hence are situated within the U.S., Rev. Rul 55-143, 1955-1 Cum. Bull. 465.

24. Sec. 2105(b)(2).

25. Under sec. 2031 the gross estate includes the value of 'all property, real or personal, tangible or intangible, wherever situated'.

26. Sec. 2103.

27. Sec. 2106(a)(1) and (2). In general, the deductions are allowed in the proportion that →

ifying charitable organizations is also allowed. The result of the subtraction of these items from the gross estate is the *taxable estate*.

The unified transfer tax rates are then applied to the sum of the taxable estate and the 'adjusted taxable gifts' (i.e., taxable gifts made by the decedent after December 31, 1976). The rates are progressive over five brackets ranging from 6% for amounts transferred up to $100,000 to 30% on amounts transferred in excess of $2 million. This 'tentative' tax is then reduced by a hypothetical tax calculated on the basis of the unified transfer tax rates applied to the adjusted taxable gifts. In effect, the amounts subject to tax in the estate are treated as coming 'on top of' the adjusted taxable gifts for purposes of determining the rate of progression.[28] The tax thus determined is then reduced by three credits against tax:

(1) The credit for death taxes paid to a State government;

(2) The credit for gift taxes paid on gifts made prior to 1977; and

(3) The credit for estate tax paid by another transferor with respect to property included in the decedent's estate where the prior transferor died within 10 years before or 2 years after the decedent.[29]

Finally, the estate is allowed a *unified transfer tax credit* in the amount of $3,600 (the equivalent of an estate tax exemption of $60,000).[30]

10.3.6. THE FOREIGN TAX CREDIT

The estates of U.S. citizens and resident aliens are allowed a foreign tax credit for 'estate, inheritance, legacy, or succession' taxes actually

→

the U.S. assets bear to the decedent's worldwide assets. The deductions are available only if the U.S. estate tax return discloses that part of the decedent's gross estate which is located outside the U.S. In general, a deduction is granted only for contributions to charitable organizations that are organized and operated in the U.S. for prescribed charitable purposes such as education, religion, scientific research, etc.

28. It should be noted that the gift tax actually paid on taxable gifts made by a nonresident alien is calculated under the rate schedule of section 2001(c). However, when calculating the transfer tax due from the estate, a 'credit' is only given for hypothetical taxes on the gifts computed by using the lower rates contained in section 2101(d). As a result, the estate will not receive a credit for the full amount of gift tax actually paid. This failure to coordinate the two rate schedules was probably unintentional. It has the effect of making a combination of lifetime and deathtime transfers by a nonresident alien decedent more costly than a transfer of the same assets which takes place only at death, assuming the assets would have been subject to a gift tax if transferred inter vivos.

29. Sec. 2102(a) and (b).

30. Sec. 2102(c).

paid to a foreign country with respect to property situated within that country. The rules discussed in 10.3.3. are applied to determine the country in which property is situated. Thus, for example, stock of a corporation is situated only in the foreign country in which the corporation is incorporated. No credit is allowed for death taxes imposed by a foreign country on property that is not situated within that country (although this result may be modified by treaty).[31]

As in the case of the income tax, the allowable foreign tax credit for estate tax purposes is subject to limitations. The maximum credit is the smaller of:

1. The foreign country's death taxes actually imposed on property in the foreign country which is included in the decedent's U.S.-computed gross estate (the so-called 'first limitation').
2. The portion of the U.S. estate tax attributable to property which is loated in the foreign country, subject to death taxes therein, and included in the decedent's U.S.-computed gross estate (the so-called 'second limitation').[32]

The limitations operate to provide a full credit for foreign death taxes where the foreign tax rate is lower than that imposed by the U.S., but the allowable credit cannot exceed the tax that the U.S. would have imposed on the foreign property.

The 'first limitation' is computed by applying a fraction to the foreign country's death taxes. The numerator of the fraction is the value of the property which is subject to the foreign country's death taxes and which is included in the decedent's U.S.-computed gross estate. The denominator of the fraction is the value of all the decedent's property subject to the foreign country's death taxes. 'Value' is determined under the foreign country's death tax rules and then converted to U.S. dollars.[33]

The 'second limitation' is computed by applying a fraction to the U.S. federal estate tax liability of the decedent. The numerator of the fraction is the 'adjusted value' of the decedent's property that is situated within a foreign country, subject to death taxes therein, and included in the decedent's U.S.-computed gross estate. The denominator of the fraction is the value of the decedent's entire gross estate minus any allowable charitable contributions deduction and marital deduction. The term 'adjusted value' refers to the value of the decedent's gross estate minus any charitable contributions deduction or marital deduc-

31. Sec. 2014(a); Treas. Reg. sec. 20.2014-1(a)(3).
32. Sec. 2014(b).
33. Treas. Reg. sec. 20.2014-2.

tion allowable with respect to, and allocable to, the foreign property.[34]

As in the case of the income tax, the foreign tax credit is allowed to resident aliens only if the country of residence allows a similiar credit to U.S. citizens who are residents in the alien's country. The limitation on resident aliens may be imposed only by Presidential proclamation after making findings like those described in 6.2.5.2.[35]

10.4. Gift tax: international aspects

10.4.1. Background

The gift tax treatment of nonresidents who are not U.S. citizens was revised in 1966 and 1976 by the legislative actions described in 10.3.1. In the 1966 legislation the U.S. relinquished more of its tax jurisdiction over transfers by gifts than it did in the case of transfers at death.

10.4.2. Gift taxation of U.S. citizens and resident aliens

The U.S. gift tax is a cumulative tax imposed quarterly on all transfers 'in trust or otherwise, whether the gift is direct or indirect, and whether the property is real or personal, tangible or intangible'.[36] For U.S. citizens and resident aliens the tax is imposed on all transfers wherever the property is situated under the rules described in 10.3.3. No foreign tax credit is allowed for transfers of property located abroad that are also subject to gift tax by a foreign country.

10.4.3. Gift taxation of nonresident aliens

Subject to the exception described in 10.4.2., the U.S. imposes a gift tax on transfers by nonresidents who are not U.S. citizens only if the subject of the gift is real property or tangible personal property physically situated in the U.S.; gifts of intangible property are therefore not subject to tax.[37] If a taxable gift is made, the full U.S. unified transfer

34. Treas. Reg. sec. 20.2014-3.
35. Sec. 2014(h).
36. Sec. 2501(a)(1), 2511(a).
37. Sec. 2501(a)(2); Treas. Reg. sec. 25.2511-3(a)(1),(b)(1).

tax rates apply; there is no reduced rate of tax as in the case of the estate tax. Gifts by nonresident aliens qualify for the $3000 annual per donee exclusion, but neither the marital deduction for inter-spousal gifts nor the unified transfer tax credit is available. A deduction for charitable contributions is available if, in general, the transfer is to a U.S. organization that will use the gifted funds in the U.S.[38]

The above rules apply irrespective of whether the donor is engaged in business in the U.S.

10.5. The generation-skipping tax: international aspects

As discussed in 10.1.4., the Tax Reform Act of 1976 introduced a tax on certain generation-skipping transfers, i.e., those in trust or a trust equivalent.

The generation-skipping tax is applicable if a nonresident who is not a U.S. citizen is the 'deemed transferor' (the person in a generation below that of the transferor but above that of the transferee) of a generation-skipping trust.[39] For example if A creates a trust for the benefit of his child B (who is a nonresident not a U.S. citizen), his grandchildren C and D, and ultimate distribution to his great grandchildren, B is a 'deemed transferor'. Upon B's death the generation-skipping tax will be imposed. The tax is computed on the basis of the unified transfer tax rates of section 2001(c) (despite the fact that, had B's estate actually been subject to estate tax on the property, the estate would have paid taxes at the lower section 2101(d) rates). The nonresident 'deemed transferor' is not personally liable for the tax, which is payable only out of the trust property. The generation-skipping tax is incurred, however, only if B would have been subject to U.S. estate tax had he been the actual transferor of the property. For this purpose Regulations to be issued by the Treasury will presumably apply rules similiar to those developed in the estate tax context as described in 10.1. (and in the gift tax context if a generation-skipping transfer occurred during B's life).

38. Sec. 2522(b); Treas. Reg. sec. 25.2523(a)-1(a).
39. Sec. 2614(b).

10.6. Expatriation to avoid transfer taxes

10.6.1. ESTATE TAX

If a decedent lost his U.S. citizenship within ten years of death and if avoidance of U.S. estate, gift, or income taxes was a principal purpose therefore, the full U.S. estate tax rates apply to the transfer of property situated within the U.S. In such cases, therefore, the reduced rates normally applicable to nonresidents who are not U.S. citizens do not apply. A unified transfer tax credit of $13,000 is allowed against the tax so computed (the equivalent of a $60,000 exemption).[40]

The tax is imposed on the taxable estate computed in the manner described in 10.1. However, a special rule requires the inclusion in the gross estate of a portion of the value of the stock owned by the decedent in a foreign corporation if:

(1) The decedent owned directly 10 percent or more of the voting power of all classes of stock of the foreign corporation; and

(2) The decedent owned directly and by attribution more than 50 percent of the voting power of all classes of stock of the foreign corporation.

The amount includible in the decedent's U.S. gross estate is determined by applying to the fair market value of the stock owned outright by the decedent a fraction, the numerator of which is the fair market value of the corporation's assets in the U.S. and the denominator of which is the total fair market value of the corporation's entire assets.[41]

The burden of proving the lack of a principal tax avoidance purpose is on the estate once the Government establishes that it is 'reasonable to believe' that the loss of citizenship would result in a substantial reduction in transfer taxes (including the transfer taxes imposed by the U.S. and by other countries).[42]

40. Sec. 2107(a), (c).

41. Sec. 2107(b) In determining the value of the stock of the foreign corporation, no reduction is allowed for corporate liabilities. Treas. Reg. sec. 20.2107-1(b)(1)(ii)(*a*). The rules of section 957, discussed in 7.3., are applied to determine if the requisite 'voting power' exists.

42. Sec. 2107(e).

10.6.2. Gift tax

The exception of intangible property from gift taxation is removed for nonresident aliens who lost their U.S. citizenship after March 8, 1965 and within ten years of the gift if the loss of citizenship had as one of its principal purposes the avoidance of U.S. gift, estate or income taxes.[43]

For purposes of this rule, special situs rules are provided for intangible property. The following property is considered situated in the U.S. and hence subject to gift tax:

(1) Shares of stock in a U.S. corporation.

(2) Debt obligations of a U.S. person, including bank deposits.

(3) Debt obligations of the U.S. or a state or local government.

(4) Intangible property of any type issued by or enforceable against a U.S. resident or corporation.

These rules apply regardless of where the stock or written evidence of the property or obligation is located. In the case of debt obligations or bank deposits, it is irrelevant that the interest thereon constituted foreign source income under the income tax rules.[44]

10.7. Estate and gift tax treaties

10.7.1. Background

The U.S. network of estate and gift treaties is substantially smaller than its income tax treaty network. Double taxation in the estate tax area can arise either because both countries claim the decedent as a domiciliary, and thus taxable on his worldwide estate, or because the decedent was domiciled in one country while holding property with a situs in the second country. The U.S. estate tax treaties in general deal with these problems by clarifying the rules with respect to the situs of property for estate tax purposes and by granting a credit for foreign death taxes paid in certain situations. Since the U.S. unilaterally grants a foreign tax credit for death taxes paid by those estates subject to its worldwide estate tax jurisdiction, the primary function of the estate tax treaties for these taxpayers is to ensure that the credit mechanism functions properly. For other taxpayers, the change in the situs rules may either eliminate assets from the reach of U.S. estate taxation or may qualify

43. Sec. 2501(a)(3)(B).
44. Sec. 2511(b); Treas. Reg. sec. 25.2511-3(b).

the U.S. tax paid on those assets for a credit in the foreign country. In any event, both classes of taxpayers are generally protected by an article which provides that the provisions of the treaty shall not be construed so as to increase the tax imposed by either country.[45]

The U.S. estate tax treaties generally apply only to federal estate taxes and do not cover state inheritance taxes. Federal gift taxes are covered only by a limited number of treaties.[46]

The estate tax treaties contain provisions for competent authority procedures and exchange of information which are parallel to those found in the income tax treaties.

10.7.2. Domicile

Under most U.S. treaties, domicile is determined in accordance with the laws of the country imposing the tax on the basis of domicile. In general no attempt is made to settle on a single domicile for the decedent and, as a result, conflicting assertions of worldwide tax jurisdiction may often take place because of differing domiciliary concepts.[47]

10.7.3. Situs rules

10.7.3.1. Real property

Real property, usually referred to in the treaties as 'immovable property', is deemed to be situated at the place where the property is located.[48]

10.7.3.2. Tangible movable property

Tangible movable property generally has its situs at the place the property was located at the time of death or, if the property was in

45. See, e.g. Canada Estate Tax Treaty, Article II (last proviso).
46. See, e.g., France Estate and Gift Tax Treaty; Japan Estate and Gift Tax Treaty.
47. The Model Estate Tax Convention of December 8, 1980, contains detailed rules aimed at arriving at the determination of a single domicile for the decedent and this will presumably be an aim of U.S. estate tax treaty negotiations for the future. The treaty with the United Kingdom follows this pattern. It also expressly covers the generation-skipping tax.
48. See, e.g., Finland Estate Tax Treaty, Article III (2) (a).

transit at that time, at the place of intended destination. Cash currency, although technically an obligation of the issuing government or central bank, is generally treated as tangible property for purposes of the situs rules.

10.7.3.3. Corporate stock

In general the treaties provide that the shares in a corporation are deemed to be situated at the place under the laws of which the corporation was created or organized. This conforms to the otherwise applicable Code rule, but is an important provision from the perspective of the nonresident estate attempting to credit the U.S. estate taxes against the death taxes in the country of domicile since it provides a U.S. situs for U.S. corporate stock.

10.7.3.4. Obligations

The treaties contain a variety of rules for debts, bank accounts, government notes and bonds, and other debt obligations. For example, government bonds have their situs at the decedent's domicile in the Greek treaty,[49] and in the country of issue in the Japanese treaty.[50]

10.7.3.5. Business assets

In general, business assets are deemed to be located where the business is carried on. The Canadian treaty specifically provides that goodwill is so situated[51] and interests in a partnership are treated in a similiar fashion.[52]

10.7.4. Exemptions and deductions

A number of treaties provide for a $60,000 level of exemption from U.S. estate tax for residents of treaty countries. Prior to the 1976 adoption of

49. Greek Estate Tax Treaty, Article IV(2)(j).
50. Japan Estate and Gift Tax Treaty, Article III(1)(c).
51. Canada Estate Tax Treaty, Article II(j).
52. Canada Estate Tax Treaty, Article II(h).

the unified transfer tax system, this was an increase over the $30,000 exemption usually available. Under current law it provides no advantage.

10.7.5. Foreign tax credit

There are two types of foreign tax credit provided for in U.S. estate tax treaties, the 'primary credit' and the 'secondary credit'. The primary credit is a credit given by the domiciliary state for taxes paid to the treaty country of situs. The secondary credit is allowed in those cases in which both of the treaty countries impose a tax on property situated outside both states or deemed to be situated within both states (because of conflicting situs rules). The secondary credit is limited to the tax of the country imposing the smaller tax and is to be divided between the two countries in the proportion of the amount of tax of each attributable to the property. In calculating the credit, however, the tax against which the credit is being taken must be reduced by other credits against, or reduction of, such tax.

To take a simple example of the secondary credit, suppose the decedent was domiciled in both Canada and the United States and property situated in a third country was subject to $10,000 of death taxes in that country, and the U.S. and Canada imposed estate taxes on that property of $6,000 and $3,000 respectively. The overall amount of secondary credit would be limited to $3,000 and of that amount $2,000 would be creditable against U.S. tax and $1,000 against Canada tax.

The Regulations specifically state that if the credit for foreign death taxes provided under an estate tax treaty is more favorable than the Code credit under section 2014, the estate may elect whichever treatment is more favorable.[53] Treaty treatment could be more favorable, for example, in a situation in which the treaty situs rules specifically provided that property was located within the foreign taxing jurisdiction, thus increasing the amount of credit for foreign death taxes available.

53. Treas. Reg. sec. 20.2014-4(a)(1).

Chapter 11
The tax expenditure concept

11.1. Introduction

The rules governing taxation of international transactions by the U.S., discussed in the preceding chapters, have been analyzed purely as tax rules. That is to say, the provisions considered have all been viewed as components of the U.S. international tax structure without any general attempt to differentiate among those provisions in terms of the role played by each in the overall system of U.S. international taxation.

However, in the decade following 1968, a method of analysis was developed and adopted by the U.S. Government which looks at the provisions in a different fashion. This analytic technique is known as the 'tax expenditure concept'.[1] The concept is based on the recognition that the U.S. income tax system, including its international aspects, is in fact composed of two different and generally contradictory structures. One structure is composed of the rules necessary to implement a tax imposed on net income; the other structure is composed of rules necessary to effect federal expenditure programs through the tax system. The first structure is generally referred to as the normative or 'normal' income tax system; the second as the 'tax expenditure' system.

The provisions discussed in the preceding chapters have been of both

1. The tax expenditure concept is described by its formulator, Professor Stanley S. Surrey, in his book *Pathways to Tax Reform* (1973). Subsequent developments are detailed in Surrey and McDaniel, The Tax Expenditure Concept and the Budget Reform Act of 1974, 17 Boston College Industrial and Commercial Law Review 679 (1976); Surrey and McDaniel, The Tax Expenditure Concept: Current Developments And Emerging Issues, 20 Boston College Law Review 225 (1979). Shorter explanations of the concept may be found in Ault, Steuervergunstigungen in der Bundesrepublik Deutschland und den USA, 1974 Steuer und Wirtschaft 335 (1974); McDaniel, The Tax Expenditure Concept: Theory and Practical Operation, Maandblad Belastingbeschouwingen, 45e Jaargang No. 12 (Dec. 1976) at p. 245; McDaniel, The Tax Expenditure Concept in the International Context, 47e Jaargang No. 2/3 (Feb./March 1978) at p. 115.

types. That is, some of the international tax rules previously considered are part of the 'normal' income tax structure; others have been identified and quantified as 'tax expenditures'.

The tax expenditure concept, and the method of analysis associated with it, have come to play an increasingly important role in U.S. tax policy discussions. Accordingly, it is useful briefly to examine the concept in terms of the tax expenditure provisions contained in the U.S. international tax rules, both to illustrate this relatively new form of analytic technique and to indicate the implications that the technique may have for the evolution of U.S. international tax policy with respect to the provisions considered in the preceding chapters.

11.2. Conceptual basis of the tax expenditure approach

The normative tax structure is composed of the statutory provisions that reflect answers to fundamental questions that must be resolved by policymakers to implement the tax. These questions include: what is the base of the tax; what rates are to be applied; what is the taxable unit; what is the time period for determination of tax liability; how are entities such as corporations, partnerships, trusts, associations, nonprofit organizations to be treated; what method will be employed to apply the tax to those engaged in international transactions? The answers to these questions and the technical rules to implement those answers form the normative structure of the tax selected.

The U.S. answers to these normative structural questions include the decision to adopt net income (gross income minus the costs of producing income) as the tax base; a progressive rate structure; an annual accounting period; the marital unit (or single persons) as the basic taxable unit; taxation of organizations, especially corporations, separately from the individuals who comprise them; and the source rules and the foreign tax credit as the mechanisms for applying the tax to those investing, working or transacting business across national borders. The technical provisions of the Internal Revenue Code required to implement these decisions form the normative structure of the U.S. income tax system.

It is obvious, however, that a great many of the provisions discussed in Chapters 2 and 6 are not responsive to these basic structural questions. Many of the provisions discussed in those chapters do not help define net income; instead certain items of income are excluded from the tax base and certain expenditures are permitted to be deducted even though they do not constitute costs of producing income. The same is true of timing issues: certain receipts are deferred to be accounted for in later periods and certain deductions are accelerated to earlier periods than those to which sound accounting principles would assign them. Some types of income qualify for rates of tax lower than those prescribed in the generally applicable rate structure. Tax credits are granted for reasons unrelated to proper determination of net tax liability.

The explanation for these special provisions thus lies not in the resolution of normative structural issues, but in the desire of the U.S. Government to provide financial incentives or assistance to induce economic actions or to provide relief from financial hardship. The investment tax credit is an example of the first type of provision; the exemption for social security benefits represents a rule of the second type. The purposes for which these provisions have been introduced are not tax collection purposes of the federal government, but are instead spending purposes of the government.

Since 1969 the U.S. Treasury Department and the Staff of the Joint Committee on Taxation of the U.S. Congress have analyzed the various provisions that fulfill functions extraneous to the resolution of normative tax structure issues as spending programs effected through the tax system. That is, a special rule that departs from the normative structure and thus causes a taxpayer to pay a tax lower than called for by that structure may be viewed as a mechanism that simultaneously effects a collection of the proper tax due and appropriation by the government to the taxpayer in the amount of the tax reduction. The funds do not physically flow into the Treasury and then back to the taxpayer, as in the case of programs financed by direct appropriations. But the economic effect of the special tax provision is otherwise identical to the direct spending process. The descriptive term 'tax expenditures' has been applied to these provisions.

Because the tax expenditure provisions cover areas similar to those involved in the direct Budget, a tax expenditure budget has been published since 1968 showing the amount expended (through foregone revenues) for each item in the tax expenditure budget. In the Budget Reform Act of 1974, Congress included tax expenditures in the normal budget process, requiring the President to include a tax expenditure budget as part of the regular direct budget submitted each year.[2] Procedures were established in the Act to try to insure that tax expenditures would be subject to the same oversight and controls that Congress applies to direct expenditure programs.

2. See, for example, Special Analyses, Budget of the United States Government, Fiscal Year 1981 – Special Analysis G, at pp. 207–238.

The listing and quantification of tax expenditures require identification of the features that constitute the normative structure of the tax under consideration and, in the context of an income tax, a definition of net income. For income definition, the U.S. tax expenditure analysis begins with the measurement as articulated in the Haig-Simons approach: Personal income (net income) is the algebraic sum of the market value of rights exercised in consumption plus the change in value of the individual's store of property rights between the beginning and end of the period in question. This definition is a beginning point for analysis and is not applied rigidly in the listing of tax expenditures in the United States. In matters of timing of income and deductions, and identification of costs of producing income, the concept refers to generally accepted accounting principles as the norm.

11.3. Tax expenditures in international affairs

The tax expenditure concept permits the identification of those provisions that have been discussed in Chapters 4 through 9 that constitute responses to the questions necessary to resolve the structural question, how is the U.S. income tax to be applied to taxpayers with investments and business transactions that cross national borders? Other provisions, however, have been identified as tax expenditures since these provisions are not responsive to the structural question, but instead perform the function of providing federal financial assistance or relief from hardship to the taxpayers whose affairs are conducted in an international setting.

The structural provisions adopted to apply the U.S. income tax to international transactions include the source rules discussed in Chapter 4; the trade or business and effectively connected concepts discussed in Chapter 5; the basic pattern of taxation of foreign corporations and nonresident aliens considered in Chapter 5; the foreign tax credit considered in Chapter 6; and the provisions necessary to insure the proper application of the U.S. tax rules considered in Chapter 8.

The following table sets forth the tax expenditures in the application of the U.S. income tax in international transactions that are listed under the budget function 'International Affairs' in the tax expenditure budget:[3]

3. Special Analysis G, note 2, at 230.

TAX EXPENDITURE ESTIMATES BY FUNCTION
(In millions of dollars)

Description	Fiscal years					
	Corporations			Individuals		
	1979	1980	1981	1979	1980	1981
International affairs:						
Exclusion of income earned abroad by United States citizens	.....	.....	.....	530	555	600
Deferral of income of domestic international sales corporations (DISC)	1,210	1,400	1,470	.....	.....	.....
Deferral of income of controlled foreign corporations	530	445	480	.....	.....	.....
Special rate for Western Hemisphere trade corporations	15	5	.....	.....	.....	.....

The tax expenditure budget does not list 'tax penalties' or 'negative tax expenditures'. Provisions that deny the applicability of the normative structural rules to a particular taxpayer for non-tax reasons can be viewed as penalties exacted by the U.S. government for prohibited activity. The denial of the foreign tax credit for foreign taxes imposed on international boycott income (discussed in 6.2.7.) is an example of such a provision. However, the denial of DISC benefits for boycott income and foreign bribes (discussed in 7.8.) is a different type of provision; it does not constitute a tax penalty, but is instead simply a mechanism for limiting the benefits of the tax subsidy program so that the subsidy is not provided to operations that conflict with overall U.S. policy.

The identification and quantification of tax expenditures do not imply any judgment as to whether a provision is desirable or undesirable. The process simply identifies those government expenditure programs that are being effected through the tax system. Once this is done, government is in a position to ask the questions that it routinely asks of direct spending programs. For example, is a government spending program needed to correct a need not being met by the market? Does the item occupy a priority status as compared to other programs? Are the benefits of the program equitably distributed by income classes in the case of individuals or by size of corporations? More specifically, the deferral of tax that is accorded by the DISC and controlled foreign corporation rules is the equivalent of a loan (in the amount of the tax deferred) granted by the government to the taxpayers benefitted. Questions appropriate to evaluate a loan program may then be asked. Why is the loan interest free? Why is there no security for the loan? Why is eligibility for the loan conditioned only on the existence of otherwise taxable income? Under cost-benefit analysis, are the amounts of foreign exports or foreign investment increased in dollar amount at least as much as the revenues foregone by the federal government? Do the loans result in increased international activity or do they merely provide a financial benefit to taxpayers to engage in activities they would engage in without the benefit of the federal subsidy?

The tax expenditure budget thus provides policymakers with a tool to evaluate expenditure programs effected through the tax system in the same manner as they evaluate expenditures made through the direct spending process. The tax expenditure concept does not imply that the government should always use the direct spending approach rather than the tax spending approach. Rather, the concept indicates that the same process of evaluation and control that applies to direct expenditures should be applied to tax expenditures as well.

Index